grow plants in pots

LONDON, NEW YORK, MUNICH,
MELBOURNE, DELHI

Project Editor Zia Allaway
Editors Sarah Ruddick, Christine Dyer
Project Art Editor Vicky Read
US Editor Rebecca Warren, Kate Johnsen
Jacket Designer Mark Cavanagh
Production Editor Joanna Byrne
DK Picture Library Jenny Baskaya,
Lucy Claxton
Managing Editor Esther Ripley
Managing Art Editor Alison Donovan
Associate Publisher Liz Wheeler
Art Director Peter Luff
Publisher Jonathan Metcalf

Additional text Zia Allaway
Photography Peter Anderson

First American Edition, 2011
Published in the United States by
DK Publishing
375 Hudson Street
New York, New York 10014

2 4 6 8 10 9 7 5 3 1
001—179522—April/2011

Published in Great Britain by Dorling Kindersley
Limited.

A catalog record for this book is available from the
Library of Congress

ISBN 978-0-7566-8250-7

Printed and bound by Star Standard, Singapore

DK Books are available at special discounts when
purchased in bulk for sales promotions, premiums,
fund-raising, or educational use. For details, contact:
DK Publishing Special Markets, 375 Hudson Street,
New York, New York 10014 or SpecialSales@dk.com.

Discover more at
www.dk.com

grow plants in pots

Martyn Cox

Contents

 indicates that plant is generally grown as a houseplant

A–Z OF PLANT ENTRIES

DESIGNING WITH CONTAINERS

Large or small, contemporary or traditional, there's a container to suit every garden, interior, and design style. Select those that match your planting theme, and combine pots in complementary materials and colors for a coordinated look. To make your home and garden stand out from the crowd, browse through this chapter for inspirational container designs and striking plant combinations.

Use bold pots of summer blooms for a modern scheme, or choose a vibrant dahlia to brighten up a border. Patterned foliage plants make exceptional specimens for the home, while herbs in crates lend a rustic note to country gardens.

Creating a design

The choice of containers for your prized plants is vast and varied. Recycled items can make quirky pots, while traditional shapes and materials suit informal and classical designs. Sleek cubes, cylinders, and conical pots made from metal, synthetics, or smooth stone are ideal for low-maintenance, contemporary gardens.

Plants have the potential to make stunning, highly valued features when teamed with the right containers, so it's well worth considering your choices carefully. By uniting plants and pots in perfect harmony, you can create a wealth of sensational displays using the myriad different styles, colors, shapes, and sizes on offer.

Materials for containers include plastic, fiberglass, terra-cotta, stone, glazed ceramic, metal, and wood, but with so many options, how do you make your choice? First, consider the overall design and style of your garden, and then think about the plants you want to display and try to match these with complementary pots. Place your plants in appropriate sites to ensure they thrive, but don't be afraid to experiment with unconventional schemes, as the beauty of container gardening is that mistakes are easily rectified.

*Above **Plant Penstemon and Ligularia** in weathered wooden crates to create a rustic design for a country or informal-style garden. The crates can be stacked and arranged to create a proportional display on varying levels.*

*Right **The brilliant red of Acer palmatum foliage** creates a striking contrast with the cobalt blue of an old oil drum. Plant creatively to add height and structure to your design.*

Eco-friendly ideas

Creating your own containers by recycling items that may otherwise become trash is good for the environment and good for your pocket, and will lend a personal touch to your garden. Just about anything that has space for compost can be turned into a plant pot, including old boots, cans, buckets, wine boxes, fruit trays, yogurt cartons, colanders, and plastic cups. Food cans of all shapes and sizes are also a great look and can often be obtained from local restaurants and delicatessens. However, before turning any item into a home for plants, drill some drainage holes in the base, and make sure there is enough space inside for your chosen plants to grow comfortably.

*Below **Grow salad crops in recycled drinks cartons** or plastic tubs. Plants with shallow roots are suitable for a wide range of containers, but remember to create drainage holes in the bottom before planting.*

*Below left **Transform decorative cans** into beautiful displays by filling them with dainty daffodils.*

*Below **These boots were made for planting** compact flowers such as Brachyscombe and Bidens.*

Cool and contemporary designs

When creating displays for a modern patio garden or a minimalist courtyard, opt for simple, elegant containers with a sculptural quality or use angular shapes that complement sharp, geometrical designs. Avoid overly ornate or traditional pots, which will clash with a modern setting. Tall, rectangular containers look great when teamed with contrasting spiky or feathery foliage, while low cubes make ideal homes for lollipop-shaped standard trees or the curved outline of a clipped box topiary. Use rectangular planters to raise vegetables, herbs, and other edibles, and try slim cylinders and tapering conical pots with trailing plants to create a striking asymmetrical display. Most plants can be grown in contemporary containers, but architectural shapes, crisp topiary, grasses, bamboos, and succulents suit them best.

Far right **Create a garden catwalk** *by lining a planked walkway with a row of tall, geometric containers. Grow colorful, spiky* Imperata cylindrica *'Red Baron' to add pizzazz.*

Right **Use a minimalist arrangement** *of box topiary and Japanese maples in large containers to frame an outside seating area and provide some privacy screening.*

Below **Choose a conical container,** *set onto a metal plate for stability, to complement the color and shape of spiky succulents and leafy trailers in a Japanese-inspired pebble garden.*

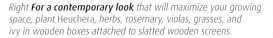

Right **For a contemporary look** *that will maximize your growing space, plant* Heuchera, *herbs, rosemary, violas, grasses, and ivy in wooden boxes attached to slatted wooden screens.*

Modern materials

Metal or synthetic materials are most commonly used to make contemporary containers because they suit modern designs. These versatile pots tend to be long lasting, lighter, and easier to clean than those made from traditional materials.

METAL

Zinc, hammered aluminium, polished steel, galvanized steel, and heavy-duty Corten steel that ages to a beautiful rusted finish are just some of the metals used for plant containers. Since metal heats up quickly, line your pots with bubble plastic before planting to keep the roots from frying. In shady areas, use shiny metals to reflect light.

Right **Create a garden hall of mirrors** *using striking pots, such as this woven aluminium container. Use the spiky leaves of a cordyline as the main focus above a skirt of colorful blooms.*

SYNTHETIC MATERIALS

Lightweight pots made from fiberglass are ideal for roof gardens, balconies, or other areas where weight is an issue. Modern plastic and polycarbonate pots can look very chic and are available in a wide range of styles and colors. Synthetics are also frost-proof and durable.

Left **Contrast fingerlike fronds** *of ferns with the sleek, modern shape of a plastic pot. This flexible material can be molded into an infinite range of modern designs.*

Above **Invest in a unique designer container** *for a modern garden, such as this sleek metal pot that looks just like a silk bag.*

Left **Underplant standard olive trees** *with a fringe of feathery blue Festuca glauca in contrasting metal pots.*

Old-world charm

Set the scene in an informal or country garden with containers made from traditional materials and molded into classic shapes, such as urns or bowls. In a country garden with deep borders, a tiny English-style garden enclosed by brick walls, or a simple yard and small patio, try warm-colored terra-cotta and clay containers to give a natural look. These materials offer the perfect backdrop for most plants because their muted tones do not overpower either flowers or foliage, and their rustic appearance improves as they weather and age. Remember that many terra-cotta pots are not frost proof, so look for those with 10-year guarantees— they are usually more expensive but can be cost effective in the long run.

Alternatively, use distressed zinc containers to add a dash of old-world charm to your design, or wooden boxes, which look fabulous in natural settings. Wicker baskets in all shapes and sizes are also charming; either line them with plastic punctured with drainage holes, or use them to hold plants potted in plastic containers.

Grow ornamental grasses and compact alpines, such as Saxifraga, in round clay pots. Larger plants, such as Mahonia, make strong sculptural displays in terra-cotta containers.

Glazed containers work well in traditional settings if you choose dark colors that complement your design. This pot lends a modern look, inspired by the graphic forms of Euphorbia characias Silver Swan ('Wilcott') and Ophiopogon.

Left **The glossy scarlet spathes** *of Anthurium create a striking contrast with the matt texture and subtle color of a wicker basket. Mix these opposites to make a bold statement in a period or traditional home.*

Below left **Plant lush ferns** *and fiery cannas in a shallow copper bowl. Treat the copper to maintain its color, or allow it to oxidize to form a patina of green-blue verdigris.*

Below **Create a striking silhouette** *in a formal garden with a Carex comans bronze form, with fountains of foliage spilling from a classic urn.*

The tight rosettes of foliage and tiny, dark pink flowers of Saxifraga x arendsii are thrown into contrast by the sharp lines and cool color of this weathered metal box, creating a decorative feature for a patio display.

Traditional materials

Containers for traditional gardens come in a wide range of natural materials, but three of the most popular are terra-cotta, stone, and wood, which blend perfectly into rustic and formal settings. Choose pots that suit the color and form of your plants, garden style, and your available budget.

TERRA-COTTA

This versatile material is used for a vast range of containers, from tiny pots to large urns, and in plain or intricately decorated styles. Terra-cotta is porous, and will crack in frigid conditions unless fired at high temperatures to make it weatherproof. Line these porous pots with bubble plastic to keep water in.

STONE

Limestone, ironstone, granite, and other types of stone make durable containers, ideal for planting trees, shrubs, and perennials. For a pot with a weathered patina, check out architectural salvage yards. If budgets are tight, opt for Terrazzo or stone resin, which are cheaper, but have the look and feel of real stone.

WOOD AND WOVEN

Versailles-style and wooden planters, and half-barrels or baskets suit informal designs and a wide variety of plants. Line containers with plastic to prevent compost from falling through the gaps, and to prevent wood from rotting. Keep them under cover in the winter and treat lumber annually with preservative.

Perfect partners

Combining pots and plants to create a balanced display is often a case of trial and error. Those with less experience may find it easier to opt for a collection of containers made from the same material, which will make a harmonious design for a formal or modern garden. A random group of pots in a variety of shapes, sizes, and materials is ideal for an English-style garden or informal space. Either set your pots out in height order in a formal fashion, or in a looser way to produce a more relaxed display.

Matching materials

A uniform group of plants growing in pots made from the same material can be a highly effective way of creating a focal point on a patio or terrace. For contemporary gardens, choose containers in colors and a design or finish that echoes your interior decoration to create a seamless flow from inside to out, or throw caution to the wind and use pots that contrast with your décor to create colorful punctuation points.

Give a sense of unity to your design by placing similar containers throughout your space to help draw the eye from one part of the garden to another. Alternatively, set identical plants and containers in a row to divide or enclose a patio, or to frame a feature or gateway. Tall, elegant containers work well in this context and ensure the materials complement your garden style.

Match galvanized containers of varying heights and widths in a contemporary space to create a raised vegetable patch of chives, peppers, leeks, strawberries, and tomatoes.

Mix the complementary hues of green Dasylirion longissimum with a set of dark red contemporary containers.

Make a feature for your home with decorative Echeveria 'Duchess of Nuremberg' housed in small metal units.

Mixing shapes and sizes

Groups of containers made from different materials and in different shapes and sizes are ideal for a relaxed flower-filled space where a natural look is required. Add movement, scale, and a sense of perspective by grouping planters by height, or raise your game and create a collection on a table, bench, or even an old ladder, using the rungs as a theater to show off the plants. Mixed pots tend to look unbalanced when arranged in a row, so try a more staggered display instead. Also include a few similar elements to unify your collection, such as pot and plant colors, foliage shapes, or a pebble mulch.

Above **A limited color palette** *of* Cosmos, Lobelia, *blue* Salvia, *white snapdragons, and* Ophiopogon *in mixed glazed pots creates a balanced display.*

Above left **Choose one material** *for your pots, but then mix and match their sizes and shapes, and the colors of your flowers.*

Far left **Use similar shades and hues** *to integrate a diverse collection of plants, including cacti, dahlias,* Echeveria, *and fountain grass in a set of mixed, neutral containers.*

Left **Contrast plant types** *to produce an exciting mixed display. Here,* Carex dipsacea, Skimmia japonica *'Rubella,'* Euonymus fortunei *'Emerald 'n' Gold,' and* Heuchera *'Silver Scrolls' make a dramatic foliage group.*

Pots in gardens

The great appeal of plants in pots is that they are versatile, adding pizzazz to an urban chill-out zone, providing a decorative touch to a flower-filled English garden, and injecting a dash of color into almost any plot. Use large containers as focal points in beds or borders, and tiny pots to help to dress up more intimate areas of the garden. Containers also allow you to celebrate the seasonal changes with spring bulbs, and summer and autumn bedding.

Traditional designs

Weathered and rustic containers lend themselves to traditional, formal, and period gardens. A large pot planted with a specimen shrub or grass makes a great focal point for the end of a grassy path or pergola, drawing the eye through the garden. Choose stone urns filled with a profusion of flowers and foliage to complement herbaceous borders or mixed beds, and raise them on platforms for added impact. Containers can also be set among plantings to heighten the sense of mystery and surprise as visitors discover them, and used to integrate seasonal color into a parterre or knot garden.

Above **Create a stately pattern** *of colorful flowers, such as scented geraniums and petunias, planted in ornate urns to frame a grass walkway and long borders.*

Left **Plant variegated ivy** *in a terra-cotta urn and squeeze it between other plants to provide a subtle focal point in a woodland garden or fernery.*

Liven up a formal parterre *with large terra-cotta containers filled with a bright mix of scented geraniums. As fall approaches, replace the summer flowers with spring bulbs and a selection of violas.*

Above **Contrast the spiky foliage and delicate petals** *of traditonal English garden irises with the bold permanence of contemporary containers in a fusion of old and new styles.*

Contemporary plans

Containers with clean, simple designs complement the elegance of a modern garden. Choose a tall slender pot made from contemporary materials, such as composite stone or metal, matched with an architectural plant and positioned in a prominent place to create an eye-catching sculpture. Minimalist planting designs also work well in chic city gardens. Try similar plants grown in identical geometric-shaped containers to add structure and movement to your garden, and use them to flank a flight of steps, add height to a low wall, or edge a pathway. Bold foliage plants will help to enhance your design. Good choices include spiky phormiums, flowing grasses, and neatly clipped box balls or lollipop-shaped bay trees, which look fantastic in elegant containers standing like sentries on either side of a front door or entrance.

Above **Mix plants and planters** *in a range of geometric shapes to create a unified display.*

Left **Select slender columns** *topped with box topiary balls, and mirror these with small rectangular containers for a neat, minimalist look.*

Edible gardens

Many edible crops have attractive leaves, fruits, or an architectural shape that will add an ornamental touch to a garden design while also providing you with tasty pickings. Crops with showy fruits, such as eggplant, chili peppers, tomatoes, and strawberries can hold their own in containers, while low-growing leafy crops like herbs are best grouped together for maximum impact. Many edibles are not ready to harvest until the end of the growing season, so create some earlier interest by combining crops with flowers or foliage plants. Dot your fruit and vegetables among permanent foliage in a border or arrange them *en masse* for a spectacle that is definitely good enough to eat. While many edible plants will hog a container, you can use the empty space below standard fruit or bay trees by underplanting with trailing fruit or low-growing herbs that enjoy similar conditions.

Far left **Interplant your crops** *with colorful flowers, such as fuchsias, for a sumptuous display. Try tomato 'Minibel' and chili pepper 'Hungarian Hot Wax.'*

Center **Arrange your pots** *of strawberries, mint, parsley, and chives at different heights to make harvesting easy and to maximize their visual appeal.*

Left **Grow eggplant** *in pots in a hot spot for an attractive display of colorful fruits. Try 'Pingtung long' (left), 'Fairy Tale' (rear), and 'Listade de Gandia' (right).*

Above **With creative planning and planting**, *a vegetable garden can be both elegant and productive. Plant underneath standard bay trees with lavender, and grow crops such as lettuce and cabbages in raised beds.*

Informal spaces

If you are aiming for an eclectic mix, just about anything goes. Plunge containers of seasonal flowers into bare patches in your borders—you could plant a series of inexpensive plastic pots with plants that bloom in succession from spring to fall to ensure there is never a gap in your display. Containers of sweet peas wound around an ornamental obelisk will bring height to your design in an English garden, or place pots on an old wooden stool or chair to create a vertical accent.

As well as recycled containers, which lend themselves to informal designs, wicker baskets, glazed urns, wooden wine crates, and distressed terra-cotta pots all complement informal spaces. You can also use walls, fences, and trees as props for your decorative designs.

Left **Elevate baskets** *by fixing them to sturdy wooden poles to create a dramatic scene-setter in an herbaceous border. Choose drought-tolerant scented geraniums and bacopa for small baskets.*

Below **Corten is weatherproof steel** *that has a rusty patina; pots made from it blend perfectly into informal spaces, such as gravel gardens. Choose plants that reflect your garden design.*

Suspend small pots of pansies, *such as Viola cornuta 'Gem Apricot Antique,' from tree branches with ribbon or twine.*

Use trailing begonias *and blue convulvulus to tumble over the sides of a terra-cotta urn in a gravel garden.*

Pots on patios

Gardeners often feel constrained by small patios, but you can grow a wide range of plants on the tiniest of terraces. Choose carefully to ensure your plants won't take over all of your available space and make it appear even smaller. Good choices include crisp topiary, scented bulbs, grasses, slimline architectural bushes, flowering annuals, edibles, and herbs. On small patios, opt for just a few sculptural pots, and use the walls and windowsills to increase your container collection.

Contemporary terraces

To create a modern look, clear your space of clutter and focus on elegant forms of both pots and plants. A minimalist approach works well; group similar pots, planted with topiary, bamboos, grasses, lavender, or regal lilies, along a boundary. Also use the vertical space to make your patio feel larger, training the eye up to the sky, rather than toward the boundaries. Select well-behaved climbers, such as *Trachelospermum* and clematis, and plant them in rustic troughs next to a wall or fence. Avoid hanging baskets and opt instead for eye-catching wall pots and simple window boxes made from modern materials. Grow sun-loving architectural plants, such as cannas, in hot spots, and use ferns, hostas, and heucheras to brighten up shady areas.

Top right **Transform a dull, shady corner** *with Japanese-inspired clouds of box and privet topiary.*

Right **Tall slim pots** *are perfect for tight spaces. Use upright plants, such as cannas, dahlias, and blood grass, with a skirt of lively red impatiens to form a head of color at the top.*

Far right **Train scented star jasmine** *on a slatted fence and use chic black planters for a trendy look.*

Left **Fill a productive patio** *with a range of pots and crops to extend your fruit and vegetable harvest. Interplant with violas, marigolds, and nasturtiums, which are also edible, and try planting tomatoes in hanging baskets to maximize your space.*

Edibles for small spaces

Long gone are the days when a vegetable plot or kitchen garden were thought to be minimum requirements for growing fruit and vegetables. Today, a vast range of compact crops have been bred specifically for growing in containers, while many other edible plants are suitable for raising in large troughs or half barrels.

  Plants on patios and terraces have to look good because they're visible whenever you step out of the door or look from your window. To address this, choose edibles with showy leaves, pretty flowers, or jewel-like fruit, such as kale, beets, frilly-leaf lettuces, peppers, and strawberries. Either arrange groups of containers alongside colorful annuals and other ornamentals, or fill large troughs with a selection of different crops. Make the most of vertical spaces, too, and plant hanging baskets with tumbling tomatoes, strawberries, and chilis. Small pots of herbs set on a garden table allow diners to pick them fresh when eating al fresco, or plant a fruit tree in a big pot on a patio for sweet treats in the late summer and fall.

Above left **Bays with braided stems** *provide an elegant addition to a patio, offering fresh leaves for the kitchen, and sophisticated focal points.*

Above **Dainty dianthus** *and flowering sages brighten up a kitchen-garden design of large galvanized containers filled with cabbages and artichokes.*

Left **Ruby-red strawberries** *hang from arched stems in a recycled colander, making a pretty display of tempting fruits ripening conveniently within reach.*

Relaxed plantings

If you don't have space for a well-filled border, or your garden is in need of a colorful lift, opt for a vibrant arrangement of plants grown with ease on your patio. Informal designs suit a collection of pots and plants with ornamental flowers and textural foliage. For a long season of interest grow heathers, evergreen grasses, and small shrubs as a backdrop to spring bulbs, summer bedding, and leafy autumn feature plants. On a large deck in the suburbs, next to your lawn and shrubs, use a range of colorful pots and flowers. For a patio in a more muted woodland or shady garden, try wooden or terra-cotta pots filled with foliage specimens, and violas, tobacco plants, and impatiens in pastel shades. Soften the edges of your pots with trailers that suit the exposure.

Far right **Vibrant pots** *filled with bright blooms produce a festive touch on a deck against a backdrop of foliage.*

Right **Petunias in raspberry hues** *enliven a glazed pot of* Hackonechloa macra 'Aureola' *and trailing* Vinca minor.

Right **Color up an autumn patio** *with a medley of heathers, cyclamens, lavender, and* Helichrysum italicum *in a clay pot. Use hardy cyclamens that will not be killed by frost.*

Far right **Re-create a summer border** *in a large glazed pot with the blue grass,* Leymus arenarius, *scented pinks, Gaura, and trailing silvery* Helichrysum petiolare.

Left **Make a stylish urban outdoor room** *ultra cool with cylindrical containers that match your furniture and complement chic limestone paving.*

Urban sanctuaries

There are no hard and fast rules about containers for urban gardens—the choice really depends on the look you're trying to achieve. You can opt for a sophisticated design by matching your pots with patio furniture, or go for galvanized metal containers to reflect light into a shady courtyard. To enhance a minimalist design, choose plants that have a crisp shape or architectural form, such as compact lavenders, grasses, bamboos, and hummock-forming hebes. Or create your own city forest with terrazzo cubes planted with multi-stemmed birch trees. These will be happy in large containers, as long as the compost is never allowed to dry out. If you want a refuge from the rigors of city life, create a cocoon of foliage by lining your patio or courtyard with a profusion of plants in tall containers. Not only will they keep your patio cool, but the foliage will help to muffle traffic noise too.

Scent your city plot *with a range of herbs, such as rosemary, marjorum, and thyme, in shiny metal pots. Use steps and walls to create a multi-layered effect, and water small herb pots every couple of days in summer.*

Combine cool greens and soft pinks *on a small paved patio, with hardy gerberas, dahlias, grasses, Phygelius, and the beautiful variegated shrub Aralia elata 'Variegata', for a relaxed vision of flowers and foliage.*

Balconies and roof terraces

Compact or slender plants are perfect for balconies since they leave you with plenty of elbow room, while those who garden up on a rooftop should choose tough plants that can cope with strong winds and sun. Despite the limitations, there are plenty of options for these difficult spaces.

Balconies

Most balconies are tiny, with just a few square feet for plants and people. To make the most of your available space, affix window boxes securely to railings, and consider installing shelving units made from treated wood or metal. Decorate your shelves with herbs, houseleeks, alpines, and a few houseplants in the summer. For year-round color, use slender conifers, and box pyramids, spirals, and other topiary forms to add lush tones. Also include a few fruits, such as strawberries and tomatoes, which will ripen quickly in a sunny spot.

Dazzle your neighbors with a bold Rhododendron yakushimanum in a glazed container. This compact type produces large clusters of pink flowers that smother the evergreen foliage to produce a spectacular display.

Create a fruitful balcony with a miniature garden encased in an assortment of rustic pots. Tiny tomatoes, such as 'Minibel,' and the fiery chili pepper 'Medusa,' together with some cut-and-come-again lettuces, will provide a feast for summer, while strawberries in window boxes and a dwarf apple tree add sweet flavors.

Left **Create a shield of plants** *to shelter a private space with summer bloomers vying with a range of leafy shrubs.*

Below **Tiers of elegant planters** *make a dramatic screen. Keep your plan simple by repeating key plants, such as phormiums, grasses, ivies, and echeverias.*

Above **Keep your design cool** *with bluish-gray hostas, silvery* Stachys byzantina *and the graceful* Miscanthus sinensis 'Morning Light' *in a metal pot.*

Roof terraces

Choose lightweight synthetic or metal containers for roof terraces where the total load-bearing weight is an issue, and make the most of any wall space by affixing pots or troughs to vertical surfaces to produce a layered effect.

High winds can cause problems, so install windbreaks to make your space more usable. Line the boundaries with tough plants, such as *Eleagnus* x *ebbingei*, the bamboo *Phyllostachys*, *Viburnum tinus,* and *Prunus laurocerasus* to create a green shelter, or use wood, woven bamboo, or metal screens, but ensure that they allow 40 to 50 percent of the wind to pass through them to prevent turbulence. With more shelter, your planting options expand, and you can include a range of flowering annuals and perennials, as well as edibles.

Before buying plants, measure door widths and stairways to ensure you can move your plants up to the roof—you may need a crane for heavy containers and large trees.

Combine a collection of green foliage plants on a city roof terrace. Choose hostas, rhododendrons, and wind-tolerant shrubs, together with sculptural pines, and plant in decorative wooden and terra-cotta containers.

Edge a terrace with a garden of flowers and foliage in pots and raised beds. Select seasonal favorites, like chrysanthemums, salvias, and sedums, and use evergreen bushes to shield your space from the neighbors' windows.

Above left **Use black-stemmed bamboo** *in three galvanized containers to create a living sculpture on a terrace. The evergreen foliage provides a year-round windbreak.*

Above **Secure wood trellis to a wall** *and suspend a series of metal troughs filled with Ophiopogon and strawberries to dress up a modern balcony.*

Left **High above the city,** *the wind can make a roof terrace uncomfortable, but a range of grasses, such as Miscanthus, Anemanthele, and Calamagrostis, planted in large metal containers, will provide some shelter.*

Decorative windowsills

Give a windowsill an instant face-lift with a collection of pots or a windowbox crammed with any compact plants that grab your interest. For a year-round display, try a selection of small bushes or a neat topiary as a backdrop to a group of ever-changing seasonal flowers and bulbs. Edibles are another possibility, with pots of herbs, salad leaves, and tomatoes taking a place of pride on a sunny sill. Remember to attach pots firmly to high windowsills to prevent accidents.

Year-round displays

South-facing or in shade, you can use any windowsill space for plants and edibles. Foodies can grow their own vegetables, herbs, and fruit, while stylish box topiary will suit a period home. Alternatively, create a cottage garden in a windowbox using tiny pinks, trailing campanulas, and a selection of herbs. The sheltered, relatively warm conditions will also allow you to experiment with tender plants that may not survive in the garden; in urban areas scented geraniums and other tender summer perennials may overwinter on a sunny sill.

Sun and shelter provide perfect conditions for ripening dwarf tomatoes, such as 'Balconi Red.' Terra-cotta pots mirror the warm tones of the tomatoes. Water them daily for good results.

Group your favorite herbs on a sill so that you can just open the window to pick a few leaves. Sage, parsley, rosemary, basil, fennel, and tarragon be happy in a warm sunny site, while lavender and scented geraniums add a splash of color.

Above **Create an elegant picture** *by decorating the front of a period house with box pyramids, white geraniums, and ivy in a black container.*

Far left **Celebrate spring with daffodils** *in a galvanized metal windowbox.*

Center **Trailing ivy** *spilling from tiny pots suspended from large hooks makes an elegant display.*

Above right **Create a simple design** *by mixing white and purple pansies.*

Left **Reflect summer's abundance** *with a large, deep window-box filled with petunias, Thunbergia, and Jamesbrittenia.*

House warmers

The easiest way to breathe life into your home is to introduce a few well-chosen houseplants. Cheaper than a makeover and instantly rewarding, there's an option for almost every room—from elegant palms in a formal living room, to a riot of spring flowers on a sunny windowsill.

Perfect pairings

Houseplants make beautiful displays when paired with the right container, so take time to find the perfect pot. Elegant modern interiors are enhanced by sleek ceramics, metallic pots, neutral tones, and simple designs, while bright colors and sculptural shapes will contribute to a funky, contemporary décor. Match your pots with foliage plants, such as ferns, elephant's ears, and succulents. If you favor shabby chic or a cozy country style, try herbs and flowering houseplants, such as primulas and African violets, in distressed galvanized pots, wicker baskets, rattan pots, or recycled containers.

Right **A classic white ceramic pot** *complements the smooth lines and fresh green and white of the peace lily,* Spathiphyllum.

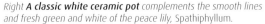

Cook's favorites, *such as basil and parsley, can be kept close at hand in the kitchen on a waterproof tray set into a rustic wooden planter.*

For a splash of 60s chic, *pair striped, glazed ceramic pots with spiky-topped spider plants,* Chlorophytum laxum.

Informal groups *of* Aeschynanthus, Begonia *Hiemalis Group,* Adiantum, Soleirolia, *and* Saintpaulia *in mixed glazed pots create a flower garden on a windowsill.*

Far left **Contrast the pink bracts** and grassy foliage of zany Tillandsia with cool, elegant white pots.

Left **Create an office setting** for a group of echeverias and other succulents in mixed pots in an old metal cabinet drawer.

Center left **Team fiery bromeliads** with ivy in rattan baskets on a well-lit windowsill out of direct sun.

Far left, bottom **A trio of distressed ceramic pots** add design magic to the flowing stems and tiny leaves of mind-your-own-business, Soleirolia soleirolii.

Left **Bring spring indoors** with a basket brimming with primulas, Hyacinthus 'Pink Pearl,' Viola cornuta 'Sorbet Coconut Duet,' Narcissus 'Inbal,' and ivy. Line the basket with plastic, and set plants in small plastic pots inside.

FOLIAGE AND FLOWERS

Whether you're looking for seasonal sensations or a container display to turn heads all year round, you'll find a wealth of ideas in this chapter. Choose bold houseplants for modern containers to inject color and texture into your home and pots of ornamental trees, shrubs, perennials, and annuals to transform outdoor spaces with fabulous flowers and lush foliage.

Create focal points with trees *in large pots, or convey a country-garden style with baskets of seasonal blooms. Orchids are a must for modern interiors, while tender foliage plants will brighten up windowsills.*

Selecting ornamental plants

Grow your plants in the conditions they enjoy, and you'll be rewarded with healthy, thriving specimens. Some prefer warm sunny sites, others do best in shade, while many are not too fussy and will cope with both. Use these checklists to help you choose plants that are best suited to your home or garden environment, and check the page references for more details.

Pairing plants with sites

Plants evolve to cope with their natural environments, and you'll get the best from yours by providing similar conditions. In most cases, plants with small, silvery, or hairy leaves are from sunny areas, such as the Mediterranean and alpine regions, where their foliage provides protection from the sun. Those with large, dark leaves have evolved to trap as much sunlight as possible in the dimly lit conditions on a forest or woodland floor and will be happiest in shade. Many flowering plants perform best in sun, as they are more visible to insects that pollinate them, while some with pale blooms become luminous in the evenings because they are pollinated by nocturnal insects.

This sophisticated arrangement *pairs* Fatsia japonica, *which thrives in partial shade, with* Pelargonium *'Lady Plymouth,' one of the few pelargoniums that can cope with some shade.* Alocasia *is also happy in filtered light and completes the plan.*

Spring displays *of violas, aubretia, and wallflowers will bloom best in a sunny place, while grassy sedges tolerate sun and shade.*

PLANTS FOR SUNNY SITES

- Aeonium pp.78–9
- *Alpines p.121, pp.134–5*
- Aster p.144
- *Bamboo pp.54–5*
- *Bananas pp.48–9*
- Caltha palustris p.137
- Canna pp.50–1
- Chamaerops humilis p.73
- Clematis pp.104–5
- Cordyline australis p.67
- Dahlia pp.130–1
- Dianthus p.41

- Echeveria pp.78–9
- Erysimum p.120
- Gaillardia p.133
- Gerbera p.132
- Graptopetalum p.84
- *Grasses pp.146–7*
- Hamamelis and Lonicera pp.44–5
- Hebe p.129
- Hedychium densiflorum p.65
- Heliotropium arborescens p.41
- Hibiscus p.129

- Ipomoea p.107
- Iris laevigata p.137
- Juncus ensifolius p.137
- Lathyrus odoratus p.109
- *Lavender pp.38–39*
- Lilium pp.42–3
- Lobelia p.137
- Lotus berthelotii p.53
- Malus p.119
- Melianthus major p.65
- Nymphaea pp.136–7

- Pelargonium p.133
- Phormium p.66
- Prunus p.119
- Rhodochiton p.106
- Roses pp.126–7
- Solenostemon p.52
- Syringa p.118
- Tetrapanax p.65
- Thunbergia p.107
- *Tulips pp.116–7*
- Viola p.120
- Yucca p.67
- Zantedeschia p.137

PLANTS FOR SHADY OR PARTIALLY SHADY SITES

- Acer palmatum pp.68–9
- Arisaema p.53
- Astilboides p.71
- Azalea pp.122–3
- Cotoneaster p.145
- Daphne tangutica p.37
- Equisetum hyemale p.137
- Eriobotrya japonica p.65
- Fatsia japonica p.64
- Galanthus p.115
- Gunnera p.70
- Hardy ferns pp.96–7
- Hardy fuchsias pp.94–5
- Heliotropium arborescens p.41
- Heuchera p.40, p.99
- Hosta p.98
- Hyacinthus p.36
- Hydrangea p.128
- Iris reticulata p.115
- Narcissus p.114
- Nicotiana p.40
- Phormium p.66
- Rhododendron pp.122–3
- Rodgersia p.71
- Sedges p.147
- Tetrapanax p.65
- Topiary pp.142–3
- Trachelospermum p.108
- Trachycarpus fortunei p.72
- Viburnum x burkwoodii p.37
- Viola p.120
- Zantedeschia p.137

Elegant Nicotiana *is happy* in some shade, while petunias prefer sun but will flower in a site that's shaded for part of the day.

PLANTS THAT TOLERATE EXPOSED SITES

- Alpines p.121, pp.134–5
- Androsace villosa var. jacquemontii p.121
- Aubrieta p.121
- Cotoneaster p.145
- Daphne p.37
- Galanthus p.115
- Gentiana acaulis p.121
- Grasses pp.146–7
- Iris reticulata p.115
- Leontopodium alpinum p.121
- Narcissus p.114
- Saxifraga p.121
- Sedum rupestre p.135
- Sempervivum p.134
- Sedges p.147

Sempervivum tectorum

PLANTS FOR THE HOME

- Abutilon x hybridum p.139
- Aechmea p.63
- Agave p.81
- Aloe p.81
- Alocasia x amazonica p.60
- Ananas comosus p.77
- Anthurium p.63
- Begonia pp.100–1
- Blechnum gibbum p.103
- Bougainvillea p.113
- Brugmansia and Gardenia augusta p. 47
- Cacti pp.82–3
- Calathea makoyana p.61
- Chamaedorea elegans p.56
- Clivia p.149
- Codiaeum p.61
- Cycas revoluta p.57
- Cyclamen persicum p.125
- Epipremnum aureum p.103
- Ficus elastica p.76
- Gloriosa p.112
- Hardenbergia p.113
- Hibiscus rosa-sinensis p.138
- Hippeastrum p.148
- Hoya p.46
- Jasminum polyanthum p.111
- Lantana camara p.139
- Medinilla p.62
- Monstera deliciosa p.59
- Narcissus and Hyacinthus pp.150–1
- Orchids pp.86–93
- Pericallis x hybrida p.125
- Philodendron p.59
- Rhapis excelsa p.57
- Saintpaulia p.141
- Sansevieria p.102
- Schefflera p.58
- Sedum morganianum p.81
- Smithiantha p.75
- Solanum p.149
- Stephanotis p.110
- Streptocarpus p.140
- Stromanthe p.77
- Tacca p.74

PLANTS THAT NEED A SHELTERED SITE

- Arisaema p.53
- Bamboos pp.54–5
- Canna pp.50–1
- Chamaerops humilis p.73
- Cordyline australis p.67
- Dahlia pp.130–1
- Echeveria and Aeonium pp.78–9
- Eriobotrya japonica p.65
- Gaillardia p.133
- Gerbera p.132
- Gunnera p.70
- Hardy fuchsias pp.94–5
- Hebe p.129
- Hedychium densiflorum p.65
- Hibiscus p.129
- Ipomoea p.107
- Kalanchoe p.85
- Lathyrus odoratus p.109
- Lotus berthelotii p.53
- Melianthus major p.65
- Pelargonium p.133
- Petunia p.40
- Rhodochiton p.106
- Solenostemon p.52
- Tetrapanax p.65
- Thunbergia p.107
- Trachelospermum p.108
- Trachycarpus fortunei p.72
- Yucca filamentosa p.67

Spring fragrance

With the darkest days of winter at an end, the new season greets us with the arrival of spring bulbs and flowering shrubs. Pots planted with those noted for their fragrance will lift your spirits further as they fill the air with sweet perfume. Place them in a prominent spot close to the kitchen door, windows, or seating areas, then get up close, breathe in deeply, and enjoy these spring treasures.

Spring bulbs

Plants used
Hyacinths, pussy willow stems

Height and spread
H 12in (30cm)
S 3in (7cm)

Exposure
Sun or partial shade

Temperature needs
Hardy to 5°F (-15°C)

Suitable pot size
8in (20cm) or larger

Suitable container material
Terra-cotta, stone, ceramic, or plastic pots placed inside decorative outer containers

Compost type
Bulb fiber

Spring bulbs are among the easiest plants to grow—plant them in the fall and simply wait a few months for them to burst through the soil. While many provide colorful flowers, some offer even better value with a beautiful scent. Hyacinths are highly fragrant and available in a wide range of colors, including white, yellow, pink, purple, and red. Some muscari or grape hyacinths are also scented—choose the yellow *Muscari macrocarpum* 'Golden Fragrance' for the best perfume. To complete your fragrant displays, add scented daffodils, such as the small-cupped jonquils and tazettas, and pheasant eyes.

SITING YOUR PLANTS
Flank your front door with pots of scented bulbs so that their fragrance greets you each time you enter the house. In the back garden, place pots on patios, close to paths, or by seating areas, raising them up on tables, chairs, or window ledges to intensify their effect.

Hyacinths have a strong fragrance and make a decorative display when planted in a cluster in a basket with stems of furry pussy willows.

TOP TIP: CARE AFTER FLOWERING

Many people treat spring bulbs like annuals and compost them once they have started to fade, but they can be retained for repeat performances year after year. To do this, remove the withered flowers, apply a liquid fertilizer to the leaves, and allow the foliage to die back naturally. Then lift the bulbs from the pot, knock off any excess compost, and allow them to dry. Store the bulbs in brown paper bags, label, and keep in a cool, dark place until fall when you can plant them out again.

Scented shrubs

Plants used
Daphne tangutica;
Viburnum x
burkwoodii

Height and spread
Daphne tangutica:
H 3ft (1m) S 3ft (1m);
Viburnum x
burkwoodii: H 5ft
(1.5m) S 5ft (1.5m)

Exposure
Sun or partial shade

Temperature needs
Hardy to 5°F (-15°C)

Suitable pot size
12–18in (30–45cm)

Suitable container material
Terra-cotta, stone,
metal, wood

Suitable compost
Soil-based compost,
e.g., John Innes No. 3

The spring shrub *Viburnum* x *burkwoodii* makes a fabulous centerpiece on a patio when grown in a contemporary gray stone pot. Evergreen in sheltered areas, its dense clusters of white, sweetly scented flowers will lift any container display. To prolong the interest, underplant with trailing plants, primroses, and evergreen grasses. Part of a large family of deciduous and evergreen shrubs, other viburnums worth growing for their scented spring flowers include *V. farreri, V.* x *juddii,* and *V. carlesii.*

FRAGRANT OPTIONS
Many daphnes are also renowned for their early scented blooms. Among the best are *Daphne tangutica*, which has pink tubular flowers and *D.* x *burkwoodii,* whose white flowers appear for a few weeks from late spring. Other fragrant shrubs to consider include *Ribes odoratum, Osmanthus delavayi,* and *Euphorbia mellifera,* a large evergreen with honey-scented flowers.

Above: **The evergreen foliage** of Daphne tangutica *provides a backdrop for the pale pink, scented flowers.*

Large shrubs *like this* Viburnum x burkwoodii *need pots filled with soil-based compost and a spring application of granular fertilizer. Planted with primulas, ivy, and the grass* Phalaris 'Dwarf Garters,' *it creates a stunning effect.*

Lavender scents

Nothing is more evocative of a summer's day than the scent
of lavender wafting across the garden on a gentle breeze.
A magnet for bees and butterflies, the perfume is also used
in aromatherapy to soothe the nerves and lower stress levels,
making lavender the perfect plant for a relaxing seating area.

Plants used
*Lavandula
angustifolia* 'Hidcote'

Height and spread
H 24in (60cm)
S 30in (75cm)

Exposure
Full sun

Temperature needs
Hardy to 5°F (-15°C)

Suitable pot size
8–15in (20–40cm)

**Suitable container
material**
Terra-cotta, stone,
metal

Compost type
Loam-based
compost, e.g., John
Innes No. 3, with
extra sand

Lavender is a welcome addition to a patio, balcony, or garden,
with aromatic foliage that releases essential oils when warmed
by the sun and scented flowers that buzz with wildlife. One of
the best compact forms for a container is *Lavandula angustifolia*
'Hidcote,' a traditional English lavender with dark, highly scented,
purple flowers and silver-gray leaves. Alternatively, choose one
from the hundreds of other varieties, available in a range of
sizes, colors, and flower shapes.

Native to the Mediterranean region, lavenders love a warm,
sunny spot and do best in light, well-drained compost—they do
poorly with wet roots. Fill a large pot with a soil-based compost,
such as John Innes No. 3, mixed with some horticultural sand.
Largely trouble-free, plants last for years with the right care, and
are best planted on their own so that you can enjoy their
rounded shape without distraction, or mix several cultivars to
produce a combination of shades and long flowering season.

CARING FOR PLANTS

Mix some slow-release fertilizer into the surface of the compost
each spring, and water plants frequently in the summer.
Lavenders hate cold, wet soil, so elevate containers in the winter
to allow excess water to drain away. Although most forms can
be left outside all year round, overwinter tender varieties in
a frost-free place. Also keep a close eye out for metallic green
and purple rosemary beetles, which strip the plants' leaves.

Center: **English
lavender***, such as
forms of* Lavandula
angustifolia, *have the
strongest scent of all
the species. Choose
a large rounded
container to balance
the mound of flowers
and foliage.*

TOP TIP: PRUNING LAVENDER

If left unpruned, lavender will
develop a mass of leggy, woody,
unattractive stems. To avoid this,
keep plants compact, bushy, and
floriferous by trimming off old
flowerheads as they fade in the
summer. Prune plants harder in
early spring, but don't cut into old,
leafless wood as it won't reshoot.

Choosing lavenders

Lavandula angustifolia *'Hidcote'* is covered with spikes of heavily scented purple flowers in midsummer.

Lavandula stoechas *'Kew Red'* is a tender form with striking cerise flowers topped with pinky-white "ears."

Lavandula angustifolia *'Loddon Pink'* is a compact shrub with soft pink flowers and narrow gray foliage.

Lavandula angustifolia *'Munstead'* is slightly shorter than 'Hidcote,' with bluish-purple blooms and gray foliage.

Lavandula *'Willow Vale'* is a French type with deep purple flowers topped by violet "ears." Likes a sheltered spot.

Lavandula x chaytoriae *'Sawyers'* has conical purple flowers on long spikes above a mass of silver foliage.

Lavandula angustifolia *'Nana Alba'* is a dwarf white form of English lavender, perfect for a small patio container.

Lavandula pinnata is a tender species with long stems of spear-shaped, purple flowerheads and furry, white leaves.

Summer perfume

For a dazzling display of scented flowers, try a few annuals, such as the tobacco plant, *Nicotiana*, and richly perfumed cherry pie, *Heliotropium*. Ideal for mixed displays, combine these scented stars with other brightly colored blooms as part of a summer plan. Where space is limited, try the spicy fragrance of alpine pinks as a decorative table centerpiece.

Tobacco plant *Nicotiana*

Plants used
Nicotiana; Petunia;
Solenostemon;
Heuchera

Height and spread
Nicotiana: H 24in
(60cm) S 10in (25cm);
Trailing petunia:
S 16in (40cm);
Solenostemon:
H 8in (20cm)
S 12in (30cm);
Heuchera: H 24in
(60cm) S 12in (30cm)

Exposure
Sun or partial shade

Temperature needs
Plants not hardy
below 32°F (0°C)

Suitable pot size
14in (35cm)

Suitable container material
Glazed ceramic,
stone, terra-cotta

Compost type
Multi-purpose

Here's a smoking hot container recipe that won't damage your health. The flowering tobacco plant, *Nicotiana*, forms the centerpiece, its trumpet-shaped, scented flowers blooming until the frost. The unusual acid-green flowers of this annual contrast dramatically with the red leaves of *Solenostemon,* or coleus, whose fiery shades echo those of the scarlet trailing petunia, which tumbles down the sides of the container. Plant this group in late spring, starting with the tobacco plant in the center, followed by the coleus, and green *Heuchera*, and finally dot the petunias in the remaining gaps. Set outside in a sunny spot when all threat of frost has passed.

COLOR CHOICES
If lime-green flowers aren't to your taste, tobacco plants are available in many other colors, including white, red, lilac, pink, and purple. However, check your seed or plant packs, since not all *Nicotiana* are heavily scented. You could also watch for dark purple petunias, most of which are fragrant.

TOP TIP: SOWING TOBACCO PLANTS FROM SEED

Nicotiana is easy to raise indoors from seed each spring. Fill small pots or cell trays with seed compost and sow seeds evenly on the surface. Do not cover. Water and place in a light spot to germinate. When seedlings are large enough to move, transfer them carefully into individual 3in (7cm) pots.

An elegant combination *of greens and pinks, this display will bloom from early summer until the frost.*

Cherry pie *Heliotropium*

Plants used
Heliotropium arborescens

Height and spread
H 18in (45cm)
S 12in (30cm)

Exposure
Light shade or full sun

Temperature needs
Not hardy below 32°F (0°C)

Suitable pot size
8in (20cm)

Suitable container material
Stone, plastic, glazed ceramic, terra-cotta

Compost type
Multi-purpose

Some plants simply don't live up to their names, but cherry pie does not fail. A bushy annual, its dark green leaves are topped with dense clusters of tiny purple flowers that pack a fruity punch that instantly reminds you of a freshly baked cherry pie. Perfect on their own in small pots or used as fillers around larger specimens, *Heliotropium* is easy to grow from seed sown indoors in early spring (*follow advice for tobacco plants in Top Tip box opposite*).

SIZE OPTIONS

One of the most popular forms, *Heliotropium* 'Dwarf Marine,' reaches 14in (35cm), while 'Baby Blue Improved' grows to just 8in (20cm) making it perfect for window boxes. For larger plants, try x Hybrid Marine, which reaches 18in (45cm).

Heliotropium x **Hybrid Marine**

Pretty pinks *Dianthus*

Plants used
Dianthus 'Devon Flores' (syn. 'Starry Night'); *Frankenia thymifolia*

Height and spread
Dianthus: H 7in (17cm) S 7in (17cm); *Frankenia*: H 8in (20cm) S 12in (30cm)

Exposure
Full sun

Temperature needs
Hardy to 5°F (-15°C)

Suitable pot size
10in (25cm)

Suitable container material
Terra-cotta, stone

Compost type
Well-drained, soil-based compost, e.g., John Innes No. 2, with added sand

Alpine pinks make great container plants, offering dainty clove-scented flowers on sturdy stems above a mat of gray leaves. Partner them with other alpines, such as the creeping *Frankenia*, whose stems of rose-pink flowers will tumble loosely down the sides of a pot. *Dianthus* 'Devon Flores' has bright magenta, double flowers that echo the warm shade of the *Frankenia* blooms.

COLOR SELECTIONS

Pinks come in many colors, from white to pink and purple, with striped, flecked, or bicolored flowers, as well as single and double blooms.

Easy to maintain, *Dianthus* are drought tolerant and need little attention, apart from watering a couple of times a week in the summer and an application of slow-release fertilizer worked into the compost in the spring. Protect plants from winter rain, and remove fading blooms to encourage more to form.

Perfect partners, Dianthus *'Devon Flores' and* Frankenia thymifolia *combine well in a small terra-cotta bowl.*

FRAGRANT FLOWERS

Elegant lilies *Lilium*

Large, dramatic flowers in an array of colors make lilies a favorite for both garden and home, but those with the added bonus of scent are the most prized. The intoxicating perfume of the Oriental hybrids will fill the air of a large garden, while the delicate flowers of some species have a more subtle fragrance.

FRAGRANT FLOWERS

Plants used
Lilium formosanum var. *pricei; Ipomoea batatas* 'Margarita;' *Gerbera* Garvinea 'Nikki'

Height and spread
Lilium: H 12in (30cm); *Ipomoea:* H 6in (15cm), S 3ft (1m); *Gerbera:* H & S 18in (45cm)

Exposure
Sun or dappled shade

Temperature needs
These lilies are hardy down to 23°F (-5°C)

Suitable pot size
12in (30cm)

Suitable container material
Glazed ceramic, terra-cotta, stone

Compost type
Soil-based compost, e.g., John Innes No. 2, with extra sand

Many lilies are towering beasts best suited to the border, but the species *Lilium formosanum* var. *pricei* is a knee-high beauty with large flowers that match those of a regal lily for size and scent. Although this compact plant looks good on its own in a container, where it will happily spread to provide a bigger and better display each summer, it is also perfect for combining with other flowers and foliage to produce a long-lasting summer design.

The blooms are the main feature of the lily, while its uninspiring foliage can be disguised with the leaves and daisy-like flowers of a hardy gerbera, and the lime-green sweet potato vine, *Ipomoea batatas* 'Margarita.' This bushy, trailing plant produces masses of lush growth throughout summer and early autumn until stopped in its tracks by frost.

CARING FOR LILIES

Its compact shape means that *Lilium formosanum* var. *pricei* doesn't need staking, but taller lilies will require stakes to support their flower stems. Water pots a few times a week in the summer, and in the fall remove and compost the frosted *Ipomoea*. Garvinea gerberas are hardy down to about 23°F (-5°C), as is the lily, and if the pot is set close to the house in a sheltered location and protected from excessive rain, it should survive the winter outside. However, if temperatures threaten to fall below 23°F (-5°C), bring the pot inside. In the spring, feed with a slow-release granular fertilizer worked into the top layer of compost.

*Center: **Mix-and-match scented lilies**, such as this Lilium formosanum var. pricei, with summer flowers, like gerberas, and trailing foliage, such as the sweet potato vine.*

TOP TIP: PLANTING LILY BULBS

Lily bulbs are best planted in the fall or spring. Fill the bottom third of a pot with compost and add 1¼in (3cm) of horticultural sand. Lay the bulbs on the sand on their sides; this allows water to drain from their scales, preventing them from rotting. Finally, top off the container with more compost.

Choosing lilies

Lilium *'Journey's End'* *is not for the faint-hearted, with large, blowsy, pink, scented flowers with white markings.*

Lilium nepalense *is ideal for a shady container. This graceful species has green flowers with swept-back petals.*

Lilium medeoloides *has short stems, ideal for pots, that bear clusters of small orange flowers. Prefers light shade.*

Lilium speciosum *var.* rubrum *has highly fragrant, recurved blooms flushed pink with crimson spots.*

Lilium martagon, *the common Turk's cap lily, is happy in sun or partial shade and has dark pink, speckled flowers.*

Lilium pyrenaicum *is grown for its scented, nodding, yellow Turk's cap flowers. Ideal for sun or dappled shade.*

Lilium *'Star Gazer'* *is tall and looks best in a big pot. Its large, red, upward-facing flowers emit a powerful scent.*

Lilium *'Sterling Star'* *is a compact lily perfect for pots, with upward-facing snow-white, slightly fragrant flowers.*

FRAGRANT FLOWERS

Winter surprise
Hamamelis and *Lonicera*

You don't need large borders to enjoy winter-flowering shrubs. Blooming when the rest of the garden is gloomy and lackluster, witch hazel, *Hamamelis mollis*, and winter honeysuckle, *Lonicera fragrantissima*, will bring it back to life. Grow them in large pots on a patio; you can then use their leafy growth later as a backdrop to spring and summer flower displays.

Plants used
Hamamelis mollis;
Lonicera fragrantissima

Height and spread
Hamamelis: H 6ft
(1.8m) S 4ft (1.2m);
Lonicera: H 4ft (1.2m)
S 4ft (1.2m).

Exposure
Sunny and sheltered

Temperature needs
Plants hardy to 5°F
(-15°C)

Suitable pot size
18in (45cm).or larger

Suitable container material
Stone, terra-cotta, plastic

Compost type
Hamamelis: John Innes ericaceous compost; *Lonicera*: soil-based compost

Winter-flowering shrubs are a luxury in a small garden where every plant must earn its keep, but you can still make space for these seasonal stars. Plants like Chinese witch hazel, *Hamamelis mollis*, can be grown in a pot on a patio or balcony and then placed in a prominent spot when the heavily scented, spidery yellow flowers appear on the naked stems. Choose a witch hazel from a palette of yellow, orange, red, or purple flowers, and look out for those with twisted or crimped petals. The winter honeysuckle, *Lonicera fragrantissima*, is another prized plant, with highly fragrant, creamy-yellow flowers, which are produced in greater numbers when it's grown in a sheltered spot.

PLANTING LARGE BUSHES IN POTS
To prevent bushes from becoming waterlogged, add a layer of broken clay pot pieces to the bottom of the container so that the drainage holes do not clog up with compost. Add a layer of compost and place your shrub on it to check that the top of the rootball is 2in (5cm) beneath the lip of the pot. Then slip the bush out of its pot, place the pot on the compost, and fill in around it with more soil. Remove the pot to leave a hole exactly the right size for the bush's rootball. Place the bush in the hole, firm around the roots with compost, water well, and add a mulch (*see p. 238*).

TOP TIP: PRUNING WITCH HAZELS

These bushes can be pruned when the flowers start to fade in early spring. First, remove dead or diseased wood, any branches that spoil the shape, or crossing stems that are rubbing against one another. *Hamamelis* are very slow growing, so avoid cutting back very hard or too frequently. Prune back shoot tips to keep plants within bounds and to encourage bushy growth.

Bring witch hazel stems indoors to enjoy their scent inside and out. Cut stems that won't ruin the overall shape of the bush when removed.

Choosing scented shrubs

Hamamelis virginiana *produces small flowers in the fall, just as the leaves are falling. Tolerant of urban pollution.*

Hamamelis x intermedia *'Pallida'* *has clusters of fragrant, sulfur-yellow flowers from mid- to late winter.*

Hamamelis x intermedia *'Jelena'* *decorates pots with large, coppery orange blooms from early to midwinter.*

Lonicera fragrantissima *is a bushy semi-evergreen. Its highly scented, creamy white flowers appear in winter.*

Hamamelis x intermedia *'Arnold Promise'* *produces bright yellow flowers throughout the winter and makes a spectacular display in a large, frost-proof terra-cotta pot.*

FRAGRANT FLOWERS

Fragrant home

Breathe new life into your interior space with a selection of scented house plants. Perfect for a light airy room, such as a sunroom, these tender beauties produce beautiful flowers that provide interest for many months from summer through to early autumn. With care, they'll repeat their perfumed performance year after year.

Wax flower *Hoya*

FRAGRANT FLOWERS

Plant used
Hoya lanceolata
subsp. *bella*

Height and spread
H & S 18in (45cm)

Exposure
Bright spot indoors

Temperature needs
Min. 41°F (5°C)

Suitable pot size
8in (20cm)

Suitable container material
Glazed ceramic, plastic

Compost type
Soil-based compost. If possible, improve drainage by adding equal parts leaf mold, horticultural sand, charcoal, and crushed bark to the compost.

Native to a large area from the Himalayas to northern Burma, the wax flower, *Hoya lanceolata* subsp. *bella*, is a shrubby evergreen that features clusters of star-shaped, white, summer flowers with red centers. Although their scent is noticeable during the day, the perfume is particularly potent when night falls. The pendulous stems make it perfect for a hanging basket, or tie them to slim stakes in a pot. Another popular wax flower, *Hoya carnosa*, has long climbing stems, which can be trained up a trellis or a similar support. It flowers slightly longer, from late spring until fall. Both plants can be grown outdoors in the summer in a sheltered sunny spot with some protection from the midday sun.

WATERING NEEDS

Water wax flowers regularly while growing, during the spring and summer, and feed every four weeks with a balanced, liquid house-plant fertilizer. Occasionally mist the leaves to increase humidity around the plant. Reduce the amount of water given in the winter.

TOP TIP: PRUNING AND TRAINING

Bushy wax flowers need supporting with frames or stakes to prevent the stems flopping over. Climbers potentially grow up to 12ft (4m) or more, but can be kept in check by training them up spiral supports or a trellis that fits within your space. Simply tie the flexible stems onto their supports with soft twine and train them to fill out the trellis. If necessary, lightly prune *Hoya* plants after flowering to keep growth controlled.

Simple ceramic containers contrast well with the Hoya's busy foliage and heads of small flowers.

Angel's trumpet *Brugmansia*

Plant used
Brugmansia x
candida 'Grand
Marnier'

Height and spread
H 6ft (1.8m)
S 3ft (90cm)

Exposure
Light spot in
direct sun

Temperature needs
Min. 45°F (7°C)

Suitable pot size
12in (30cm)

**Suitable container
material**
Glazed ceramic,
plastic, metal

Compost type
Well-drained,
loam-based compost

Brugmansia x *candida* 'Grand Marnier'

Angel's trumpet is a large, dramatic plant, ideal as a focal point in a sunny room. Often grown as a standard, the form 'Grand Marnier' produces a bushy head of green leaves that provide a foil for the heavily scented, pale peach, trumpet-shaped flowers that drip from its stems from summer until fall. You can display *Brugmansia* outdoors in summer, but bring it back inside when night temperatures start to fall. Also keep it away from children and pets, as both the plant and its blooms are poisonous.

ANNUAL CARE
Keep the compost on the dry side over the winter, then increase watering when the plant is in growth. *Brugmansia* is a heavy feeder and responds well to a liquid fertilizer every two weeks in summer. In late spring, prune to keep it in shape, and trim off dead or spindly growth.

Cape jasmine *Gardenia augusta*

Plant used
Gardenia augusta

Height and spread
H 24in (60cm)
S 18in (45cm)

Exposure
Bright, but not in
direct sun

Temperature needs
Summer:
Daytime: 70–75°F
(21–24°C)
Nighttime: 59–65°F
(15–18°C)
Winter: 61°F (16°C)

Suitable pot size
8in (20cm)

**Suitable container
material**
Glazed ceramic,
plastic

Compost type
Soil-based
ericaceous compost

Not for the beginner, the Cape jasmine requires a lot of care and attention, but get its growing conditions right and you'll be rewarded with large, waxy, white, heavily scented flowers from summer until fall, held against a backdrop of glossy green leaves. *Gardenia* dislikes direct sunlight, so place plants on a west-facing windowsill during the summer and a south-facing windowsill over the winter.

TEMPERATURE REGULATION
The Cape jasmine is a bit of a diva and conditions must be right for it to perform. To guarantee a flower display, plants need a nighttime temperature of 59–65°F (15–18°C) and daytime temperature of 70–75°F (21–24°C). In the winter, plants prefer cooler conditions of around 61°F (16°C). Fluctuating temperatures can upset flowering, and plants should not be moved when in bud, as this may cause them to drop prematurely.

**Use soft water or
rainwater** to prevent
Gardenia leaves from
yellowing, and apply
fertilizer for lime haters.

Go bananas

Create your own leafy jungle with pots of bananas. The plants boast huge leaves that unfurl majestically from spring until fall, and they are ideal for large containers. If you place them in a sunny, sheltered location, and feed and water them regularly, bananas will put on an exotic display for many years. Plants will also need protection from frost in the winter.

Plant used
Ensete ventricosum 'Maurelii' (Abyssinian banana)

Height and spread
H up to 7ft (2.2m)
S up to 6ft (2m)

Exposure
Full sun

Temperature needs
Not hardy below 32°F (0°C)

Suitable pot size
Min. 18in (45cm)

Suitable container material
Stone, terra-cotta

Compost type
Soil-based compost, e.g., John Innes No. 3

Although these ornamental bananas won't produce edible fruit if you grow them outside in your garden, the foliage more than makes up for it. Huge paddle-shaped leaves unfurl during the growing season from the top of a stout trunk to form a leafy, palm-like canopy. Natives of China, Japan, and other parts of Asia, bananas fall into three groups: *Musa, Ensete,* and *Musella.* Most have plain, jade-green foliage, but the leaves of some are attractively blushed or striped red, or variegated.

To prevent them from blowing over in strong winds, bananas are best grown in large, heavy containers filled with soil-based compost. Place pots in a warm, sunny, sheltered spot—the leaves of bananas shred easily if they are in a wind tunnel. Water plants regularly, but guard against waterlogged compost.

FEEDING PLANTS

Bananas are greedy plants and will grow taller and produce more leaves when given copious applications of fertilizer. Get the plant off to a flying start in the spring by applying a general fertilizer, and then add a liquid feed every time it is watered. Supplement this every month during the growing season by sprinkling blood, fish, and bone over the compost surface, and water it in well.

TOP TIP: OVERWINTERING

If you have the space, bring bananas into a heated greenhouse, cool room indoors, or sunroom. If you have no space indoors, the hardier types can remain outside if you cover the compost with a layer of bark mulch and wrap the pot with bubble plastic or fabric. Cut off all the leaves, then stack lengths of duct tubing around the stem, filling the gap with straw. Cover the top with plastic or a tile to keep rain out.

*The **Abyssinian banana** produces magnificent, paddle-shaped, green and maroon leaves. Place it in a sheltered spot to protect the leaves from wind.*

Banana choices

Ensete ventricosum *is the green form of Abyssinian banana. Its long leaves are held upright like a shuttlecock.*

Some hybrid bananas *are attractively variegated—ideal for adding interest to a foliage display.*

Ensete ventricosum *'Tandarra Red' is a choice plant that carries huge red-flushed foliage.*

Musa basjoo *is the Japanese root-hardy banana. Widely available, it grows quickly and has massive green leaves.*

Team a colorful banana *with an underplanting of lime-green Ipomoea and Celosia argentea var. plumosa, which has dark red foliage to match the Ensete, and pinkish-red flowerheads.*

Colorful cannas

Turn up the heat in summer with tropical cannas. These sizzling sun lovers flower continuously from midsummer until fall, but their foliage provides a spectacular feature long before the blooms unfold. Both leaves and flowers come in many fiery shades reminiscent of carnival costumes from their native Brazil.

Plant used
Canna 'Durban'

Height and spread
H 5ft (1.5m)
S 16in (50cm)

Exposure
Full sun

Temperature needs
Not hardy below
32°F (0°C)

Suitable pot size
12in (30cm) or larger

Suitable container material
Stone, terra-cotta, glazed ceramic, plastic

Compost type
Soil-based compost, e.g., John Innes No. 3

Ideal in the center of a display of annual bedding plants, cannas look equally effective in pots on their own, or combined with containers of *Crocosmia, Colocasia,* and bananas to create a leafy, colorful, tropical design. Cannas are frost-tender perennials grown from rhizomes and produce tall stems of magnificent iris-like flowers in hot reds, oranges, and yellows. The blooms are often paired with equally flamboyant brightly colored or variegated foliage. *Canna* 'Durban' is one of the best, and features a combination of large, luminous orange flowers and dark red foliage with flamelike markings in red, pink, and orange. Others are grown for their dark leaves. *C.* 'Black Knight', for example, has sultry burgundy foliage that makes a great foil for its own deep red flowers and other summer blooms.

PROMOTING FLOWERING

Given a warm sheltered site where they can bask in full sun, cannas provide a long-lasting display, blooming from mid- to late summer, depending on the variety, and continuing to send out new flower shoots until the middle of autumn. However, if you attempt to grow them in even light shade, they are unlikely to bloom. As well as heat, plants enjoy moist conditions and must be watered frequently from spring to fall and never allowed to dry out. They are also extremely hungry, so for robust growth and optimum flower production, feed them every two weeks during the growing season with a balanced liquid feed. Also remove fading blooms, which helps to promote more to form.

Center: **Flickering like flames** *from an ornate pot, the leaves of Canna 'Durban' are set ablaze with an underplanting of fiery red impatiens and Cuphea.*

TOP TIP: OVERWINTERING AND DIVIDING CANNAS

To protect your plants over the winter, before the first frost in the fall cut back the leaves and flower stems to 1¼in (3cm) from the soil surface and move the pot to a frost-free shed or greenhouse. Keep the compost damp, but not overly wet, in the winter and then move plants back outside in late spring or early summer. Spring is also the time to divide rhizomes to make new plants. Clean the rhizomes of compost, then, using a clean sharp knife, cut them into sections, each with a bud, or eye. Pot the rhizome sections in fresh compost.

Canna choices

Canna *'Assaut'* is a tall plant, bearing dusky purple foliage and long stems of scarlet flowers from midsummer.

Canna *'Richard Wallace'* (syn. 'King Midas') is a robust plant with dark green leaves and golden yellow blooms.

Canna *'Black Knight'* has deep red flowers that stand out dramatically against a foil of dark burgundy foliage.

Canna *'Rosemond Coles'* produces vibrant red flowers with golden yellow margins above dark green leaves.

Canna *'Striata'* bears blazing orange flowers that sit above broad, oval, green leaves with bright yellow stripes.

Canna speciosa *'Tropical Rose'* is a dwarf form, with green leaves and pink flowers on knee-high stems.

Canna *'Durban'* produces bright orange flowers above bronze leaves with red, orange and pink stripes.

Canna *'Cleopatra'* is a compact plant with green leaves and flashy red and yellow flowers with contrasting flecks.

TROPICAL EFFECTS

Bright highlights

If your garden is in need of a lift, inject some color with tropical-looking flowers and foliage plants. Flame nettles are perfect for filling gaps in borders when spring or summer flowers have faded, or use them in a mixed container display. Parrot's beak provides interest at head height in baskets or flowing over the sides of tall pots, while *Arisaema* will brighten up shady spots.

Flame nettles *Solenostemon scutellarioides*

Plant used
Solenostemon
(mixed)

Height and spread
H 8in (20cm)
S 8in (20cm)

Exposure
Sun or partial shade

Temperature needs
Min. 60°F (15°C)

Suitable pot size
4in (10cm)

Suitable container material
Plastic, metal, stone, terra-cotta, baskets

Compost type
Multi-purpose compost

Known to generations of gardeners as coleus, and often sold as such, these leafy plants were long considered outdated, but are now back in vogue thanks to striking new forms with colorful and patterned foliage. Their vibrancy gives patio displays a lift, or use them to add color to border designs. Another idea is to use pots of flame nettles as underplanting around the stems of trees or shrubs in large containers.

Easy to grow from seed, young plants are also available from nurseries. Keep them well watered and repot young plants several times during the growing season. Prune stems to maintain a bushy shape and remove flowers, as the foliage loses intensity when plants bloom.

TOP TIP: PROTECTING PLANTS

In early autumn, place plants in a light, frost-free place where the temperature does not fall below 60°F (15°C). A warm windowsill or heated greenhouse is ideal. Cut back stems by about half and allow the compost to almost dry out between waterings; too much moisture at this time of year can lead to fungal diseases.

Buy young plants in spring and pot them in larger containers for a long display of vibrant foliage from summer to fall.

Parrot's beak *Lotus berthelotii*

Plant used
Lotus berthelotii

Height and spread
H 8in (20cm)
S indefinite

Exposure
Full sun

Temperature needs
Not hardy below
32°F (0°C)

Suitable pot size
12in (30cm)

Suitable container material
Plastic, terra-cotta, baskets

Compost type
Soil-based compost, e.g., John Innes No. 2

Lotus berthelotii **filling a large hanging basket.**

A close look at the red flowers that cover this evergreen plant immediately reveal how the parrot's beak got its common name. The other feature that makes it so popular is the trailing stems of gray ferny foliage, which makes it ideal for a hanging basket display or tumbling over the sides of a large container. Although it needs protection from frost in the winter, Parrot's beak is perfectly happy outside in the summer.

FLOWERING NEEDS
For maximum flower power, plants need around six to eight hours of sunlight each day, so place them in a warm, bright spot. Water plants regularly during the spring and summer, and feed with a liquid fertilizer every couple of weeks during the spring. Keep plants frost free in the winter and reduce watering (*follow advice for Flame nettles in the Top Tip box opposite*).

Arisaema *Arisaema candidissimum*

Plant used
Arisaema candidissimum

Height and spread
H 16in (40cm)
S 6in (15cm)

Exposure
Dappled shade

Temperature needs
Hardy down to 23°F (-5°C)

Suitable pot size
8in (20cm)

Suitable container material
Plastic, terra-cotta

Compost type
Soil-based compost, e.g., John Innes No. 3

A group of tuberous spring- and summer-flowering perennials originating from China, Japan, North America, and the Himalayas, arisaemas have curious flowers that in some species resemble the head of a cobra about to strike. The flowers are generally held on long stems and are often teamed with large leaves. Their sinister appearance is perhaps a hint that the plants are poisonous, but not all look quite so gruesome. *Arisaema candidissimum* appears more like whipped ice cream with its pink and white flowerhead, which are also delightfully scented.

SITING PLANTS
Arisaemas prefer the shade and are perfect for small, sheltered, urban gardens where they can survive the winter outside. Either display a group of plants together or use them to plug gaps in a bed or border. You can then whip the pots out of the border when they've finished flowering and the leaves have died back. Water regularly during the growing season, but keep compost just moist when plants are dormant in winter.

Elegants spathes in ice-cream colors protect the tiny flowers of Arisaema candidissimum.

Graceful bamboos

Bamboos instantly add a lush, tropical effect to gardens, patios, and balconies, and include many different varieties, with tall types suitable for large containers and more compact forms ideal for small spaces. Easy to look after and reliably hardy, these elegant evergreens provide interest all year round.

TROPICAL EFFECTS

Plant used
Pseudosasa japonica

Height and spread
H 10ft (3m)
S 4ft (1.2m)

Exposure
Full sun or partial shade

Temperature needs
Hardy to 5°F (-15°C)

Suitable pot size
18–24in (45–60cm)

Suitable container material
Metal, plastic, glazed ceramic

Compost type
Soil-based compost, e.g., John Innes No. 3

Bamboos are versatile plants and suit a range of garden styles and uses, whether you're looking for a focal point, backdrop, specimen to disguise an eyesore, or an airy screen to divide your space. Their main attractions are their decorative stems, which come in a range of colors, including golden yellow, black, green, and striped. Thriving in soil-based compost, such as John Innes No. 3, the larger bamboos, including *Pseudosasa, Sasa, Fargesia,* and *Phyllostachys,* need roomy pots that provide space for plants to spread. Containers made from metal, plastic, or with glazed finishes are ideal, but avoid terra-cotta, as this permeable material sucks moisture from the compost, which can cause bamboo foliage to dry out and turn yellow. Although some bamboos are rampant thugs in the garden, spreading via underground root systems, when grown in pots even vigorous species won't turn into unwanted guests. However, it is still wise to avoid plants that grow very quickly and require frequent repotting or dividing; all of those shown here are well behaved, requiring the minimum of maintenance, apart from watering.

CARING FOR BAMBOOS
Bamboos are thirsty plants and need regular watering to prevent the loss of foliage. If you have a number in pots, consider installing an automatic irrigation system to maintain moisture levels. Also apply a balanced fertilizer in the spring or early summer to promote a mass of new canes and healthy leaves. As plants mature, thin out heavily congested clumps by removing some of the thinner canes or older shoots that look beat up. Stripping leaves from the bottom third of the plants also helps to show off the canes.

TOP TIP: APPLY A DECORATIVE FINISH

Add interest to your container display and prevent weeds from growing on the compost around bamboos by covering the surface with an ornamental mulch. Choose a material that contrasts with the container and sets off the bamboo, such as pebbles, slate, colored gravel, or glass beads.

Tall and graceful, Phyllostachys bambusoides *'Castillonii' makes a beautiful screen if given a large container and plenty of water.*

Choosing a bamboo

Fargesia murielae produces masses of elegant, slim canes covered with lush green foliage. It also tolerates dry soils.

Sasa veitchii is a bushy bamboo with purple canes and variegated leaves that bleach to pale brown in the winter.

Phyllostachys vivax f. aureocaulis is a tall plant with bright yellow canes occasionally striped green.

Pleioblastus variegatus is happy in sun or shade. It forms knee-high stems of creamy-white and green foliage.

Contemporary galvanized containers filled with the arrow bamboo, Pseudosasa japonica, and topped with a gray slate mulch, make a sophisticated boundary for a modern city garden.

Potted palms

Elegant, happy in low light, and easy to look after, tropical palms make great specimens for clean, simple containers that show off their architectural forms. Use them as focal plants or as the backdrop for a group of indoor pots. Palms also make a good foil for exotic blooms and most are happy to spend the summer outside lending a hint of the tropics to a warm, sheltered patio.

Parlor palm *Chamaedorea elegans*

Plant used
Chamaedorea elegans

Height and spread
H 8ft (2.4m)
S 5ft (1.5m)

Exposure
Bright, but away from direct sunlight

Temperature needs
Min. 64°F (18°C)

Suitable pot size
12in (30cm)

Suitable container material
Glazed ceramic, stone, plastic

Compost type
Well-drained, multi-purpose compost

Popular in homes since Victorian times, and known by a number of common names, including parlor and table-top palm, this bushy plant is still widely grown for its exotic appearance and long fronds of shiny green leaves. Small specimens can be used to brighten up shelves or gaps in bookcases, while larger plants are ideal for livening up a shady corner or as focal points where their attractive fronds are on show. Plants are fairly slow growing, so buy a plant of a size that matches your space.

CARING FOR PARLOR PALMS
One of this plant's charms is that it is relatively undemanding. Water it regularly while in growth, keeping the compost on the moist side, but allow it to dry out between each watering in the winter. Feed your parlor palm every month during the spring and summer with a balanced liquid feed to keep the foliage lush and healthy. It will also enjoy a vacation outside on the patio in the summer and makes a great foil for colorful bedding and tropical blooms.

> **TOP TIP: KEEPING FRONDS HEALTHY**
>
> If the tips of fronds turn brown, you probably need to raise the humidity around the palm. Spray plants regularly with a mister or sponge the leaves—the latter also helps to remove any dirt. Conversely, this type of damage can be caused by root rot due to overwatering, so check that the bottom of the container is not filled with water. Brown leaves are sometimes the result of scorching; keep parlor palms in a cool, shady spot away from the midday sun.

Fronds of tropical-looking foliage lighten gloomy corners and lend a touch of class to a minimal interior décor.

Sago palm *Cycas revoluta*

Plant used
Cycas revoluta

Height and spread
H & S 5ft (1.5m)

Exposure
Bright, but out of
direct sunlight

Temperature needs
Min 50°F. (10°C)

Suitable pot size
12–18in (30–45cm)

**Suitable container
material**
Terra-cotta, stone,
plastic, ceramic

Compost type
Soil-based compost
e.g., John Innes
No. 3

Despite its ferny appearance, this slow-growing palm
has tough fronds with spine-tipped leaves and is best
placed where you will not accidentally snag your clothes as
you brush past. It likes bright light but not direct sun, making
it ideal for a partially shaded area in a sunroom. Young plants
have a bushy appearance, but over time the sago palm forms
a distinctive trunk, giving it a passing resemblance to a tree fern.

WATERING AND AFTERCARE
Although these palms like moist compost, be careful not
to overwater them or the leaves may turn an unsightly yellow.
Also, reduce watering in the winter when temperatures fall.
Avoid changing the position of sago palms when new growth
appears in spring; as the fronds unfurl they follow the sun, so
moving plants around at this time can result in palms with
crooked stems and an unbalanced shape.

*A container made from bamboo makes the
ideal partner for this exotic-looking palm.*

Fan palm *Rhapis excelsa*

Plant used
Rhapis excelsa

Height and spread
H & S 5ft (1.5m)

Exposure
Partial shade

Temperature needs
Min. 59°F (15°C)

Suitable pot size
6–8in (15–20cm)

**Suitable container
material**
Metal, glazed
ceramic, terra-cotta

Compost type
Multi-purpose
compost

Dramatic fans of glossy leaves carried on upright stems
make this clump-forming palm a real eye-catcher. It
hails from subtropical East Asia and looks stunning
in an ornate, Asian-style container. Really easy
to grow, fan palms thrive in the shade of a north-
facing room and enjoy some time outdoors in
the summer, as long as they are brought
in again long before the first frost.
Keep plants well watered during
the growing season, but reduce
moisture levels in the winter. Also, mist
the foliage every week to increase humidity.

FAN PALM OPTIONS
There are dozens of cultivars of
Rhapis excelsa that are highly prized
by collectors. Many are attractively variegated,
including 'Taiheinishiki,' which has boldly
striped yellow and green leaves, and 'Variegata'
with white-striped foliage. For a smaller form,
try 'Zuikonishiki,' which grows to just 24in (60cm)
in height and has yellow variegated leaves.

*Forest-floor dwellers,
fan palms prefer shade
and fertilizer every two
weeks when in growth.*

Foolproof foliage

Some houseplants need careful pampering and attention to detail to thrive, but these foliage species are almost foolproof. Their bold leaves may look exotic, adding a tropical touch to interiors, but umbrella plants, philodendrons, and Swiss cheese plants are tough and resilient, putting on a show even when they have been neglected for a while.

Umbrella plant *Schefflera*

Plants used
Schefflera arboricola
'Gold Capella;'
Ficus pumila 'Sunny'

Height and spread
Schefflera: H 5ft
(1.5m) S 3ft (1m);
Ficus: S up to
3ft (1m)

Exposure
Good light, but not
in direct sun

Temperature needs
Min. 55°F (13°C)
in winter

Suitable pot size
12in (30cm) or larger

**Suitable container
material**
Any

Compost type
Multi-purpose
compost

Handsome specimens grown for their glossy leaves held high on slender stalks, umbrella plants are widely available and require very little care. You can buy green plants, but the variegated types are much showier and add more interest to a room. *Schefflera arboricola* 'Gold Capella' is one of the best and can reach 10ft (3m) high, with a similar spread, in warm climates. However, it is unlikely to reach such heights in a pot and can be kept within its designated area by pruning in the spring. The main stem is weak, so provide a suitable support, such as a cane pole.

WATERING REQUIREMENTS
Keep the compost damp during the growing season, from spring to early autumn, but avoid overwatering, which may result in root rot. Reduce the watering frequency in the winter, allowing the compost to dry out completely between each application. Feed umbrella plants every few weeks during the growing season with a balanced liquid fertilizer.

TOP TIP: RETAINING VARIEGATION

Growing variegated plants in poor light often results in sparse growth and loss of variegation. In addition, colorful *Schefflera* may revert to the parent plant's coloring and produce plain green leaves. These tend to grow faster than the variegated shoots and should be cut out completely when you see them.

A frill of the trailing fig, Ficus pumila *'Sonny,' softens the edge of the pot and contrasts well with the umbrella plant.*

Swiss cheese plant *Monstera deliciosa*

Plant used
Monstera deliciosa

Height and spread
H 6ft (1.8m)
S 24in (60cm)

Exposure
Light, but not in
direct sunlight

Temperature needs
Min. 59°F (15°C)

Suitable pot size
12in (30cm) or larger

**Suitable container
material**
Any

Compost type
Multi-purpose
compost

A tropical climber, the Swiss cheese plant produces massive glossy green leaves, which sometimes grow up to 36in (90cm) in length. The foliage is deeply lobed and often punctured with elliptical holes that increase in size as the leaves expand. Train plants up a moss pole or other form of support, and feed regularly in the summer with a balanced liquid fertilizer.

WATER AND LIGHT NEEDS

Water plants regularly, but allow the compost to almost dry out between applications, and reduce the frequency in the winter. Clean the leaves to remove dust, spray to increase humidity levels, and prune plants to keep them right sized. Although Swiss cheese plants will cope with dark corners, plants may not do well, producing tiny leaves on leggy shoots. To thrive, they require some light but not direct sun, and you may need to move plants to a brighter spot in the winter when light levels are lower.

Monstera deliciosa

Philodendron

Plant used
*Philodendron
bipinnatifidum*

Height and spread
H & S up to 5ft (1.5m)

Exposure
Light, but not in
direct sunlight

Temperature needs
Min. 59°F (15°C)

Suitable pot size
18in (45cm) or larger

**Suitable container
material**
Plastic, placed in a
decorative container

Compost type
Multi-purpose
compost

Provide this stately tropical shrub with plenty of space in a light room, and it will become a striking specimen. A large architectural plant, it produces huge, deeply lobed leaves that provide glossy, verdant color all year round. Water and feed plants regularly during the growing season, and allow the compost to dry out between waterings in the winter. Clean the leaves with a soft, damp cloth, and spray them occasionally to raise humidity levels.

CHOOSING VARIETIES

There are many other types of philodendron available. Among the best are *P. hederaceum*, which has glossy heart-shaped leaves, and *P. angustisectum*, with its deeply divided foliage similar to a palm. *P. melanochrysum* produces dark green, arrow-shaped leaves that have a velvety texture. All of these are climbers and need a moss pole support.

Philodendron bipinnatifidum has magnificent foliage.

TROPICAL EFFECTS

Dramatic hothouse foliage

If you're fed up with the monotony of a neutral room, inject a dash of dazzling color with tropical foliage plants grown in contemporary containers. Their flamboyant good looks make them eye-catching focal points and they are best displayed in pots on their own, rather than in mixed groups where they will fight against others for the limelight.

Elephant's ear *Alocasia x amazonica*

Plant used
Alocasia x amazonica

Height and spread
H & S 24in (60cm)

Exposure
Light, but not
in direct sun

Temperature needs
Min. 59°F (15°C)

Suitable pot size
8in (20cm)

Suitable container material
Plastic, stone,
ceramic, metal

Compost type
Multi-purpose
compost with added
bark or perlite

With leaves that measure a whopping 18in (45cm) long, this plant's common name is no exaggeration. Held on sturdy stems, the arrow-shaped, glossy, dark green foliage is truly spectacular, with its bright silver veins creating a beautiful pattern. Ideal for a bright location indoors away from full sun; it will not do well and start to lose its intense color in a gloomy corner. It also requires heat to thrive and will drop its leaves in cool conditions, but if you restore warm temperatures, within a day or two the plant will recover and produce new foliage.

PLANT CARE
Keep the compost moist at all times, but avoid overwatering, which could lead to root rot. In the winter, allow the compost to dry out completely before watering again. During the growing season, mist plants regularly to raise humidity levels, and feed every month with a balanced liquid fertilizer. Prevent the plants from looking untended by snipping off dead, dying, or damaged leaves.

A bright bathroom is the ideal location for an elephant's ear, which will appreciate the warmth and humidity.

TOP TIP: MAINTAINING HEALTHY FOLIAGE

Misting leaves with a handheld sprayer to raise humidity levels will help to prevent dust from settling on the foliage, but you will still need to clean the leaves from time to time to ensure they keep their luster. Wipe the surface with a soft, damp cloth, and do not press too hard or you may bruise the leaves.

TROPICAL EFFECTS

Peacock plant *Calathea makoyana*

Plant used
Calathea makoyana

Height and spread
H 18in (45cm)
S 9in (22cm)

Exposure
Bright, but not
in direct sunlight

Temperature needs
Min. 61°F (16°C)

Suitable pot size
6in (15cm)

Suitable container material
Ceramic, glazed
terra-cotta, stone,
metal

Compost type
Multi-purpose
compost

For a spectacular display of variegated foliage, try the peacock plant. Native to Brazil, it is a bushy clump of paddle-shaped leaves with dark green edges and ovals of dark green marking the surface. Turn the leaf over and the same pattern is repeated in purple, while the silvery effect is produced by netlike, see-through areas on the foliage. Plants are shown off to their best advantage in a neutral or light-colored pot, and will enjoy a sheltered, bright spot away from drafts, with high humidity.

CARING FOR PEACOCK PLANTS
Water plants regularly, but allow the compost to almost dry out between each application, and reduce watering even further in winter. Spray the leaves during the summer to raise humidity levels, and feed monthly with a balanced liquid fertilizer to boost growth.

Calathea makoyana has peacock-patterned foliage.

Croton *Codiaeum*

Plant used
*Codiaeum
variegatum* var.
pictum 'Gold Star'

Height and spread
H 3ft (1m)
S 24in (60cm)

Exposure
Full light, shaded
from hot sun

Temperature needs
Min. 59°F (15°C)

Suitable pot size
8in (20cm)

Suitable container material
Stone, ceramic,
metal, plastic

Compost type
Soil-based compost,
e.g., John Innes No. 2

Codiaeum variegatum var. *pictum* 'Gold Star.'

Among the most spectacular foliage plants you can grow in the home, crotons come in a range of colors and leaf shapes. Originating from Malaysia and the islands of the East Pacific, they are grown for their leathery leaves, which are splashed, dotted, or flushed with the bright colors you find in a child's crayon box.

In their native environment they grow into large trees, but they make compact plants when grown in containers in the home. To thrive, water plants regularly, reducing the frequency in the winter. Mist leaves with a handheld sprayer, and feed every month or so during the growing season with a balanced liquid fertilizer.

CHOOSING CROTONS
C. variegatum var. *pictum* 'Petra' has spear-shaped green leaves with dramatic yellow veins, while 'Gold Star' produces gold-splashed foliage. For bolder colors, try 'Excellent,' which has large, forked leaves marked with green, yellow, and red patterns.

Tropical blooms

Create a tropical paradise in your home with some exotic blooms. If you can provide the conditions that these plants enjoy, you will be rewarded with an enviable display. Medinillas are stately queens, with large leaves and spectacular flowers, while the flamingo flower is adorned with eye-catching waxy blooms. The vase plant's sculptural leaves and flowers are also guaranteed to turn heads.

Medinilla *Medinilla magnifica*

TROPICAL EFFECTS

Plant used
Medinilla magnifica

Height and spread
H & S 4ft (1.2m)

Exposure
Bright, but not direct sun

Temperature needs
Min 59–68°F
(15–20°C)

Suitable pot size
8in (20cm)

Suitable container material
Ceramic, stone, metal

Compost type
Orchid compost

A magnificent plant, *Medinilla* is worth growing for its large, glossy leaves with attractive veins, but it really comes into its own during spring and summer when long stems bend under the weight of lush, deep pink blooms. A native of the Philippines, this plant prefers a warm, bright environment, such as a heated sun porch or greenhouse, but shelter it from direct sun. Don't allow the compost to dry out while growing and mist the leaves frequently to provide the humidity it needs to thrive. Also, wipe the foliage occasionally with a soft cloth to remove dust.

As flower buds appear, *feed* Medinilla *every couple of weeks with a liquid fertilizer to ensure they fulfil their promise and open to reveal the exotic blooms.*

TOP TIP: PROMOTING NEW BLOOMS

Plants may be slow to flower, but you can encourage them to bloom by lowering the temperature slightly in the winter, and reducing the amount of water you apply. Wait until the compost is almost dry and give the plant just enough to prevent it from wilting. In the spring, resume more frequent watering, feed every two weeks with a liquid fertilizer and raise the humidity by misting the foliage.

Vase plant *Aechmea*

Plant used
Aechmea fasciata

Height and spread
H & S 20in (50cm)

Exposure
Bright, but not
in full sun

Temperature needs
Min. 59°F (15°C)

Suitable pot size
6in (15cm)

**Suitable container
material**
Plastic, set inside
a decorative outer
container

Compost type
Well-drained,
multi-purpose
compost

Showy bracts last for up to two months.

Known as the vase or urn plant, *Aechmea fasciata* is a native of South America. It is admired for its upright rosette of leaves, which are attractively marked with silver bands and provide a feature in themselves. However, when mature it performs its star turn as a stem rises from the center of the foliage carrying a large head of pink bracts and small blue flowers.

WATERING NEEDS

As well as keeping the compost damp around the plant, use fresh rainwater to fill up the "vase" that forms in the center of the leafy rosette. If you live in an area with soft tap water, this will be fine, but hard water leaves deposits that spoil the foliage effect. Empty the "vase" and refill with fresh water every month or so to prevent the plant rotting and producing an unpleasant smell.

Flamingo flower *Anthurium*

Plant used
Anthurium
andraeanum

Height and spread
H & S 20in (50cm)

Exposure
Bright. Avoid
south-facing
windowsills
in summer

Temperature needs
Min 59°F. (15°C)

Suitable pot size
6in (15cm)

**Suitable container
material**
Plastic, set inside
a decorative outer
container

Compost type
Use a mix of 1 part
soil-based
compost, 1 part
sharp sand and 3
parts leaf mold.

Reminiscent of elaborate headgear you might see at a Mardi Gras festival, the decorative flowers of *Anthurium* bloom from spring until late summer, providing a long season of interest. Rising above spear-shaped glossy leaves, the "flowers" are actually the finger-like spadix that emerges from a waxy spathe. The spathes come in a range of colors, including white, yellow, green, pink, orange, and red.

Flamingo flowers like bright conditions out of direct sunlight and away from drafts, although when the sun is weaker in the winter, move them to a sunnier location. Ensure the compost never dries out, but guard against waterlogging, which can damage the roots.

REPOTTING FLAMINGO FLOWERS

Plants will need repotting every couple of years into slightly larger containers. Position the rootball so the roots that grow above the surface of the compost are exposed. Cover these with a layer of damp moss. Mix sharp sand and leaf mold with the compost to improve drainage and provide the acidic conditions that these plants prefer.

*Spray flamingo
flowers regularly to
create the humid
conditions they enjoy.*

Sculptural leaves

Foliage plants with leaves of different shapes, sizes, and colors create long-lasting, dramatic container displays. Many are perfect for a shady location and suit small urban gardens and contemporary designs, but there are plenty to choose from for any exposure. Some of the most dazzling foliage plants are tender and will require winter protection.

DRAMA QUEENS

Plant used
Fatsia japonica; *Alocasia sanderiana*; *Pelargonium* 'Lady Plymouth'

Height and spread
Fatsia: H & S 5ft (1.5m); *Alocasia:* H & S 3ft (1m); *Pelargonium:* H 16in (40cm) S 8in (20cm)

Exposure
Dappled shade

Temperature needs
Protect from frost in the winter

Suitable pot size
18in (45cm)

Suitable container material
Stone, metal, glazed terra-cotta

Compost type
Mix of multi-purpose and soil-based compost

The bright green, glossy leaves of *Fatsia japonica*, or false castor oil plant, provide a striking focal point for a jungle-inspired container plan, either as a single specimen or matched with other tropical-looking plants, such as *Alocasia sanderiana*, (*see also p. 60*). Most frequently grown as a house plant, *Alocasia* will also add pizzazz to outdoor summer designs with its dark green, arrow-shaped leaves and bold silver veins, while variegated pelargoniums provide contrast and scented foliage.

Fatsia prefers a shaded spot and is hardy to 23°F (-5°C), but if you grow it in a container with tender plants, bring the display indoors over the winter. It can then be taken outside again after all danger of frost has passed in the spring. Add some slow-release granular fertilizer to the compost in early spring, and keep the container well watered during the growing season, but allow the compost to dry out between waterings in the winter.

RESTRICTING GROWTH

If your *Fatsia* becomes too tall for its container, prune it in spring or summer. Cut the main stem down to a more desirable height so that it balances the size of your pot. Lower branches can stifle the plant's grown beneath, so raise the canopy by removing a few stems to give plants at the base space to flourish.

TOP TIP: WRAPPING UP TENDER PLANTS

If you are growing a false castor oil plant in a pot on its own, you can protect it from the worst winter weather by moving it to a sheltered area, wrapping the container with insulated or bubble plastic, and then covering the plant with fabric when very low temperatures are forecast. Other plants that can be treated in this way include the loquat, *Eriobotrya japonica*, the ginger plant, *Hedychium densiflorum*, and *Tetrapanax*. *Alocasia*, pelargoniums, and *Melianthus* are all too tender to survive the winter outside and must be moved to a light, frost-free place indoors until late spring.

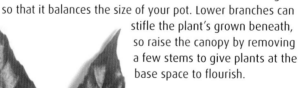

*Fatsia **has glossy dark green leaves**, accompanied in the fall by white spherical flowerheads followed by shiny black fruits.*

The different foliage shapes and textures in this combination are shown off to perfection in a white stone container.

OTHER LARGE-LEAF OPTIONS

Melianthus major, *known as the honey bush, has large, bluish-gray, serrated leaves that smell like peanut butter. Protect the pot and plant from frost over the winter.*

Eriobotrya japonica *will produce fruit if grown in the ground, but in a pot enjoy this small tree for its architectural shape and deeply ribbed, large, dark green leaves.*

Hedychium densiflorum, *or perennial ginger, makes a large clump of long, lance-shaped leaves topped by perfumed orange flowers at the end of summer.*

Tetrapanax *has huge evergreen leaves carried on long stalks, and can be grown outside in mild areas with some winter protection. The cultivar 'Rex' is one of the hardiest.*

Spiked statements

There's not a flamboyant flower in sight, but these eye-catching plants still demand attention, thanks to their vibrant, spiky foliage. Single plants make fantastic living sculptures or they can be mixed together with a selection of other architectural plants in pots to create an arresting display of contrasting textures, colors, and shapes.

New Zealand flax *Phormium*

Plant used
Phormium 'Jester'

Height and spread
H & S 3ft (1m)

Exposure
Sun

Temperature needs
Hardy to 23°F (-5°C)

Suitable pot size
12in (30cm)

Suitable container material
Terra-cotta, stone, metal

Compost type
Soil-based compost, e.g., John Innes No. 3, with extra drainage material

New Zealand flaxes are easy-to-grow architectural plants with striking sword-shaped leaves that provide colorful focal points in tall containers. All these evergreen, clump-forming perennials need to thrive is free-draining, moisture-retentive compost, a sunny location, and regular watering, especially during hot, dry summers. Apply a slow-release granular fertilizer in late spring. Although most are hardy to 23°F (-5°C), in harsh winters you'll need to protect pots with bubble plastic and cover plants with garden fabric.

PLANT CHOICES
Phormium varieties related to *P. cookianum* have cascading foliage, while those bred from *P. tenax* have a upright habit. *P.* 'Platt's Black' has deep purple leaves, *P.* 'Jester' produces pink leaves with green margins, and the foliage of *P.* 'Pink Panther' has red edges with a pink stripe; the cascading habit of all three suits tall pots.

New Zealand flax makes an attention-grabbing statement plant for a sunny spot in your garden.

TOP TIP: MAINTAINING HEALTHY FOLIAGE

To keep *Phormium* foliage at its best, remove any dead or dying leaves, as well as those around the base of plants that have become frayed. Thin leaves are easy to snip off with shears, but thicker plant material may need to be cut off with a sharp gardening knife. Keep the compost moist. Avoid splashing plants with water on hot, sunny days or you may scorch the foliage.

Cabbage palm *Cordyline australis*

Plants used
Cordyline australis
Purpurea Group

Height and spread
H 5ft (1.5m)
S 24in (60cm)

Exposure
Full sun

Temperature needs
Not reliably hardy
below 32°F (0°C)

Suitable pot size
12in (30cm)

Suitable container material
Terra-cotta,
stone, metal

Compost type
Soil-based compost,
e.g., John Innes No. 3

Try pairing a **Cordyline** *with colorful flowering plants such as* Agastache *for a pleasing contrast to its spiky foliage.*

Cordyline makes a great focal point with its upright rosette of spear-shaped leaves. Tough and easy-going, plants can easily cope with a salty blast in a seaside garden and do best in full sun. There are many different colored plants to choose from; all do well in pots for a few years, but will eventually need to be planted in the flowerbeds, since they are very fast-growing and will start to wilt if their roots are restricted for too long. Set plants in a light area in a cool room indoors, or in a frost-free greenhouse over the winter.

PLANTING PARTNERS
Cabbage palms have a bare trunk that can be hidden by careful underplanting. Here, a mass of orange *Agastache* softens the architectural leaves of the *Cordyline*, alongside a lavender's purple flowers and silver-gray foliage.

Yucca *Yucca filamentosa*

Plant used
Yucca filamentosa
'Bright Edge'

Height and spread
H 3ft (90cm)
S 5ft (1.5m)

Exposure
Full sun

Temperature needs
Fully hardy

Suitable pot size
18in (45cm)

Suitable container material
Plastic, stone, metal,
terra-cotta

Compost type
Soil-based compost,
e.g., John Innes No. 2

The stiff rosette of sword-shaped leaves on this ornamental, evergreen shrub will provide stunning year-round interest in a sunny part of the garden or on a south-facing patio or balcony. Masses of pendulous cream flowers appear on a 10ft- (3m-) tall flower stem in early summer. Although it makes a great statement plant on its own, its structural shape looks fantastic when displayed alongside other spiky plants, such as *Agave* and cabbage palms, in a summer display.

PLANT CARE
Keep plants looking good by watering regularly and feeding monthly during the growing season with a liquid feed. Remove any dead, diseased, or damaged leaves from the base of plants, and cut off the flower stalks as blooms start to fade. A large group of plants, some yuccas are hardy, but others will need to be given a sheltered site or be brought indoors to survive the winter.

Yucca filamentosa 'Bright Edge'

Magnificent maples
Acer palmatum

Grown for their graceful foliage, Japanese maples create a sophisticated statement on a patio or in a garden. These compact trees are ideal for pots, where they provide a decorative canopy in spring and summer, followed by a spectacular autumn display of sparkling yellow, orange, and red leaves.

DRAMA QUEENS

Plant used
Acer palmatum

Height and spread
H 6ft (2m)
S 5ft (1.5m)

Exposure
Best in sheltered, dappled shade

Temperature needs
Hardy to 5°F (-15°C)

Suitable pot size
12–18in (30–45cm)

Suitable container material
Terra-cotta, stone, Asian-style pot, plastic

Compost type
50/50 mix of soil-based compost, e.g., John Innes No. 3, and ericaceous compost

Many trees are too vigorous or grow too large for pots, but most Japanese maples are either slow-growing or naturally compact and make beautiful container specimens. Japanese maples or acers comprise a large group of plants, but most coveted are forms of *Acer palmatum*, which create low hummocks or rounded domes of arched branches clothed in elegant lobed foliage. While maples are undoubtedly prized for their blazing autumn tints, the plants provide interest all year-round. Stripped of foliage, they create architectural shapes in the winter garden and some also feature colorful stems. Spring foliage is often bright and changes color as the leaves mature in the summer.

Maples can be used as focal points, specimens on a lawn, or as features next to a pond. Their Asian origins make them perfect companions for bamboos, Oriental grasses, pebbles, and Japanese ornaments in a Zen-inspired patio or garden display.

PREVENTING SCORCHING

Although Japanese maples are very hardy, their foliage is vulnerable to frost, wind, and strong sun, any of which can cause them to scorch, shrivel, desiccate at the edges, and fall prematurely. To prevent problems, do not place pots in frost pockets, wind tunnels, or open, south-facing locations. Their ideal home is in a sheltered spot in dappled shade.

Center: **Maples with red summer foliage** *add drama to a patio setting and combine well with foliage plants and colorful seasonal flowers.*

TOP TIP: KEEPING MAPLES HEALTHY

Japanese maples require little pruning. In the spring, remove the top layer of compost and replace it with fresh compost mixed with slow-release fertilizer granules. Add a mulch to the surface to retain moisture. Keep well watered, and cover the pot with bubble plastic in the winter.

Maple options

**Acer palmatum *var.* dissectum
'*Filigree*'** *has feathery green foliage
that changes to yellow in the fall.*

Acer palmatum '*Chitose-yama*' *has
deeply lobed green leaves that start
turning deep red in late summer.*

Acer palmatum '*Sango-kaku*' *has
bright pink shoots and pink fall leaves
that then turn yellow.*

**Acer palmatum *var.* dissectum
'*Garnet*'** *has finely divided, dark red
leaves that turn scarlet in the fall.*

Acer palmatum '*Bloodgood*', *a bushy
tree with dark purple leaves, turns
a dramatic shade of scarlet in the fall.*

Acer palmatum '*Linearilobum*' *has
deeply cut leaves that turn from bronze
to orange, then yellow before falling.*

Acer palmatum '*Nicholsonii*' *has olive
green, lobed leaves that brighten up fall
pots with shades of orange.*

Acer palmatum '*Katsura*' *has red-
edged, orange new leaves that fade to
green, then turn yellow, red, and orange.*

DRAMA QUEENS

Big and bold bog plants

Not for the faint hearted, these moisture-loving perennials are guaranteed to create impact, with giant jungly leaves that would look at home on the set of a dinosaur movie. Despite their potential to grow into large beasts, these monsters can be tamed in containers if you are prepared to water them regularly during the growing season and never let them dry out.

Massive sculptural leaves *create an arresting focal point in a contemporary design with other foliage plants.*

Gunnera

DRAMA QUEENS

Plant used
Gunnera manicata

Height and spread
H 5ft (1.5m)
S 6ft (1.8m)

Exposure
Partial shade

Temperature needs
Hardy to 5°F (-15°C),
but vulnerable
during prolonged
cold periods

Suitable pot size
18in (45cm) or wider

**Suitable container
material**
Plastic, and other
non-porous
materials

Compost type
Soil-based compost
with added leaf
mold

Prized for its huge leaves that can reach 6ft (2m) in diameter, *Gunnera* makes large clumps when grown in moist soil by a pond, but its size is severely curtailed when confined to a pot. Happy in a shady spot, it can be used as a focal point or as a backdrop to other shade-loving foliage plants in containers on a patio or deck. In early summer, a long, conelike spike of tiny red flowers rises from the center of the clump, adding to the dramatic effect. The smaller species, *G. tinctoria,* is a great choice for a more confined spot. Feed *Gunnera* plants with a slow-release granular fertilizer in the spring and apply a liquid feed every month in the summer. Never allow the compost to dry out.

PRUNING PLANTS
An overly wide *Gunnera* will soon outgrow its welcome in a small garden, while top-heavy plants can cause their pots to topple over. Remove wayward leaves to keep plants in check, and don't be afraid to prune hard; this treatment will not affect the plant's health.

TOP TIP: OVERWINTERING PLANTS

Gunnera is fully hardy, but the crown of the plant (where the stems meet the root system at ground level) is vulnerable to damage when temperatures are below freezing for prolonged periods. When frost damages the top growth, remove and place the leaves over the crown to provide some insulation. Alternatively, cover the top of the pot with a layer of straw pinned down with wire pegs. Remove these layers in the spring when the worst frosts are over.

Rodgersia

Plants used
Rodgersia pinnata
'Superba'

Height and spread
H 4ft (1.2m)
S 30in (75cm)

Exposure
Partial shade

Temperature needs
Hardy to 5°F (-15°C)

Suitable pot size
12–18in (30–45cm)

Suitable container material
Plastic, and other non-porous materials

Compost type
Soil-based compost with added leaf mold

The *Rodgersia*'s tall plumes of white or pink flowers are beautiful in the summer, but even before they appear, the plant's architectural shape and handsome palmate leaves make it an impressive feature. Up to 36in (90cm) long, the leaves are flushed bronze when young and then darken to a deep green. They are also heavily textured and beg to be touched. Plants add a stately form to container arrangements of ferns, lilies, and hostas, which enjoy similar cool, shady conditions and regular watering.

CONTROLLING PESTS
Although this plant is rarely troubled by pests, it is vulnerable to slug and snail damage when new leaves appear in the spring. Protect plants with copper rings, organic pellets, or take other measures to prevent the plant being harmed at this critical stage.

Tall spikes of pink frothy flowers appear in the summer.

Astilboides

Plants used
Astilboides tabularis

Height and spread
H 4ft (1.2m)
S 36in (90cm)

Exposure
Partial shade

Temperature needs
Hardy to 5°F (-15°C)

Suitable pot size
12–18in (30–45cm)

Suitable container material
Plastic, and other non-porous materials

Compost type
Soil-based compost with added leaf mold

Leaves the size of a small tabletop create drama.

If you're looking for a plant that will get people talking, try this shade-lover; its huge round leaves with scalloped edges sometimes reach 36in (90cm) across and are perfectly supported on strong stems. Worth growing for its foliage alone, *Astilboides* has the added bonus of small white flowers which appear on arching stems in midsummer. A native of boggy areas, use it in containers close to water features, and mix with other moisture lovers, such as feathery-plumed *Astilbe* and purple loosestrife, *Lythrum salicaria*.

WATERING NEEDS
Astilboides is very sensitive to drought and does not tolerate dry soil conditions, which will quickly cause a check on growth and brown leaves. To keep compost moist, line a pot with plastic and perforate it around the sides, about 1½in (3cm) from the base of the container. This will create a reservoir, while allowing excess moisture to drain out. Alternatively, install an automatic watering system.

DRAMA QUEENS

Palms for the garden

If you need a quick and easy way to add an exotic touch to your garden, pot up a palm. Architectural and evergreen, their spiky fronds make great partners for a contemporary container in a minimalist design, or use them to dress up a display of vibrant blooms and luxuriant foliage to transform your patio into a tropical paradise.

Chusan palm *Trachycarpus fortunei*

DRAMA QUEENS

Plant used
Trachycarpus
fortunei

Height and spread
H 6ft (1.8m)
S 3ft (1m)

Exposure
Sun or dappled
shade

Temperature needs
Hardy to 5°F (-15°C)

Suitable pot size
18in (45cm)

**Suitable container
material**
Plastic, stone,
terra-cotta

Compost type
Soil-based compost,
e.g. John Innes No. 2

You would expect such an exotic-looking plant to need careful pampering, but the Chusan palm is remarkably easy to look after in cool climates, requiring virtually no maintenance apart from watering, feeding while it's actively growing, and occasional trimming with garden shears. Best of all, it's tough and can cope with temperatures down 5°F to (-15°C).

Although it's a robust plant, the Chusan palm performs best when grown in a sheltered location, because it needs protection from strong winds, which batter the leaves, giving them a ragged appearance. Choose a large, sturdy container filled with soil-based compost, such as John Innes No. 2, and feed plants annually in the spring with a slow-release granular fertilizer. Water your palms regularly in summer, but ensure the compost does not become waterlogged in winter by raising pots on "feet."

Use plants as focal points on a sunny or partially shaded patio or in a garden; they look particularly effective as part of a tropical design.

KEEPING PLANTS NEAT

To maintain the appearance of your palms, remove the lower fronds as they start to turn brown and die, which is a natural aging process and not usually a sign of disease or stress. Cut back the stems so that the stumps are as flat as possible to the trunk. Although not strictly necessary, you can also strip the hairy growth from the trunk if you want a smooth stem. To do this, remove the hairy fiber at the base with your hands and then cut it off, together with any old leaf stumps. Continue like this up the rest of the trunk.

Spiky fans of glossy green leaves look impressive when silhouetted against a plain backdrop.

TOP TIP: OVERWINTERING PALMS

Although hardy, the Chusan palm benefits from extra care to get it through the winter. Its worst enemy is soggy compost, so move it to a sheltered spot close to a house wall where rain will not drench the soil, and do not water your palm when temperatures fall in the winter. You may also need to protect the pot, especially if it is made from porous terra-cotta. Wrap it up in a sheet of bubble plastic and secure with string.

Dwarf fan palm *Chamaerops humilis*

Plant used
Chamaerops humilis

Height and spread
H & S 4ft (1.2m)

Exposure
Full sun

Temperature needs
Hardy to 16°F (-9°C)

Suitable pot size
12–18in (30–45cm)

Suitable container material
Terra-cotta, plastic, stone

Compost type
Well-drained, soil-based compost, e.g. John Innes No. 2 with added grit

This very slow-growing palm with fans of stiff leaves may eventually grow to 4ft (1.2m), but it can take several decades to achieve this height, so buy a plant of the size you require. Fairly low growing, it makes a bushy specimen when young, eventually forming a distinct trunk as it matures and the lower leaves die back.

Although not as hardy as the Chusan palm, its robust, dense growth is better equipped to cope with wind, and it even thrives in pots in coastal areas. The palm's compact size also makes it easy to move indoors when extremely low temperatures are forecast.

WHEN TO WATER

Water your palm regularly in the summer and while in active growth until it is well established, when you should allow the compost to dry out between waterings. In the winter, do not water plants grown outside, and move containers to a sheltered spot protected from heavy rain.

Three palms in a row produce a contemporary effect.

Positioned in a place of pride on a patio, the dwarf fan palm makes an elegant feature in a clean, white ceramic pot.

DRAMA QUEENS

Striking flowers

These indoor plants require a little more care and attention to detail than most, but you'll be amply rewarded for your efforts. Nurture them well, and they will produce breathtaking flowers that make stunning indoor features. Use them to add drama to a modern interior and choose colorful glazed containers to match them or to provide a striking contrast to the blooms.

DRAMA QUEENS

Bat flower *Tacca*

Plant used
Tacca chantrieri

Height and spread
H & S 3ft (1m)

Exposure
A bright spot, out of direct sunlight

Temperature needs
Min. 55°F (13°C)

Suitable pot size
8in (20cm)

Suitable container material
Plastic, metal, glazed terra-cotta

Compost type
Multi-purpose compost with added soil-based compost, e.g., John Innes No. 2

There are lots of unusual-looking flowers you can grow, but *Tacca chantrieri* is perhaps the most peculiar. A native of India and parts of Southeast Asia, it's commonly known as the bat flower thanks to its nodding maroon blooms and threadlike "whiskers" that hang from large, winglike bracts. The flowers are held on lofty stalks that rise above a cluster of lush, corrugated, green leaves. The bat flower likes a warm spot indoors, but can be placed outside in a sheltered location for several weeks in the summer.

GROWING FROM SEED

Ready-grown plants are available from garden centers, but it's satisfying to raise your own from seed. Sow seeds ¼in (5mm) deep into small pots filled with seed compost, water them, and place in a heated propagator. After germination, which can take anywhere from one to nine months, move seedlings into 3in (7.5cm) pots when large enough to handle; you should have a flowering plant within three years.

TOP TIP: LONG-TERM CARE

To keep the bat flower looking good, ensure the compost never dries out and mist the leaves regularly to raise humidity in summer. It's a hungry plant, so feed monthly by spraying with a foliar liquid feed. When your plants fill their original containers, move them into larger pots, or divide plants in spring. The plants will enter a dormant period in the autumn, and should be kept dry and warm until spring, when you can resume watering.

***The unique flowers of** Tacca chantrieri are held on tall stems and provide a dramatic focal point in a bright room.*

Temple bells *Smithiantha*

Plant used
Smithiantha 'Little One'

Height and spread
H 8in (20cm)
S 4in (10cm)

Exposure
Bright, but out of direct sunlight

Temperature needs
Min. 59°F (15°C)

Suitable pot size
6in (15cm)

Suitable container material
Plastic, ceramic, glazed terra-cotta

Compost type
Multi-purpose compost

A close inspection of the flowers of this Mexican perennial reveal why it is often called "temple bells"—the brightly colored, pendulous blooms that drip from long stems in the summer and fall are perfectly bell-shaped. These delicate house plants prefer a bright location away from direct sunlight and enjoy humid conditions. While they are growing, water the plants well, but allow the compost to dry out completely before watering again. Add a liquid feed with every watering, but don't overdo it— a quarter-strength dilution is ideal.

PLANT CHOICES

There are several named varieties of *Smithiantha* that are worth tracking down. 'Little One' is a dwarf form, and produces sprays of bright orange flowers and velvety purple leaves, while 'Extra Sassy' has pink flowers that rise above large red leaves. *Smithiantha cinnabarina* grows to about 24in (60cm) and has hairy red leaves and red flowers.

The dark velvety leaves of Smithiana *plants need high humidity levels to thrive. Set pots in a tray of moist gravel to create the right conditions.*

TOP TIP: OVERWINTERING

In the winter, *Smithiantha* plants become completely dormant and the leaves and flowers die back. Remove the dead growth from the plant and allow the compost to completely dry out. Do not water the plants again until spring, at which time move them into a larger container of compost, and water lightly until the plant is back in full growth.

Dramatic foliage

If you're searching for a house plant that blends into the background, look away now. These leafy lovelies are most definitely not shrinking violets; their bold, colorful foliage cries out for attention and will provide a talking point all year round. Try combining a few of them in a group for a dramatic display of foliage shapes and forms.

Rubber plant *Ficus elastica*

DRAMA QUEENS

Plant used
Ficus elastica
'Tineke'

Height and spread
H 6ft (1.8m)
S 36in (90cm)

Exposure
Bright, but not in
direct sunlight

Temperature needs
Min. 59°F (15°C)

Suitable pot size
12in (30cm)

**Suitable container
material**
Plastic, ceramic,
glazed terra-cotta,
metal

Suitable compost
Soil-based compost,
e.g. John Innes No. 2

When grown in a sleek, dark purple, contemporary container, this well-known, easy-to-grow house plant is given a new lease on life and brought up to date—no longer a throwback to the interiors of the 1960s and 70s. Many attractive rubber plant cultivars are now available, in addition to the commonly found green form of *Ficus elastica*. 'Doescheri' produces large, elliptical leaves with gray patches and creamy edges, 'Tineke' has a similar camouflaged leaf pattern overlaid with pinkish-red, and 'Decora' bears dark green, broad leaves that are flushed bronze when young.

WATERING AND FEEDING
Water rubber plants all year round, but allow the compost to dry out between waterings. For plenty of healthy growth, apply a liquid feed that is high in nitrogen every month. If plants become too tall or leggy, keep them in check by pruning.

TOP TIP: CLEANING FOLIAGE

The smooth leaves of *Ficus elastica* attract dust like a magnet, so clean them regularly This helps to keep the foliage healthy by allowing maximum light penetration, and improves its appearance. There are many commercially produced sprays and wipes, but these are not necessary unless you really want to add an artificial shine to the surface of the leaves. Simply wipe them with a soft damp cloth to remove dust, and add a little milk to make the leaves shine.

Variegated rubber plants, such as 'Tineke', thrive in good natural light with a monthly dose of liquid fertilizer.

Stromanthe *Stromanthe sanguinea*

Plant used
Stromanthe sanguinea 'Triostar'

Height and spread
H 20in (50cm)
S 18in (45cm)

Exposure
Bright, filtered light

Temperature needs
Min. of 59°F (15°C)

Suitable pot size
8in (20cm)

Suitable container material
Plastic, glazed terra-cotta, ceramic, metal

Compost type
Multi-purpose with added soil-based compost, e.g., John Innes No. 2

Vibrantly colored 'Triostar' produces green, cream, and red variegated leaves, given a bright spot out of direct sunlight.

Perfect for adding a touch of the tropics, this exotic plant makes a clump of technicolored leaves that can be used to brighten up a shady spot indoors. The long, lance-shaped, variegated leaves are smooth and glossy, and splashed with green, pink, dark pink, burgundy, and white brush strokes. As an added bonus, the plant boasts clusters of tiny pink flowers in the spring.

MAINTENANCE TIPS
Keep the compost moist at all times; the leaves will start to curl if it's allowed to dry out. However, guard against overwatering as this may cause the stems to rot. In hot summers, mist the leaves to raise humidity levels and prevent them browning. Give plants a boost with a soluble fertilizer every four weeks in the spring and summer. Congested plants can be divided before new growth starts in spring.

Pineapple plant *Ananas comosus*

Plant used
Ananas comosus var. variegatus

Height and spread
H 3ft (1m)
S 20in (50cm)

Exposure
Light spot in sun

Temperature needs
Min. 59°F (15°C). Above 75°F (24°C) is best for flower formation

Suitable pot size
8in (20cm)

Suitable container material
Plastic, glazed terra-cotta, ceramic, metal

Compost type
Orchid compost

Closely related to the edible pineapple, this large, showy plant from South America makes a rosette of brightly colored, variegated, arching leaves edged with spines. In the summer the plant is topped by a flower followed by a small, bright red fruit that perches on a stout stem. The fruit can remain on the plant for around ten months. If you have the space for it, the pineapple plant makes a striking addition to a mixed display of bromeliads.

CARING FOR PINEAPPLES
This plant likes a sunny location, ideally in a sunroom, and needs high humidity to do well. Mist leaves regularly with a hand sprayer and keep the "well" at the center of the rosette topped up with water. However, the compost should not be too wet—a free-draining orchid compost should help to provide the right conditions. Pineapples also require heat to flower, and when buds appear, feed every couple of weeks with a liquid plant food.

The pineapple plant grows all year round, and can reach a spectacular size in the right conditions.

Easygoing drought busters
Echeveria and *Aeonium*

Some plants need lots of care, but *Aeonium* and *Echeveria* are easygoing and trouble free. Native to dry, sunny climates, they are drought tolerant, slow growing, and require virtually no pruning, making them perfect for those short of time. Their sculpted leaves and unusual flowers also make decorative displays.

DESERT DWELLERS

Plants used
Mixed *Aeonium* and *Echeveria*

Height and spread
H 1½in–6ft (4cm–2m)
S 5in–6ft (13cm–2m)

Exposure
Aeonium: partial shade to full sun; variegated forms need good light for best color
Echeveria: full sun

Temperature needs
Aeonium: 50°F (10°C)
Echeveria: 45°F (7°C)

Suitable pot size
3–9in (7.5–22cm)

Suitable container material
Terra-cotta, glazed ceramic, plastic

Compost type
Soil-based compost, e.g., John Innes No. 2 with added grit

In the past *Echeveria* and *Aeonium* would have been seen gathering dust on window ledges indoors, but these attractive tender plants are perfect for garden displays from late spring to the first frost in the fall, after which they'll need some protection to survive the cold months ahead.

These decorative succulents encompass a great range of sizes and appearances. Some are large multi-branched shrubs grown for their purple, bronze, green, blue, or variegated rosettes; others produce cascading stems or form a single flat rosette. A number have leafy rosettes as large as dinner plates, while diminutive types are the size of a thumbnail. Despite their diversity, all thrive in gritty, soil-based compost and look particularly effective in terra-cotta or glazed containers. Water plants every two weeks in the summer and shelter them from long wet periods. Top-heavy plants or those that produce a single main stem may need staking to prevent them from toppling over.

GROUPING PLANTS

Although solitary specimens can look good, you can create a more striking display by grouping them together. Combine different colors, shapes, and sizes, placing larger succulents in the center and low-growing ones toward the outside of the group to achieve a 3D effect. Top-dress the pots with gravel or an ornamental mulch to complete the effect.

*Center: **Create a striking display** by grouping succulents together on a simple wooden table on a sunny patio.*

TOP TIP: WINTER CARE

Protect these succulents from frost damage by placing them on a light windowsill indoors or by draping a sheet or two of garden fabric over containers and storing them in a heated greenhouse for the winter.

Apply a small quantity of water when the compost dries out completely, and remove any dead or diseased leaves as soon as you see them. Control mealybug where necessary (*see p. 243*).

Echeveria and *Aeonium* options

Echeveria agavoides *is a clump-forming succulent with tight rosettes of narrow, tapering leaves with red tips.*

Echeveria gibbiflora *var.* **metallica** *produces short spikes of red flowers in the summer above huge purple rosettes.*

Echeveria secunda *var.* **glauca** *is a clump-forming plant with small rosettes and red and yellow flowers.*

Aeonium haworthii *'Variegatum' has bright, light new leaves, with yellow and green variegation, edged with red.*

Aeonium *'Zwartkop', a multi-branching succulent, adds a dramatic note with its near-black rosettes.*

Aeonium arboreum *is a fast-growing shrub valued for its architectural shape and numerous pale green rosettes.*

Aeonium *'Ballerina' forms a neat mound of rosettes with narrow, grayish-green leaves with white edges.*

Aeonium haworthii *forms masses of small grayish-blue rosettes that cover the wiry branches of this compact shrub.*

DESERT DWELLERS

Textured sun-lovers

Whether armed with spines, edged with teeth or clothed in masses of small rounded leaves, these succulents offer exciting texture and form, which can be heightened further with contrasting smooth or simple containers. Traditionally these plants have been displayed indoors, but all can be grown outdoors in summer on a sunny sheltered patio, balcony, or deck.

Agave

DESERT DWELLERS

Plant used
Agave americana
'Mediopicta Alba'

Height and spread
H & S: up to 5ft
(1.5m)

Exposure
Full sun. Light
location indoors

Temperature needs
Min. 41°F (5°C)

Suitable pot size
8–24in (20–60cm),
depending on
plant size

**Suitable container
material**
Terra-cotta, stone,
plastic, metal,
ceramic

Compost type
Well-drained,
soil-based compost,
e.g., John Innes No. 2

Prized for their architectural rosettes, *Agave* are low-maintenance plants that complement contemporary containers and modern designs. Best displayed individually, select a contrasting pot, such as a cool, white ceramic container with a white-striped type like 'Mediopicta Alba.'

Agave make excellent house plants, but place them carefully to prevent clothes from catching on the tooth-edged leaves. Allow the compost to dry out between waterings, and keep plants even drier in winter. Fast-growing species will need moving into larger pots every few years, or remove young shoots to keep them in check.

AGAVE OPTIONS
There are many *Agave* varieties to choose from. *Agave parryi* var. *truncata* has neat blue rosettes with wide leaves, while *A. stricta* is a dangerous looking plant that forms a sphere of slender spiky leaves. *A. schidigera* is compact and produces upright leaves edged with wispy white filaments, while *A. victoriae-reginae* is small and tender with stiff, white-edged, green leaves.

TOP TIP: GROWING AGAVES OUTSIDE

Agave are ideal for growing in a sunny spot outdoors over the summer months, but most need to be moved to a light, frost-free place indoors for the winter. Large specimens of *Agave americana* that are too large to bring indoors will survive winters outside if you live in a mild area or have a sheltered garden. To increase survival rates, bring plants up close to the house, cover with fabric and tip the containers on their sides to keep the compost dry.

Agave americana 'Mediopicta Alba' *produces rosettes of striking white-and-green striped leaves.*

Donkey's tail *Sedum morganianum*

Plant used
Sedum morganianum

Height and spread
H: 12in (30cm)
S: 24in (60cm)

Exposure
Light location

Temperature needs
Min. 41–45°F (5–7°C)

Suitable pot size
4–6in (10–15cm)

Suitable container material
Terra-cotta, plastic, ceramic

Compost type
Well drained, soil-based compost, e.g., John Innes No. 2

With its pendulous stems heavily weighed down by cylindrical gray-green leaves, this sedum is a curious sight. In the spring and summer, small pink flowers may appear at the end of stems. Other than watering and repotting from time to time, donkey's tail needs very little attention, but take care not to break off the delicate leaves. Allow the compost to almost dry out before watering, and water less in the winter.

PLANTING IDEAS
While the plant is young it can be grown in a small, decorative pot, but once the stems have reached their full length, it needs to be raised off the ground to prevent the leaves being damaged. It's ideally suited to a hanging basket or wall-mounted pot, or set it in a container on a bookcase or shelf where you can appreciate its cascading stems of beadlike leaves.

The leaves of Donkey's tail resemble strings of beads.

Aloe

Plant used
Aloe ferox

Height and spread
H & S up to 3ft (1m) in a pot

Exposure
A light location indoors, full sun in the garden

Temperature needs
Min. 50°F (10°C)

Suitable pot size
4–24in (10–60cm), depending on plant size

Suitable container material
Terra-cotta, stone, plastic, metal, ceramic

Compost type
Gritty, soil-based compost, eg, John Innes No. 2

Everyone has heard of *Aloe vera*, a plant famed for the healing properties of its sap, but there are many others worth growing too. Most come from Africa and encompass a huge and varied range of plants, including dwarf, smooth-leaf varieties suitable for a south-facing windowsill indoors, and large plants, such as the heavily armored *Aloe ferox*. Many can be placed in a sunny location outdoors in the summer, as long as they are moved back inside before the frost returns. Keep the compost just moist in the summer, and do not water the leafy rosettes. In the winter, keep the compost almost dry.

ALOE SELECTIONS
Indoors, grow the smooth-leaf *A. vera* or the partridge-breasted aloe, *A. variegata*, which boasts rosettes of green leaves decorated with white bands. *A. ferox* is an architectural plant with steely-blue leaves edged with red teeth, while *A. arborescens* 'Variegata' is a large plant with sword-shaped, yellow-striped leaves.

Aloe ferox's spiny foliage has architectural appeal.

DESERT DWELLERS

Prickly partners

A well-lit spot in a warm house is the perfect place for a low-maintenance display of prickly plants. Fascinating, architectural, and virtually indestructible, they look stylish in modern ceramic containers, and you can choose from a wide range of species to create a decorative group of colors and textures.

DESERT DWELLERS

Plant used
Euphorbia trigona;
Crassula;
Aeonium;
Pachypodium;
Opuntia

Height and spread
Euphorbia trigona:
H 5ft (1.5m) S 30in
(75cm); *Crassula:* H &
S 3ft (1m); *Aeonium:*
H & S 24in (60cm);
Pachypodium:
H 5ft (1.5m) S 18in
(45cm); *Opuntia:*
H & S 3ft (1m)

Exposure
Sunny, warm
location

Temperature needs
Min. 59°F (15°C)

Suitable pot size
Large cactus or
succulents 12–18in
(30–45cm)

**Suitable container
material**
Stone, ceramic,
plastic

Compost type
Well-drained,
soil-based compost,
e.g., John Innes No.
1, with added sand

*Center: **Ideal for a
centrally-heated
home**, this group of
cacti and succulents
thrives in a warm,
sunny environment.*

If you're looking to add sculptural interest to a modern interior, forget about ornaments and snap up some architectural plants. Great choices include *Euphorbia trigona*, a statuesque, South African succulent whose tall, green, columnar stems have attractive black spines and small leaves. Add to this an *Opuntia,* with its classic cactus shape and spines, the dramatic treelike *Pachypodium,* armed with a vicious-looking stem, and a bushy *Crassula* to provide a visual contrast.

When putting a display like this together, choose plants of different heights and shapes, with compact and clump-forming types set against tall and slender specimens. Include enough plants to make an impact, but ensure that the room does not feel cluttered. Also, give your cacti and succulents plenty of space so that each is displayed to full advantage, and place them where they won't be in your way or catch your clothes when you walk past. Remember, too, that they like a bright, airy location, so avoid pushing them back into dark corners.

WATERING NEEDS
They may hail from some of the most parched landscapes in the world, but this does not mean that you can completely ignore cacti. In the summer, allow the compost to completely dry out between waterings, and for the rest of the year, water less frequently, but enough to prevent plants from withering. Succulents need just a little more water (*see plants on pp. 80–81*).

TOP TIP: PAIN-FREE PLANTING

The tiny hairlike spines on cacti can be very painful if you get them on your hands, so wear a pair of tough leather gloves when planting. In addition, handle plants by wrapping them in folded strips of newspaper or thin card stock, but don't squeeze too tightly or you will damage the delicate spines.

Choosing cacti

Notocactus magnificus *(syn.* Parodia magnifica*) is a compact, grayish-blue, spherical cactus with golden yellow spines on pronounced ridges. It readily produces offshoots to form large clumps and suits a large shallow bowl.*

Mammillaria zeilmanniana *is a clump-forming cactus armed with a combination of small spines and those that look like fishing hooks. Its barbed good looks are softened in the summer by a profusion of bright pink flowers.*

Echinocereus *encompasses a large group of column-forming or cylindrical cacti, renowned for the rich colors of their bright, showy flowers that appear in the spring and summer. Most are low-growing and suit small spaces.*

Opuntia microdasys *var.* albispina *is related to the large, imposing prickly pear, but this dwarf* Opuntia *is perfect for small pots in the home. It has oval-shaped, dark green pads studded with groups of white spines.*

Rebutia krainziana *produces dark green stems that resemble flattened spheres and provides a great backdrop to tiny silver spines that are arranged in a spiral pattern on the surface. Scarlet flowers appear in summer.*

Schlumbergera truncata*, commonly known as the Christmas cactus, is perfect for a tall pot or a hanging basket, where the long, bright green stems terminating in pink flowers can rain down in the fall and winter.*

DESERT DWELLERS

Flowering succulents

Most succulents are grown for their architectural foliage, but there's a group that sports equally eye-catching flowers. Easy to grow, these drought-loving plants thrive in sunny areas and produce richly colored blooms over many weeks. The flowers of *Graptopetalum bellum* look like tiny shooting stars while *Kalanchoe* comes in many different forms.

Graptopetalum

Plant used
Graptopetalum bellum

Height and spread
H 9in (23cm)
S 6in (15cm)

Exposure
Sunny windowsill

Temperature needs
Min. 41–50°F
(5–10°C)

Suitable pot size
4–8in (10–20cm)

Suitable container material
Terra-cotta, ceramic

Compost type
Well-drained, soil-based compost, e.g., John Innes No. 1, with added sand

At first glance, the flat rosette of leaves formed by this succulent are attractive, yet fairly unremarkable, but the plant transforms when short spikes of flowers rise up in summer. The star-shaped blooms are shocking pink, instantly bringing to mind the color of a 1950s Cadillac. Native to Mexico, this plant gives its best performance in a bright, sunny spot indoors.

Graptopetalum is drought tolerant, and you should allow the compost to dry out between waterings in the summer, and water sparingly in the winter, giving plants just enough moisture to prevent them from drying out. Overwatering can result in root rot, so check that the plant is not standing in a pot of water. Plants spread easily and over time form a cluster of white-edged rosettes. When the original pot has been filled, either move the plant into a larger container or divide the rosettes up and replant them in small pots.

PLANTING PARTNERS

Graptopetalum is a decorative feature on its own, but can look a little underwhelming when not flowering. To maintain interest, group a few plants together or combine it in a bowl with other succulents that require similar growing conditions. Team it up with *Crassula, Echeveria,* or a small *Aloe.* Alternatively, combine it with trailing *Graptopetalum paraguayense,* alongside the reddish rosettes of *Graptopetalum rusbyi.* Add a decorative mulch to the surface of the compost (*see p .239*).

Graptopetalum bellum *flowers more profusely when grown in bright, sunny conditions. Feed plants monthly with a half-diluted cactus fertilizer to keep it thriving.*

Kalanchoe

Plant used
Kalanchoe pumila

Height and spread
H & S: 18in (45cm)

Exposure
Bright, sunny spot

Temperature needs
Min. 50°F (10°C)

Suitable pot size
6in (15cm)

Suitable container material
Terra-cotta, plastic, ceramic

Compost type
Well-drained, soil-based compost, e.g., John Innes No. 1, with added sand

The powdery-gray scalloped leaves of Kalanchoe pumila provide an excellent foil for the pale pink flowers that appear on slender stems during the spring and summer. Its spreading habit makes this succulent an ideal candidate for a hanging basket or wall-mounted container, and it will be happy outside on a warm, sunny sheltered patio or deck in the summer.

Kalanchoe is a large family of succulents, and includes a range of plant sizes and habits. Others to try include forms of K. manginii, which have large, bell-shaped, suspended blooms held on long stems, and varieties of Kalanchoe blossfeldiana, or Flaming Katy, the most popular and widely available species, with green leaves and upward-facing blooms.

CARING FOR KALANCHOE

Keep plants on the dry side and do not water the leaves. Allow the compost to dry out between waterings and water sparingly in the winter. Kalanchoe plants will flower well on a sunny windowsill, but they need encouragement to bloom again after their initial burst. When the flowers start to fade, cut off the stalks at the base and move the plant to a shady windowsill for four weeks. Don't water during this time, then bring the plant back to a sunny sill and water as usual. Feed plants every two weeks in the spring and summer with a liquid fertilizer.

Delicate pink flowers and pale gray leaves suit a pastel-colored glazed container that won't overpower them.

CHOOSING VARIETIES OF KALANCHOE

Kalanchoe 'Tessa' has dark green, fleshy foliage that provides a contrasting backdrop for masses of orangey-red, tubular flowers held on pendulous stems in the spring.

Kalanchoe 'Wendy' produces scalloped leaves and wiry stalks topped with dramatic flowerheads of up to 15 pink, bell-shaped blooms edged with yellow ruffles.

Kalanchoe blossfeldiana 'Calandiva White Monroe' has white flowers that resemble rosebuds. They open from greenish buds above large glossy leaves.

Kalanchoe blossfeldiana Pink Form is one of the most widely available varieties, with large heads of tiny, star-shaped, pink flowers that appear in the spring.

EASY ORCHIDS

Moth orchids *Phalaenopsis*

This orchid's popularity is well deserved. Plants bear lots of elegant flowers on branched stems that last for months and will often produce several flushes of blooms throughout the year. Best of all, they are not picky about temperatures and will flourish in the average centrally heated family room.

Plant used
Phalaenopsis hybrid

Height and spread
H & S 12in (30cm)

Exposure
Light, but not in direct sun

Temperature needs
68°F (20°C) or higher in daytime;
61°F (16°C) or higher at night

Flowering time
Any

Suitable pot size
6in (15cm)

Suitable container material
Plastic, placed inside a decorative pot

Compost type
Orchid compost

With exotic blooms in just about every color imaginable, which remain on the plants for months and will often reward you with repeat flowering during the year, you'd expect there to be a catch, but there isn't one. *Phalaenopsis*, or moth orchids, will perform well in any room that is unheated in the summer and kept warm by a central-heating system during the winter.

Flowers usually appear on multi-branched stems that will need supporting with small stakes. Plants bloom at any time of year, and by selecting a few varieties, you can enjoy a continuous floral display. Moth orchids are ideally placed on an east-facing windowsill or in another bright spot out of direct sunlight. To ensure they perform well, water regularly to keep the compost damp, but avoid overwatering to prevent roots from rotting. They enjoy high humidity, so stand pots on a shallow pebble tray half-filled with water, or mist leaves with a handheld sprayer. Do this in the morning so the moisture can dry before evening. A layer of moss placed on top of the compost will help to retain moisture, as well as giving your arrangement an attractive finish.

ENCOURAGE REPEAT FLOWERING
After the flowers start to fade, cut the stalk back to the second leaf joint from the bottom. A further stalk should form from this point and carry more buds to give you another show of flowers. Use a liquid orchid fertilizer when you water your plants (following the instructions) to encourage flower production.

TOP TIP: TRY PHALAENOPSIS HYBRIDS

If you can grow *Phalaenopsis*, you can't fail with *Doritaenopsis* orchids, a cross between *Phalaenopsis* and *Doritis*. There is a huge range of colorful hybrids, such as the striking *Doritaenopsis* Taida Sweet Berry (left), and they're grown in exactly the same way as *Phalaenopsis*.

Centre: **Phalaenopsis hybrids** *are widely available at reasonable prices. Group several plants together for an elegant arrangement.*

Moth orchid varieties

P. cornu-cervi *is a beautiful species that will fill a room with scent from its speckled, star-shaped flowers.*

P. Brother Little Amaglad *is a compact moth orchid with subtle, pale pink flowers with a pale orange lip.*

P. violacea *is a compact, fragrant beauty with star-shaped flowers, vividly marked purple, in spring and summer.*

P. I-Hsin Black Tulip *is a very desirable orchid thanks to its beetroot-red flowers that are edged with white.*

P. stuartiana *produces white flowers, with a lower lip that is attractively speckled red, on tall stems in the winter.*

P. Doris *is grown for its large pink flowers that appear throughout the year on 12in (30cm) stalks.*

P. Brother Pico Sweetheart 'K&P' *is a diminutive orchid topped with masses of pale pink, red-lipped flowers.*

P. Lundy *is a compact orchid, growing to 6in (15cm), with spectacular greenish-yellow flowers with red veining.*

Intricate blooms

An orchid covered with flowers is an impressive sight, but get up close and personal with these plants and you'll see the beauty of their individual blooms, which are elaborately patterned or flushed with other shades, producing a breathtaking display. *Dendrobium* likes cool temperatures, while striking *Oncidium* thrive in a range of conditions.

Oncidium

Plant used
Oncidium
Sharry Baby

Height and spread
H 24in (60cm)
S 12in (30cm)

Exposure
Light, but not
in direct sun

Temperature needs
64–75°F (18–24°C) in
the day and 55–61°F
(13–16°C) at night

Flowering time
Several times during
the year

Suitable pot size
6in (15cm)

Suitable container material
Plastic, placed inside
a decorative
container

Compost type
Orchid compost

Although famed for their dazzling yellow flowers, *Oncidium* is a large and varied tribe with flowers in white, cream, pink, and red. In addition, some are short and compact, while others produce a robust fan of leaves and flower stalks over 3ft (1m) long that have to be staked. Most bloom in the fall, but there are plants that will bloom in the spring, summer, and winter. Some species need a fair bit of attention, but hybrids, such as Sweet Sugar and the chocolate-scented Sharry Baby, are perfect for beginners. Place in a light location, out of direct sunlight.

TEMPERATURE CONTROL
Depending on the variety, *Oncidium* needs either cool, intermediate, or warm conditions, so check that you can provide the right environment before buying. Cool-loving plants need a temperature of 61°F (16°C) during the day and a minimum of 50°F (10°C) at night, while intermediates thrive in 64–75°F (18–24°C) during the day and 55–61°F (13–16°C) at night. Warm-loving plants need at least 70°F (21°C) during the day and 61°F (16°C) at night.

TOP TIP: ENCOURAGING FLOWERING
Oncidium are generally floriferous, but some people find that plants bought in flower are difficult to coax into bloom again. To ensure they thrive, make sure the temperature range is correct and that the plants are getting enough light. Water regularly, but less in the winter, and use a liquid orchid feed (following the instructions on the pack) with every other watering to encourage flower production.

Oncidium *Sharry Baby's* *spikes of dark red, pink, and white flowers are long-lasting and beautifully scented.*

Dendrobium

Plant used
Dendrobium
Momozono 'Princess'

Height and spread
H 24in (60cm)
S 12in (30cm)

Exposure
Bright, but not in
direct sun

Temperature needs
Cool conditions, with
a minimum of
50°F (10°C)

Flowering time
Spring

Suitable pot size
6in (15cm)

**Suitable container
material**
Plastic, placed inside
a decorative
container

Compost type
Orchid compost

Thousands of these show-stopping divas are available, with plants varying in size, from those that grow to ankle height to lofty specimens that soar well above 3ft (1m). These orchids are recognizable by the cluster of slender, canelike structures (pseudobulbs) that either produce flowers and leaves down their length or hold clusters of blooms on top. Most *Dendrobium* plants like cool conditions, with a daytime temperature of about 61°F (16°C) and a minimum nighttime temperature of 50°F (10°C). However, there are some that need warmer temperatures to thrive.

MAINTAINING PLANTS

Dendrobium plants prefer a light location with shade from direct sunlight; an east-facing windowsill is ideal. Water plants regularly from spring to fall, but less in the winter. It's important not to overwater or the roots can rot. Like most orchids, they are fairly hungry and need a liquid feed with every third watering. To raise the humidity around them, either grow several plants on a pebble tray filled with water, making sure the level is below the top of the pebbles, or mist in the morning with a hand sprayer, leaving plenty of time for the moisture to dry out before evening.

D. ***Momozono 'Princess'*** *bears heads of eye-catching pink, yellow, and white flowers.*

EASY ORCHIDS

CHOOSING DENDROBIUMS

D. nobile *produces large, pale pink flowers with darker pink marks and a yellow throat. These sit on top of 18in (45cm) cylindrical stems and appear in the spring.*

D. Sonia *is an exotic beauty, the flowers of which are often used to make floral garlands in Hawaii; they are an intense pink with contrasting cream-colored markings.*

D. Sweet Dawn *fills a room with natural floral fragrance. The star-shaped white flowers with a yellow center are generally produced from fall to spring.*

D. fimbriatum *produces pretty fringed flowers the color of orangeade, with a dark brown center, which appear in spring. This orchid likes cool conditions.*

Cool cymbidiums

These showy orchids are among the easiest to grow, because they thrive at normal indoor temperatures and will flower for months in the winter when little else is in bloom. The flowers come in many striking shades and grow in large sprays on slender spikes, while some are fragrant. They also require very little care and attention.

Plant used
Cymbidium Lisa Rose

Height and spread
H 24in (60cm)
S 36in (90cm)

Exposure
Partial shade in summer; bright light in winter

Temperature needs
Varies and depends on variety—most will die below about 45°F (7°C), and will not thrive above 77°F (25°C).

Suitable pot size
6in (15cm)

Suitable container material
Plastic, placed inside a decorative pot

Compost type
Orchid compost

Valued for their large sprays of colorful flowers, *Cymbidium* bloom for up to ten weeks, usually during winter and spring. New breeding has led to thousands of vibrant varieties with flowers in shades of white, yellow, red, pink, and green, many of which are attractively speckled. Some have whopping flower stalks 3ft (1m) high, but there are plenty of compact varieties for small spaces that grow to no more than 12in (30cm).

Although they are easy to care for, the compost must be kept moist during the growing season—but do not overwater; this can cause rotting. In the winter, reduce watering to keep plants on the dry side. For the best floral display, add a few drops of specialist liquid orchid feed to every other watering. Support flower spikes with a stake to prevent them from flopping, and cut back stems almost to the base when the blooms have faded.

TEMPERATURE REQUIREMENTS

In the summer, a temperature of 61-77°F (16-25°C) is perfect for a *Cymbidium*. You can set them in a bright location in a cool room, out of direct sunlight, or place them outside, as long as they are in a sheltered spot protected from the sun. Remember to bring them back indoors well before frost threatens in the fall. In the winter, lower the temperature to 50-57°F (10-14°C); a place in a cool greenhouse, sunroom, or on bright windowsill is ideal.

A huge variety of Cymbidium *are available in a vast range of colors, including this pink* Cymbidium Lisa Rose

---

TOP TIP: REPOTTING ORCHIDS

Orchid roots will soon fill a container, and plants will need repotting every few years to prevent stunted growth. *Cymbidium* flower best if a little pot-bound, so will not need repotting as frequently as other plants. Choose a pot that's just about an inch wider than the original. First, prepare the root ball: slide it out of the original container and remove any dead or shrivelled growth and dead roots. Tap the root ball gently to dislodge loose compost. Put a handful of compost in the bottom of the new pot, place the plant on top, and then fill in around it with orchid compost, up to the original level.

Cymbidium selections

C. hookerianum *is a stunning species with delightfully scented, apple-green flowers that appear in the winter.*

C. *Showgirl* *boasts pink-blushed, white flowers that are speckled red; they are produced throughout winter and spring.*

C. *Pontac 'Mont Millais'* *is a tall variety with dramatic, dark maroon-red flowers that appear in the winter.*

C. *Portelet Bay* *produces large white flowers with broad petals and bright red centers in the winter.*

C. *Golden Elf* *is a summer-flowering variety with large bright yellow flowers that are sweetly scented. Plant it in a contrasting contemporary black container to create a stylish arrangement.*

Slipper orchids *Paphiopedilum*

At first glance you could be forgiven for thinking that these flowers look too perfect to be real. Intricately patterned, they come in a wide range of colors and shapes, all with an unusual slipperlike pouch. To enjoy these long-lasting blooms at home, just give them the growing conditions they need to thrive.

Plant used
Paphiopedilum hybrid

Height and spread
H & S 6–12in (15–30cm)

Exposure
Bright, but not direct sunlight

Temperature needs
Varies, depending on variety

Suitable pot size
6in (15cm)

Suitable container material
Plastic, placed inside a decorative pot

Compost type
Orchid compost

Slipper orchids are extremely popular thanks to their showy, colorful flowers and their foliage, which is sometimes attractively spotted. Although not the easiest orchid to grow, it's certainly not the most challenging and will thrive with a little care and attention. There are many different varieties of slipper orchid worth growing, ranging in height from 6–12in (15–30cm) when in flower. The blooms are either borne singly or in clusters and are highly distinctive, comprising an upper sepal, two swept-back petals, and a pouch at the front that gives this orchid its common name.

Water plants regularly, allow the compost to almost dry out between waterings, but don't overwater. They like humidity, so either group plants together and stand them on a gravel tray filled with water or wipe down leaves with a soft damp cloth.

LIGHT AND HEAT REQUIREMENTS

Slipper orchids like a light location out of direct sun, such as an east-facing window. They fall into three groups, each relating to temperature requirements, so check that you can give the plant what it needs before you buy. Those that like cool conditions need a temperature of 61°F (16°C) during the day and a minimum temperature of 50°F (10°C) at night; intermediates prefer a daytime temperature of 64–75°F (18–24°C) and 55–61°F (13–16°C) at night; and warm-loving plants require a daytime temperature of at least 70°F (21°C), and 61°F (16°C) at night.

Center: **Feed your slipper orchids** *every two weeks with half-strength orchid fertilizer and reduce to monthly in the fall and winter.*

TOP TIP: DIVIDING SLIPPER ORCHIDS

After several years the roots of your *Paphiopedilum* will have filled its container, and it will need to be repotted into a larger pot with fresh orchid compost. Alternatively, you can divide your plant in the spring, when it's not in flower, to produce two plants. Remove the orchid carefully from its pot. Loosen the congested root ball and look for a natural break between the leaves of the plant. Then gently ease the root ball apart to produce two plants. Remove any dead roots and repot one section into the original pot with fresh compost and the other into a new container.

Choosing slipper orchids

P. *Clair de Lune* is a highly prized hybrid with a single lime-green and white flower on each stem.

P. **callosum** is extremely easy to grow and boasts a tall flower spike emerging between heavily mottled leaves.

P. **fairrieanum** bears a single purple-veined flower that rises above a clump of strap-shaped leaves in the fall.

P. **insigne** is a compact orchid with pale green leaves and single flowers that appear from fall to spring.

P. **venustum** produces very exotic-looking flowers on slender stems from winter to spring.

P. **villosum** is a compact orchid, bearing stems of 6in (15cm) reddish flowers with light-green pouches.

P. *Pinocchio* is a small orchid whose flower spike holds several yellow-green blooms with pinky-yellow pouches.

P. *Maudiae 'Coloratum'* produces 12in (30cm) stems, bearing single dark red flowers that are attractively striped.

EASY ORCHIDS

Frost-proof fuchsias

Blooming continuously from midsummer until well into fall, hardy fuchsias are among the few flowering container plants that are happy in some shade. Choose from elegant single bells to fat, blowsy, frilly-skirted blooms, and team them with impatiens and foliage plants. Their leaves need to be cut down before it frosts, but plants should revive again in spring.

PLANTS FOR SHADE

Plant used
Fuchsia 'Genii;'
Chlorophytum comosum;
purple Heuchera;
plain-leaf ivy

Height and spread
Fuchsia: H 36in (90cm) S 30in (75cm);
Chlorophytum H 6in (15cm) S 12in (30cm); Heuchera H & S 20in (50cm); ivy S 24in (60cm)

Exposure
Partial shade or full sun

Temperature needs
Ivy and heuchera are fully hardy.
Fuchsia 'Genii:' min 23°F. (-5°C).
Chlorophytum: min. 45°F (7°C).

Suitable pot size
12in (30cm)

Suitable container material
Stone, terra-cotta, metal

Compost type
Soil based compost, e.g., John Innes No. 2

Tall and elegant, or compact and floriferous, there are many hardy fuchsias to choose from. *Fuchsia* 'Genii' has the added bonus of golden-yellow spring foliage that turns bright green as it matures. Use its decorative leaves and flower-laden stems to form a colorful centerpiece in a container arrangement, matched with metallic purple-leaved heucheras, variegated spider plants, and trailing ivy.

Although hardy fuchsias are much tougher than bedding varieties, most lose their top growth after a sharp frost, but they are easily rejuvenated by pruning back to undamaged growth in the spring—you will see green shoots appearing along the lower stems as temperatures rise. Remove any weak, damaged, or diseased stems at the same time. Also place pots of fuchsias close to house walls or in a sheltered site to protect plants from the worst of the winter weather.

HARDY FUCHSIA OPTIONS
Whatever your garden style, there's a fuchsia to match. For a dwarf type, try 'Tom Thumb,' with its red and mauve flowers, or its cousin 'Lady Thumb' (*see opposite*), which is about the same size. If you want a slightly larger plant, look out for 'Alice Hoffman,' which has semi-double pink and white flowers, or 'Mrs Popple' (*see opposite*). Dark purple and crimson 'Riccartonii' is a taller type, and makes a striking feature in a large mixed container, or keep it compact by pruning the stems back in the spring.

> **TOP TIP: CREATING BUSHIER PLANTS**
>
> Hardy fuchsias respond well to pruning when young, which encourages bushy growth and more flowers. Using your fingers, pinch off the leading shoot at the top of the plant when it has developed three sets of leaves. This will result in a number of sideshoots developing. Pinch these back when they too have developed three sets of leaves. As the plant grows, remove wayward shoots to keep a bushy shape.

Forms of **Fuchsia magellanica** *are reliably hardy and produce red, pink, or white single flowers.*

Hardy fuchsia choices

Fuchsia magellanica *var.* molinae *is a large plant with delicate, single, pale pink flowers from midsummer.*

Fuchsia *'Lena'* *is a very hardy selection with double white and magenta flowers held on lax arching stems.*

Fuchsia *'Mrs Popple'* *is almost fully hardy. An upright bushy shrub, it has rich scarlet and purple single flowers.*

Fuchsia *'Lady Thumb'*, *a tiny form ideal for windowboxes or wall pots, has semi-double pink and white blooms.*

A colorful medley of flowers and foliage, *this combination of* Fuchsia *'Genii,' dark-leaf heuchera, spider plant, and ivy will produce the best display when given a liquid fertilizer every month in summer.*

PLANTS FOR SHADE

Mini fernery

Don't let a dank spot in the shade get you down. Make the most of it with a pot of tactile, leafy ferns guaranteed to transform the gloomiest of corners with year-round color and texture. Choose a selection of different foliage types and mix evergreens with deciduous types for a variety of winter shades.

Plant used
Asplenium scolopendrium Cristatum Group;
Athyrium niponicum var. *pictum*;
Polystichum makinoi

Height and spread
Asplenium scolopendrium Cristatum Group:
H 24in (60cm)
S 32in (80cm)
Athyrium niponicum var. *pictum*: H & S 8in (20cm)
Polystichum makinoi:
H & S 24in (60cm)

Exposure
Sheltered, shady

Temperature needs
Hardy to 5°F (-15°C)

Suitable pot size
12–18in (30–45cm)

Suitable container material
Terra-cotta, stone, glazed terra-cotta, metal

Compost type
Grow in a mix of 3 parts multi-purpose compost, 1 part soil-based compost, and 1 part sharp sand.

Center: **Group ferns together** *in a shallow container to create a focal point in a shady corner of the garden.*

Most gardens have a difficult shady area where nothing seems to grow, but a container of mixed ferns will provide lush, verdant hues in these unpromising sites. Good choices include the hart's tongue fern, *Asplenium scolopendrium,* with its leathery, wavy-edged leaves, the feathery evergreen holly fern, *Polystichum makinoi,* and the Japanese painted fern, *Athyrium niponicum* var. *pictum,* whose fronds are blushed pinky red. Although these three ferns work well together in a container, there are many others you can use but aim to achieve a combination of different leaf shapes, shades, and textures. Robust, vigorous, and tall-growing ferns, such as *Matteuccia struthiopteris,* or the shuttlecock fern, are best given a pot of their own.

When choosing containers for ferns, opt for something clean and simple; these plants are not garden divas and anything too fancy will draw attention away from their subtle good looks. Ferns are also not deep rooted and do well in shallow pots.

CREATING A MICROCLIMATE

Most ferns enjoy damp, shady conditions that mimic those on the forest floor where they grow in the wild. Avoid open, exposed locations, as the sun and wind will scorch their leaves. To ensure plants thrive, keep the compost damp at all times, summer and winter, and feed plants annually in the spring with a slow-release granular fertilizer. Choose your ferns carefully to ensure they all prefer the same conditions; those here enjoy damp shade, but the male fern, *Dryopteris filix-mas,* suits dry shade.

TOP TIP: SPRING CARE

Most ferns are tough, fully hardy plants that more or less take care of themselves. However, the outer fronds of some evergreens may look a bit battered or tired after a long winter, so tidy them up by removing old leaves before new fronds unfurl in spring. Leave the dried bronze leaves of deciduous ferns to provide color and contrast in the winter, and then cut these off when you see new growth appearing at the base of the plant in the spring. Also remove weeds and any debris lodged between the leaves.

Hardy fern options

Adiantum venustum, *the evergreen Himalayan maidenhair fern, has bronze-pink new growth in the spring.*

Asplenium scolopendrium, *or hart's tongue fern, forms dense clumps of evergreen, leathery, upright fronds.*

Dryopteris affinis, *the golden male fern, is a semi-evergreen, waist-high plant with long feathery fronds.*

Dryopteris erythrosora *has knee-high stems of beautiful fine fronds. It is a deciduous plant and new growth is red.*

Matteuccia struthiopteris, *the stately shuttlecock fern, is a robust, tall, upright deciduous fern that suits a large pot.*

Polypodium vulgare 'Cornubiense' *is the common polypody fern. A compact plant, it bears glossy evergreen fronds.*

Polystichum setiferum *Divisilobum Group* *is a bushy evergreen with tall, tapering fronds with brown midribs.*

Polystichum polyblepharum, *known as the Japanese tassel fern, is a compact evergreen with yellowish fronds in spring.*

Foliage collections

Hostas and heucheras thrive in containers and look stunning when combined with colorful flowers or grouped together on their own. There are hundreds of different types of both plants in a wealth of colors, shapes, and sizes. Try a collection of hostas for a cool leafy display, or heucheras in a rainbow of colors for a bolder design.

Hostas

Plants used
Hosta 'Francee;'
Hosta 'Krossa Regal;'
Hosta fortunei var. albopicta f. aurea;
Hosta 'August Moon'

Height and spread
H & S 8–30in (20–75cm)

Exposure
Shade

Temperature needs
Hardy to -10°F (-23°C) or lower

Suitable pot size
8in (20cm)

Suitable container material
Any

Compost type
Soil-based compost, e.g., John Innes No. 3

Hostas make elegant foliage groups for shady sites. To create the best show, choose varieties with different shapes and leaf colors and make a tiered display with larger plants at the back and more compact types toward the front. Plants range in height from mound-forming miniatures an inch or so tall, such as *H. fortunei* var. *albopicta* f. *aurea,* to those whose foliage reaches over 24in (60cm).

Water hostas regularly in the spring and summer, and feed in early spring with a slow-release granular fertilizer. Plants spread slowly to form large clumps over time; either move them into larger pots or divide them up and replant healthy sections in pots of fresh compost.

Group together hostas for a rich mix of colors, shapes, and types. Those here are H. *'Francee,'* H. *'Krossa Regal,'* H. fortunei *var.* albopicta *f.* aurea, *and* H. *'August Moon.'*

TOP TIP: SLUG DETERRENT

Hostas are magnets for slugs and snails, but you can easily protect plants in pots by sticking a band of copper tape around the outside. Widely available at garden centers, the copper emits a tiny electrical charge that deters leaf-munching pests trying to cross it.

Heucheras

Plants used
Heuchera 'Can-can;'
Juncus effusus f.
spiralis (corkscrew
rush); *Teucrium
scorodonia* 'Crispum'

Height and spread
Heuchera: H & S
20in (50cm);
Juncus: H 18in (45cm)
S 24in (60cm);
Teucrium:
H 14in (35cm)
S 10in (25cm)

Exposure
Partial shade

Temperature needs
Fully hardy

Suitable pot size
12in (30cm)

**Suitable container
material**
Terra-cotta, plastic,
stone

Compost type
Multi-purpose with
added soil-based
compost, e.g., John
Innes No. 3

Heucheras, or coral plants, produce lively displays in partially shaded areas with their evergreen leaves and spires of tiny bell-shaped flowers in the spring and summer. While they look great on their own or displayed as a collection, they also make good companions for other plants in a container design. For example, the metallic purple 'Can-can' contrasts beautifully with a backdrop of crinkle-leaved *Teucrium*, while the spiral leaves of a corkscrew rush echo the tall stems of the heuchera.

To maintain your displays, water heucheras regularly and ensure that the compost does not dry out over the summer. Feed plants in early spring with a slow-release granular fertilizer. Pots can be left outside all year, but store them in a sheltered spot in the winter to protect them from excessive rainfall. Heucheras will be happy in their pots for several years, but may eventually need to be divided or moved into a larger pot.

EVIL WEEVIL

Heucheras are largely trouble-free, but can be damaged by vine weevils; the adults eat notches around the leaves, while the grubs munch on the roots, causing plants to wilt and die. Protect plants by drenching containers with a biological control containing nematodes that eat vine-weevil larvae (*see also p.245*).

Blend Heuchera *'Can can' with the corkscrew rush,* Juncus effusus f. spiralis, *and* Teucrium scorodonia *'Crispum' to produce a mound of colorful foliage and spires of flowers.*

PLANTS FOR SHADE

CHOOSING HEUCHERA VARIETIES

H. *'Amber Waves'* *makes a compact clump of scalloped-edged leaves that are golden yellow and pink. In spring they are topped with sprays of dainty cream flowers.*

H. *'Plum Pudding'* *has rich purple leaves that look good all year, but are particularly appealing in the winter. The foliage makes a great foil for the pink summer blooms.*

H. *'Silver Scrolls'* *bears masses of pink summer flowers on red stems above a mound of heavily veined, burgundy, evergreen leaves overlaid with shades of metallic silver.*

H. brizoides *may not be as brightly colored as other heucheras, but it has a clump of rich green leaves that shows off its sprays of white flowers to perfection.*

Beautiful begonias

If you're looking for plants that provide exotic foliage and color all year, nothing beats begonias. This decorative tribe of house plants is blessed with striped, streaked, swirled, or splashed foliage in the most amazing hues, and dainty blooms that are generally less flamboyant than their summer-bedding cousins.

PLANTS FOR SHADE

Plants used
Begonia rex hybrids; Pilea depressa

Height and spread
Begonia rex: H 10in (25cm) S 12in (30cm); Pilea depressa: S 8in (20cm)

Exposure
Bright location out of direct sun

Temperature needs
Min. 50°F (10°C)

Suitable pot size
12in (30cm)

Suitable container material
Metal, plastic

Compost type
Multi-purpose compost

Modern breeding has resulted in a raft of striking new begonia cultivars, producing bright, cheery, exciting plants that deserve a place of pride in a modern home. Until recently begonias suffered from an image problem and were widely thought of as old-fashioned and sort of dreary. Most of the plants under attack were the dark-leaved varieties of *Begonia rex*, and although some of those melancholic varieties still exist, new hybrids look anything but antiquated and suit contemporary galvanized containers, whose unfussy style helps to show off the foliage to its best advantage. Choose selections with large leaves emblazoned with silver and metallic purple markings that shimmer in the light, or in colors to suit your decor, and team them with trailing plants, such as the tiny-leaved *Pilea depressa*, to soften the edges of the display.

Begonias aren't particularly deep-rooted, so if you are using tall containers, plant them in plastic pots that fit snugly inside your decorative ones. Then fill the base of the tall containers with pieces of broken styrofoam or pebbles to help build up the height, and pop the begonias in their plastic pots on top.

WATERING NEEDS
Begonias will soon wilt or lose their luster if you neglect watering them. Water the compost carefully from above with a long-necked watering can. It's important to avoid splashing the leaves as they are quite sensitive and easily damaged. Allow the surface of the compost to dry out before watering again.

Center: **Pair begonias with trailing plants** *in tall contemporary containers to brighten a modern décor with color and texture.*

TOP TIP: YEAR-ROUND CARE

Begonias are hungry plants that will not perform well if deprived of food. To keep them happy and to ensure they produce lots of colorful leaves, feed them every two weeks from spring to fall with a general-purpose liquid fertilizer. They also like to be kept warm all year round, ideally between 64–70°F (18–21°C), and they need a bright location out of direct sunlight, which may scorch their leaves. Remove any fallen flowers or damaged leaves to prevent them from rotting on the surface of the compost.

Choosing begonias

Begonia aconitifolia *has canelike stems, deeply lobed leaves flecked with silver, and pendulous pink flowers.*

Begonia benichoma *is a bushy begonia with serrated pink leaves that take on a silvery sheen as they mature.*

Begonia masoniana *is often called the iron cross begonia due to the distinctive dark markings on the textured leaves.*

Begonia serratipetala *is a shrublike begonia with long serrated leaves with pink spots and clusters of pink flowers.*

Begonia 'Merry Christmas' *is closely related to* Begonia rex, *with huge leaves adorned with rich pink markings.*

Begonia 'Silver Queen' *is an upright begonia with pink autumn flowers and leaves embellished with silver marbling.*

Begonia 'Fire Flush' *has deep-green and maroon leaves highlighted with fine red hair and scented pink flowers.*

Begonia 'Plum Rose' *has large leaves enriched by a glitzy combination of silver, pink, and green markings.*

PLANTS FOR SHADE

Foliage for a shady spot

Every home has its share of low-lit areas, where most flowering houseplants fail to prosper. However, there are some tough, resilient types grown for their attractive foliage that will thrive in gloomy sites. These three offer contrasting forms and appearances, and would look great as a group.

Mother-in-law's tongue *Sansevieria*

PLANTS FOR SHADE

Plant used
Sansevieria trifasciata 'Laurentii'

Height and spread
H 24in (60cm)
S 12in (30cm)

Exposure
Shade, although will grow equally well in direct light.

Temperature needs
Min. 50°F (10°C)

Suitable pot size
6–8in (15–20cm)

Suitable container material
Plastic pots inside decorative outer containers of any material

Compost type
Well-drained, soil-based compost, e.g., John Innes No. 2

Grown for its sword-shaped leaves that boast dark horizontal stripes and gold edges, this succulent is a great choice for a shady spot. With a reputation for being virtually indestructible, it will put up with drafts, dry air, and drought. A single plant can look a little lonely, so turn these architectural plants into a feature by displaying them in groups. Despite growing fairly tall, these plants do well in small containers and do not need frequent repotting. To keep them looking good, water when the compost has dried out, and dust the leaves occasionally.

TOP TIP: MAKING NEW PLANTS

Mother-in-law's tongues spread readily, sending up new leaves from underground stems. In time, dense clumps form that may become too large for their pots. To keep plants in check, tease the rootball apart to make several smaller plants; replant these in fresh compost.

Spiky tongues of variegated foliage create a dramatic focal point on a table, sideboard, or shelves.

Devil's ivy *Epipremnum aureum*

Plant used
Epipremnum aureum

Height and spread
S 5ft (1.5m)

Exposure
Best with some indirect light

Temperature needs
Min. 59°F (15°C)

Suitable pot size
8in (20cm)

Suitable container material
Plastic, ceramic, glazed terra-cotta

Compost type
Well-drained, multi-purpose compost

The devil's ivy can be grown as a climbing plant up a large support, or allow its long stems to cascade over the sides of a container raised up on a wooden stand, small table, or shelf. Alternatively, try growing it in a hanging basket or wall-mounted container where you can appreciate its glossy, heart-shaped, yellow-splashed leaves.

Not for the darkest corner, this plant needs some light or the variegation will fade. For the best performance, clean the leaves every few weeks to remove any dust, and mist them occasionally with a handheld sprayer. If the stems become too long, pinch them back to keep the plant right-sized and to encourage bushy growth. Water whenever the compost dries out during the growing season, but reduce the amount you give over the winter. Feed monthly in the summer with a foliage feed.

Trail the leaves of a devil's ivy over the sides of a stand, and place it in an area where it gets some indirect light.

Hard fern *Blechnum gibbum*

Plant used
Blechnum gibbum

Height and spread
H & S 24in (60cm)

Exposure
Partial shade

Temperature needs
Min 59°F (15°C)

Suitable pot size
6–8in (15–20cm)

Suitable container material
Plastic, metal, glazed terra-cotta

Compost type
Soil-based compost, e.g., John Innes No. 2

Ferns are among the most forgiving plants for a shady room, and the hard fern is one of the most desirable. Boasting long, leathery, deeply divided fronds, it produces a mass of stiff foliage. As the fern ages, it forms a distinctive black trunk, giving rise to its other common name, the dwarf tree fern.

WATERING NEEDS
Hailing from the tropics, this fern predictably likes warmth and humidity, making it a good choice for a bathroom, although it won't be very happy next to a drafty window. If you don't have a humid area for your plant, raise moisture levels by misting the leaves every few days with a handheld sprayer, which will also remove dust from the foliage. Ensure the compost is always moist, using warm water, and feed with a slow-release granular fertilizer in the spring.

Large, deeply divided fronds produce a beautiful display in a simple terra-cotta container.

Colorful clematis

Most people think of clematis as rampant climbers, only suitable for growing through trees or adorning house walls and pergolas, yet there are many compact varieties that can be grown in large pots. Train these colorful climbers up ornamental supports and use them to decorate patios and to add height to borders.

Plant used
Clematis Ooh La La

Height and spread
H 3–4ft (90–120cm)
S 24in (60cm)

Exposure
Sun or dappled shade

Temperature needs
Hardy to 5°F (-15°C)

Suitable pot size
18in (45cm)

Suitable container material
Use plastic pots set in outer containers of wood, stone, metal, or terra-cotta

Compost type
Soil-based compost, e.g., John Innes No. 3

If you don't have any space in a border close to a wall, fence, or house, you can still enjoy clematis by growing those that are naturally compact or have been bred specifically for containers. Both types need a large pot and a place in the sun or partial shade. Although their vigor may be curtailed in cramped quarters, these Lilliputian climbers are as floriferous as their larger relatives, and the new varieties will be covered from top to bottom in blooms during the summer. One such plant is *Clematis* Ooh La La, from the Evipo Boulevard patio range; its large pink flowers, with a darker stripe running down each petal, look stunning in a classic wooden planter.

PRUNING AND TRAINING

You can grow compact clematis up a wigwam of canes, an obelisk, or a fan-shaped trellis panel pushed into the container. Cover supports by regularly tying in new shoots with soft twine. To keep clematis within bounds and flowering prolifically, give them an annual prune. Spring- and early summer-flowering clematis should be pruned when the blooms fade, cutting to just above a leaf joint. Double-flowering varieties and those that flower twice in the summer need pruning in the winter or early spring; shorten long stems and remove weak or dying shoots. Cut all the stems of late summer- and early fall-flowering clematis to healthy buds just above the compost in late winter or early spring.

*Center: **Modern hybrids**, such as the pink-striped C. Ooh La La, have been bred to thrive in large patio containers.*

TOP TIP: MIX AND MATCH VARIETIES

Clematis look great on their own, but you can create an even more eye-catching display by growing two different varieties together. Pink flowers go well with white, dark blue, or purple blooms, or try an elegant white and purple mix, such as Ice Blue, with its blue-flushed white flowers, and King Fisher, as shown here.

Clematis for containers

Clematis *'Vyvyan Pennell'* is a very showy clematis for midsummer interest with large, double, lilac flowers.

Clematis *Fleuri* is a bushy little climber with a profusion of violet flowers from late spring until mid-fall.

Clematis *'Fireworks'* produces glowing purple and magenta flowers that adorn plants from early to midsummer.

Clematis florida *var.* florida **'Sieboldiana'** bears large white /flowers from late spring to fall.

Clematis *'The President'* is a summer-flowering variety with large flowers that are a rich shade of bluish-purple.

Clematis *'Niobe'* bears single, velvety red flowers with a cluster of yellow stamens from late spring to fall.

Clematis *Chantilly* has pale pink flowers with a darker stripe that appear from summer to early autumn.

Clematis *'Arabella'* has small, mauve and purple flowers. Its non-climbing stems need tying in to their supports.

Soaring annuals

Some of the greatest spectacles are short lived, and these annual climbers are a case in point. They last just one season, but in that time produce a blaze of beautiful flowers on twining stems. Use them in combination with other annual flowers and foliage plants, or create a profusion of color by planting two together.

Rhodochiton

Plants used
Rhodochiton atrosanguineus; *Cerinthe major* var. *purpurascens*; *Plectranthus zatarhendii*

Height and spread
Rhodochiton: H 3ft (1m); *Cerinthe*: H & S: 12in (30cm); *Plectranthus*: S: 24in (60cm)

Exposure
Sun or partial shade

Temperature needs
Not hardy below 32°F (0°C).

Suitable pot size
18in (45cm)

Suitable container material
Ceramic, terra-cotta, stone

Compost type
Soil-based compost, e.g., John Innes No. 3

Stems of earthy red, pendulous *Rhodochiton* flowers make a striking statement when wrapped around a wigwam of bamboo canes. The bare stems at the base of the plant can be hidden by the silvery-blue bushy foliage of *Cerinthe* plants, and the sides of the pot softened with trailing *Plectranthus*. Perfect as a focal point or to break up a sea of patio slabs, *Rhodochiton* will provide a sophisticated splash of color from summer to fall. Add some slow-release granular fertilizer to the compost when planting, and keep plants well watered during the summer. If your display starts to wilt in the summer, give it a boost with a tomato feed.

TRAINING PLANTS

Rhodochiton has twining leafstalks and will climb naturally when established, but it needs a helping hand to get started. After erecting your wigwam of canes in a large pot, plant a climber at the foot of each, and secure stems to the canes with soft twine. Plant the other annuals between the bamboo canes.

TOP TIP: SAVING SEED

Although it is a perennial, *Rhodochiton* is often grown as an annual, because it is not frost hardy. It is best started from seed each year, and you can save your own seeds from old plants. Allow the pods to dry out, then break them open to extract the seeds. Store seeds in a labeled jar until spring.

Create an exciting arrangement with color and height by grouping Rhodochiton with Cerinthe and trailing Plectranthus.

Morning glory *Ipomoea* and *Convolvulus*

Plant used
Ipomoea purpurea

Height and spread
H 6ft (1.8m)

Exposure
Full sun

Temperature needs
Min. 45°F (7°C)

Suitable pot size
12–18in (30–45cm)

Suitable container material
Terra-cotta, metal, ceramic, wood

Compost type
Soil-based compost, e.g., John Innes No. 3

Ipomoea is an easy-to-grow annual climber, known as morning glory, which produces masses of delicate flowers from summer until the first frosts. Growing to 6ft (2m) or more, it is perfect for training up supports in large pots. Dwarf morning glory, *Convolvus tricolor*, is also an annual, but reaches just 14in (40cm) and can be tied in to a low support, or allowed to scramble through other plants. Both *Ipomoea* and *Convolvus* are best combined with other flowers, as their blooms often close during the hottest part of the day. Water plants freely, and apply a balanced liquid fertilizer every month.

COLOR OPTIONS
There are many morning glories to choose from, and flowers vary in shape from trumpets to tubes, and colors include white, pink, purple, and blue, while many are bicolored.

Convolvulus tricolor

Black-eyed Susan *Thunbergia*

Plant used
Thunbergia alata

Height and spread
H 6ft (1.8m)

Exposure
Sun

Temperature needs
Min. 50°F (10°C)

Suitable pot size
12–18in (30–45cm)

Suitable container material
Terra-cotta, metal, ceramic

Compost type
Soil-based compost, e.g., John Innes No. 3

Cheery yellow flowers with a distinctive black "eye" cover this vigorous climber from midsummer to autumn. Superb in a large container, where it can be grown up a wigwam of canes, trellis, or an ornamental obelisk, this plant needs a sunny spot and regular watering to thrive. Apply a balanced liquid fertilizer every month. Although it's a perennial, black-eyed Susan is usually grown as an annual from seed each year. Seeds germinate easily; you can start them off indoors in early spring so that the young plants will be good sized and ready to start flowering soon after you plant them outside when the risk of frost has passed.

PLANTING PARTNERS
Black-eyed Susan looks great as a centerpiece among white petunias, yellow nasturtiums, and the yellow foliage of trailing *Ipomoea batatas* 'Margarita.' Alternatively, mix yellow *Thunbergia* with orange- or white-flowered varieties, or even plant them with green beans (*see pp. 176–7*).

Thunbergia alata creates an impressive summer show.

HIGH CLIMBERS

Fragrant climbers

Bring flowers and scent up to nose level with these fragrant climbers.
Both produce small blooms that belie their heavy perfume, which is
guaranteed to give your garden a lift all summer long. Star jasmine
also sports glossy evergreen foliage that turns bronze in the winter,
and sweet peas can be grown easily from seed each spring.

Star jasmine *Trachelospermum*

Plant used
Trachelospermum jasminoides

Height and spread
H up to 8ft (2.5m) if pruned

Exposure
Sun or partial shade

Temperature needs
Hardy to 23°F (-5°C)

Suitable pot size
12in (30cm)

Suitable container material
Stone, terra-cotta, ceramic, metal, wood

Compost type
Soil-based compost, e.g., John Innes No. 3

Star jasmine, *Trachelospermum jasminoides*, is a strong evergreen with glossy dark green leaves that make the ideal backdrop for its small, heavenly-scented, white summer flowers. The plant can grow to 28ft (9m) in the ground, but with regular pruning it is easy to keep in check in a large pot. The more compact *Trachelospermum asiaticum* is a good alternative, and has similar foliage and jasmine-scented flowers. Happy in sun or partial shade, both are frost hardy, but will need protecting in harsh winters. Water plants regularly in the growing season, and feed annually in the spring with a slow-release granular fertilizer.

SUPPORTING PLANTS
Plants in pots can be pushed up against a wall, fence, shed, or the leg of a pergola and trained against wires fixed to the support. Alternatively, place a trellis, an obelisk, or a wigwam of canes in a pot to provide a free-standing support, or train the stems over a sturdy metal arch set between two pots of star jasmine.

TOP TIP: PRUNING STAR JASMINE
Star jasmine grows very rapidly and will soon look unkempt unless it's given an annual trim. Prune plants in the spring. First, cut out any dead, diseased, or congested growth. Then prune out any wayward shoots to maintain a tight, compact shape. You may also need to thin out new shoots as they appear later in spring and throughout the summer. Although plants are self supporting, you can tie in shoots with soft twine to fill gaps on your support.

Trachelospermum jasminoides *provides a tower of scented starry flowers in summer.*

Sweet peas *Lathyrus odoratus*

Plant used
Lathyrus odoratus

Height and spread
H 6ft (2m)

Exposure
Full sun

Temperature needs
Hardy to 5°F (-15°C)

Suitable pot size
12in (30cm) or larger

Suitable container material
Terra-cotta, stone, ceramic

Compost type
Soil-based compost, e.g., John Innes No. 3

Native to southern Italy, sweet peas comprise a large clan of annuals that will fill your garden with color and scent from early summer to the first frost in the fall. Perfect for large pots, where their stems can be trained up cane supports or an ornamental obelisk, sweet peas come in shades of pink, red, blue, purple, and white, with two-tone flowers also available.

Although seedlings can be readily purchased in the spring, you'll have a greater choice if you raise your own from seed. In the spring, sow seeds ½in (1cm) deep in tall cell trays, and place them in a coldframe, greenhouse, or cool room to germinate. Keep the compost moist, and when seedlings have four leaves, pinch off the top pair with your fingers, which encourages side-shoots to form. The well-rooted sweet peas can be planted in pots outside from mid-spring.

PROLONGING FLOWERING
Although sweet peas can flower continuously until autumn, they need nurturing to ensure a long-lasting display. Water plants regularly, and drench the compost with a weak solution of liquid fertilizer every two weeks. Also remove blooms as soon as they start to fade, or regularly pick bouquets for your home, to prevent the plant from diverting its energy into making seeds, which halts flower production.

Make a rustic support for sweet peas by twisting flexible willow stems around a pyramid of sturdy poles.

HIGH CLIMBERS

CHOOSING SWEET PEA VARIETIES

'Blue Ripple' *is a stunning type with long slender stems of highly scented, white, frilly-edged flowers with distinctive blue markings on the edge of the petals.*

Heirloom Mixed *is a showy mixture of heavily scented, old-fashioned varieties with large flowers in a wide range of eye-catching colors.*

'Matucana' *is a dark and desirable climber. An old-fashioned sweet pea that has been grown since the 18th century, it produces strongly scented maroon and purple flowers.*

'Jayne Amanda' *is a Spencer cultivar with large frilly flowers that characterize this group. It has warm pink blooms 1½in (3.5cm) across, which are perfect for cutting.*

Jasmines for the home

Covered with masses of small starry flowers that emit a heady perfume, tender climbing jasmines put on a vertical show to delight the senses for much of the year. Plant them in large pots and train their long trailing stems along a wall, or twine them around a plant support to fill your home with the natural scent of these sophisticated climbers.

Madagascar jasmine *Stephanotis*

Plant used
Stephanotis floribunda

Height and spread
H 24in (60cm)
S 6ft (2m) in a large pot

Exposure
Sun or partial shade

Temperature needs
Min. 55°F (13°C)

Suitable pot size
8in (20cm)

Suitable container material
Glazed terra-cotta, ceramic

Compost type
Soil-based compost, e.g., John Innes No. 2

This evergreen climber makes an attractive houseplant all year round. Its dark green, leathery leaves provide a dramatic foil for the waxy white flowers which appear in large clusters from spring until fall.

Widely available, Madagascar jasmines are often sold in small pots, already trained with their long stems twisted around a hoop of wire. Although the hoop will suffice for a while, it will eventually become overcrowded, at which point the plant will need a larger support structure and a bigger container. Repot by carefully removing the ties and unwinding the stems. Plant the jasmine in the center of the new pot, secure a piece of trellis or an obelisk in it, and wind the stems around the uprights, tying them in with soft twine. If necessary, cut back long shoots after flowering.

To keep the plant happy, keep the compost moist at all times, decreasing the watering in the winter. From time to time, wipe the leaves with a damp cloth to remove dust, and mist the foliage occasionally to increase humidity.

POSITIONING PLANTS

This plant loves a bright location, but should be kept out of direct sunlight in summer. A light, airy living room where you can get maximum enjoyment from the scented flowers is an ideal location, but do not place it in the bedroom because the perfume can be a little too strong. Avoid moving it around when in bud or bearing flowers; the sudden changes of temperature can cause both to drop prematurely.

Ideal in a partially shaded site, Stephanotis *thrives when fed monthly while in growth with a balanced liquid feed.*

White jasmine *Jasminum polyanthum*

Plant used
Jasminum polyanthum

Height and spread
H & S 5ft (1.5m)

Exposure
Bright light, away from direct sun

Temperature needs
64°F (18°C)

Suitable pot size
8–12in (20–30cm)

Suitable container material
Plastic, stone, glazed terra-cotta, ceramic

Compost type
Soil-based compost, e.g., John Innes No. 2

Its flowers may be small, but what they lack in size they make up for in fragrance. Borne in prolific numbers during winter and spring, the white star-shaped blooms open from pink buds and have a knock-out scent. Although jasmines are often sold trained on a metal hoop, this is rarely adequate for this vigorous evergreen plant. Pot it into a large container and retrain the stems up a more substantial support, such as an obelisk or wigwam. To keep it healthy, ensure the compost never dries out, and feed every month with a balanced liquid fertilizer while in active growth. This plant grows quickly and can become straggly and choked with stems if left to its own devices. Prune annually after flowering to control its size and maintain a tidy plant.

TEMPERATURE CONTROL

Keep jasmines in a cool room with temperatures of around 64°F (18°C); any warmer and it will produce lots of growth at the expense of flowers. In early fall, encourage the formation of new buds by placing it outside during the day for about four weeks, bringing it back inside n late afternoon to avoid frost damage. After this, return it to a cool room.

Single, white, highly scented flowers appear in late winter and early spring, brightening up the gloomy months.

HIGH CLIMBERS

TOP TIP: REMOVING DEAD BLOOMS

Faded jasmine flowers tend to stick to the plant, giving it an undesirable appearance. It's a time-consuming job, but removing the dead blooms with a pair of sharp scissors will keep the plant looking good and encourage the production of more blooms. Cut the old flower stalks back to the main stem.

Flying colors for the home

Let these flowering exotics paint walls of color in your home with their exquisite blooms and green foliage. They are tender climbers and produce an abundance of flowers along their twining stems over many months. Purple coral peas bloom from late winter to early summer, while the glory lily and bougainvillea are both flower in summer.

Glory lily *Gloriosa*

Plant used
Gloriosa superba 'Rothschildiana'

Height
H 6ft (2m)

Exposure
Sunny, but shaded from direct sun

Temperature needs
Min. 46°F (8°C)

Suitable pot size
12in (30cm)

Suitable container material
Plastic inside a decorative pot

Suitable compost
Multi-purpose compost

Few climbing plants make a more arresting sight than the glory lily in summer, when its slender stems are festooned with large red flowers. Measuring 3in (8cm) across, each bloom consists of six wavy, swept-back petals with yellow margins. Native to the tropics of Africa, this self-clinging climber can easily scale 6ft (2m) and will happily scramble through a tall obelisk or other robust support in a large container. Place your plant in a sunny, light, warm sunroom or kitchen.

WINTER CARE
After the glory lily's flowers start to fade, stop feeding and reduce watering (*see Top Tip box below*). The leaves will then turn yellow, and the plant will become dormant over winter. Remove the dead growth from the surface of the container, and do not water your glory lily again until new shoots start to appear above the surface of the compost the following spring.

Create a tower of vibrant flowers by weaving stems of Gloriosa superba 'Rothschildiana' through an obelisk.

TOP TIP: ENCOURAGING FLOWERING

To flower well, the glory lily needs a location in a warm, light place with some protection from the sun in summer. Water well during the growing season, and give plants a boost by feeding with a balanced liquid fertilizer every two weeks. Raise humidity levels by misting the leaves occasionally—do this in the morning so that the plant can dry out before evening.

Bougainvillea

Plant used
Bougainvillea glabra

Height
H up to 25ft (8m),
but can be restricted
to size of support

Exposure
Full sun—shade will
cause leaves to drop

Temperature needs
Not reliably hardy
below 32°F (0°C)

Suitable pot size
Min. 6in (15cm)

**Suitable container
material**
Plastic inside a
decorative pot

Suitable compost
Multi-purpose
compost

A sun lover for a windowsill or sunroom, there are many fabulous *Bougainvillea* forms to choose from. As well as *B. glabra*, which comes in pink, purple, and white, try *B.* x *buttiana* with cream flowers, the pale yellow *B.* x *buttiana* 'Enid Lancaster', or, for the most eye-catching display, select bright pink *B.* x *buttiana* 'Raspberry Ice,' which also sports variegated foliage.

GROWING BOUGAINVILLEA
Trim back plants to suit your space, and grow up frames, around hoops, or along wires as an espalier. Water and feed plants regularly in the growing season. *Bougainvillea* can flower for up to ten months a year in a sunroom, and will be happy outside on a patio in the summer, but it needs a frost-free place for the winter. Forms of *B.* x *buttiana* also become dormant in winter and lose their leaves, which then reappear in spring.

Bougainvillea glabra *produces white blooms.*

Purple coral pea *Hardenbergia violacea*

Plant used
*Hardenbergia
violacea*

Height
H up to 6ft (2m)

Exposure
Light, out of
direct sun

Temperature needs
Not reliably hardy
below 32°F (0°C)

Suitable pot size
12in (30cm)

**Suitable container
material**
Plastic inside a
decorative pot

Suitable compost
Soil-based compost,
e.g., John Innes No. 3

Hardenbergia violacea *has delicate purple flowers.*

Between late winter and early summer, this evergreen climber makes itself a welcome house guest by providing an amazing show of small purple flowers held in long clusters. The wiry branches of this Australian native are self-climbing, but you may need to tie in the shoots with soft twine to train them evenly over a support, such as an obelisk or trellis.

CARE FOR CORAL PEAS
Grow plants in a light area indoors, but make sure they have some protection from direct sun. A sunroom or large family room that receives plenty of natural light is perfect.

Although they are very drought tolerant when grown in the ground in their native environment, plants need watering regularly when in pots, but allow the compost to almost dry out between each watering. Feed monthly in the growing season with a liquid fertilizer, and restrict the height of the plant to keep it within bounds by pruning after flowering.

Early bulbs

Perfect for chasing away those winter blues, daffodils, dwarf irises, and snowdrops are the earliest plants to flower, appearing when there's little else of interest in the garden. Plant your favorite bulbs in the fall to guarantee an early flush of color, but wait until spring to plant snowdrops when they are in leaf. This produces better results.

Daffodils *Narcissus*

Plants used
Narcissus 'Salome'
Myosotis scorpioides

Height and spread
Narcissus 'Salome':
H 18in (45cm)
Myosotis:
H & S 8in (20cm)

Exposure
Sun or dappled shade

Temperature needs
Hardy to 5°F (-15°C)

Suitable pot size
8in (20cm)

Suitable container material
Terra-cotta, stone, plastic, metal, wicker baskets, recycled containers

Compost type
Bulb fiber

Rustic woven willow baskets and terra-cotta pots make ideal containers for daffodil displays. Choose a tall variety, such as *Narcissus* 'Salome,' as a centerpiece and underplant with white forget-me-nots whose tiny white flowers and foliage complement those of the daffodil.

Plant daffodil bulbs in the fall 4in (10cm) deep and place pots in a sunny or semi-shaded, sheltered spot. If squirrels or cats are a problem, secure a piece of chicken wire over the top until growth appears in late winter. Pots should not need watering over winter, but water during dry spells when they are in bud and flower. Feed with a liquid fertilizer when blooms have faded, and allow foliage to die down naturally.

GOOD VARIETIES FOR POTS

There are thousands of daffodil varieties to choose from, with tiny or tall types, and single or double flowers. Among the best low-growing daffodils are 'Jack Snipe,' 'Hawera,' 'Pipit,' and 'Tête-à-Tête,' or try taller forms, such as 'Acropolis,' 'Ice Follies,' and 'Carlton.'

Narcissus **'Salome'** *makes a beautiful display of white petals and peachy-yellow trumpets.*

TOP TIP: PLANTING PARTNERS

Create striking combinations by underplanting daffodils with other spring-flowering plants. A carpet of white grape hyacinths (*Muscari*) and white daffodils make pretty partners, or use contrasting purple crocuses, dwarf irises, or violas. Blue *Corydalis* and grape hyacinths work well with yellow daffodils.

Dwarf iris *Iris reticulata*

Plant used
Iris reticulata

Height and spread
H 4in (10cm)

Exposure
Full sun

Temperature needs
Hardy to 5°F (-15°C)

Suitable pot size
4–6in (10–15cm)

Suitable container material
Terra-cotta, stone, recycled containers

Compost type
Well-drained, soil-based compost, e.g., John Innes No. 3

Iris reticulata lifts the spring garden with dainty blooms.

Irises are usually associated with borders, but there are a number of ankle-high plants that are perfect for spring pots. Native to mountainous regions of Europe and Asia, *Iris reticulata* grows to just 4in (10cm) and looks sharp when planted clustered in a terra-cotta bowl. Plant bulbs in early fall 2in (5cm) apart and about 2in (5cm) deep, and place containers in a sunny spot to flower. Apply a liquid fertilizer when flowers fade and allow foliage to die down naturally.

DIFFERENT COLORS
Dwarf irises come in many different colors. *I. reticulata* 'Cantab' has pale blue flowers, and *I. reticulata* 'J.S. Dijt' is deep purple. For pale primrose flowers, choose *I. winogradowii*, or try *I. danfordiae* with its bright yellow, sweetly scented blooms. Another perfumed iris, 'Edward,' has orange-marked blue flowers.

Snowdrops *Galanthus*

Plant used
Galanthus nivalis

Height and spread
H 3–12in (8–30cm)
S 2–3in (5–8cm)

Exposure
Dappled shade

Temperature needs
Most are hardy to 5°F (-15°C)

Suitable pot size
4–6in (10–15cm)

Suitable container material
Terra-cotta, stone, recycled containers

Compost type
Soil-based compost, e.g., John Innes No. 3

Grown for their instantly recognizable nodding white flowers, snowdrops are the first flowers to appear in late winter and early spring. There are hundreds of different types to choose from, varying in height from 3in (8cm) to 12in (30cm), with flowers in many shapes and sizes. Many have exquisite green markings beneath their white petals, and plants are best displayed on tables or ledges so you don't have to stoop to fully appreciate their hidden petticoats.

PLANTING SNOWDROPS
Snowdrops will grow quickly if they are bought and planted in the spring while actively growing, or "in the green," as it is often called. Ensure the snowdrops are planted at the same depth as they were before they were taken from the ground—the point where the green leaves start to turn yellow should be level with the surface of the compost. Dried bulbs are available in the fall, but snowdrops may not establish well from them.

Plant snowdrops in small pots for early spring color.

SPRING SPECTACLES

Elegant tulips

With a vast array of colors and styles to choose from, you can create dramatic tulip displays from mid- to late spring, brightening up patios and adding punch to border designs. These seasonal stars make beautiful focal points in tall pots of mixed plants, or use smaller types *en masse* in bowls or baskets.

Plant used
Tulipa 'Abu Hassan;'
Erysimum cheiri
(wallflower);
Myosotis scorpioides
'Royal Blue'
(forget-me-nots)

Height and spread
Tulipa 'Abu Hassan'
H 20in (50cm);
Erysimum
H & S 8in (20cm);
Myosotis H 12in
(30cm) S 8in (20cm)

Exposure
Full sun

Temperature needs
Hardy to 5°F (-15°C)

Suitable pot size
12–18in (30–45cm)

Suitable container material
Stone, terra-cotta, plastic, wood, baskets

Compost type
Multi-purpose compost

Icons of the spring garden, tulips are incredibly versatile and provide exceptional value in the spring garden. Choose from elegant double flowers in pastel shades that resemble peonies, simple cups of rich color, or frilly-petaled "parrots", which mimic the feathers of exotic birds. For a dramatic patio display, plant the eye-catching *Tulipa* 'Abu Hassan,' with its mahogany-red goblets, above a sea of burnt orange, red, and yellow wallflowers and clouds of tiny blue forget-me-nots in a range of Victorian chimney pots. Alternatively, create a more subtle vista with pale pink *Tulipa* 'Angélique,' white forget-me-nots, variegated thyme, and purple violas.

To produce dazzling tulip displays, plant the bulbs at a depth of 4in (10cm) in plastic pots in the fall, and then in early spring fill the gaps around the edges with other spring flowers. The utilitarian pots can then be placed into an earthenware pot or other decorative container and set in a sunny location to bloom.

CARING FOR TULIPS
Protect bulbs from foraging squirrels by covering the compost with chicken wire, tucking it down in the sides to keep it in place, and remove it in spring when shoots appear. Keep the compost moist during dry spells, and deadhead flowers as they start to fade. Once the plants are done blooming, you can remove the plastic pots and replace them with summer-flowering plants.

*Center: **Tall chimney pots** raise tulips up closer to eye level, allowing a better appreciation of their colorful flowers.*

TOP TIP: LAYERING TULIPS WITH OTHER BULBS

Tulips make great partners for other bulbs, such as daffodils and grape hyacinths. First, add a layer of compost to the bottom of the pot and plant the biggest bulbs, followed by a 2in (5cm) layer of compost and the next-largest bulbs. Add another layer of compost, plant the smallest bulbs, and cover them with compost.

Tulip options

Tulipa *'Artist' is a viridiflora type, with shapely flowers decorated with green, pink, and orange markings.*

Tulipa *'Estella Rijnveld' is a parrot tulip that produces a globe of intricately fringed petals in red and white.*

Tulipa *'China Pink' produces lilylike candy pink flowers on tall, graceful stems from mid- to late spring.*

Tulipa *'Ballerina' is a scented lily-shaped tulip bearing orange flowers with pointed petals.*

Tulipa *'Queen of Night' has deep purple-black single flowers that contrast well with light blue forget-me-nots.*

Tulipa *'Spring Green', a viridiflora tulip, produces slightly feathered ivory white flowers with green stripes.*

Tulipa clusiana *is a desirable species whose small white flowers marked with a dark pink stripe appear in late spring.*

Tulipa *'West Point' is a clear lemon yellow, lily-flowered tulip with graceful, swept-back, pointed petals.*

Blossoms in pots

There's nothing shy and retiring about a shrub or tree laden with spring blossoms. The flowers, some of which are sweetly scented, are borne in great profusion, and provide head-height displays on a patio or deck. Choose dwarf forms of trees, because these will be the happiest in containers, and keep plants well fed and watered.

Lilac *Syringa*

Plants used
Syringa vulgaris 'Andenken an Ludwig Späth;'
Viola cornuta;
Hedera helix (ivy)

Height and spread
Syringa: H 6ft (2m) S 3ft (1m);
Viola: H 6in (15cm) S 16in (40cm);
Hedera: S 18in (45cm)

Exposure
Full sun

Temperature needs
Hardy to 5°F (-15°C)

Suitable pot size
18in (45cm)

Suitable container material
Stone, glazed terra-cotta

Compost type
Soil-based compost, e.g., John Innes No. 3

Much admired for their long sprays of heavily scented late-spring flowers, lilacs are most often thought of as border plants. However, those that have the potential to reach 22ft (7m) in open ground, such as the reddish-purple-flowered 'Andenken an Ludwig Späth,' will grow to just a fraction of that size when confined to a pot. Add interest to your displays with a skirt of ivy and perennial horned violet (*Viola cornuta*), which produces a carpet of tiny lilac flowers. Keep plants well watered throughout the growing season, and feed annually in spring with a slow-release granular fertilizer.

DWARF OPTIONS FOR CONTAINERS
Large lilacs can be grown in containers, but those that are naturally dwarf or slow growing will generally perform better and be happiest for longer in a pot. Among the best are the pale-pink dwarf Korean lilac, *S. meyeri* 'Palibin,' and purple *S. pubescens* subsp. *patula* 'Miss Kim.' The cut-leaf lilac, *S.* x *laciniata*, is another option; it grows to just 6ft (2m) and bears purple flowers.

TOP TIP: PRUNING LILACS

Avoid deadheading lilacs until you can see two shoots beneath the fading flowerheads—removing them before this could jeopardize next year's display. To maintain an open, bushy shape, remove one or two old stems in the winter, cutting them to the base. This will result in a flush of new growth in the spring.

Glorious, sweetly scented purple blossoms adorn Syringa *'Andenken an Ludwig Späth'* in late spring.

Crab apple *Malus*

Plant used
Malus 'Adirondack'

Height and spread
H: 5ft (1.5m)
S: 3ft (1m)

Exposure
Full sun

Temperature needs
Hardy to 5°F (-15°C)

Suitable pot size
18in (45cm)

Suitable container material
Stone, glazed ceramic

Compost type
Soil-based compost, e.g., John Innes No. 3

If you only have space for one tree on your patio, a crab apple is hard to beat. Naturally compact, it is a rounded or narrow, upright tree that is easy to maintain with minimal pruning. To keep plants in good condition, water pots regularly and remove some of the old soil in early spring, replacing it with slow-release granular fertilizer added to fresh compost.

TWO SEASONS OF INTEREST

Crab apples are a great value, providing two seasons of interest. In the spring their branches are covered with blossoms, followed in fall by round or oval fruits that last for a few months. The crabs come in many sizes and colors: 'Red Sentinel' has glossy red fruit, while 'Butterball' bears golden-yellow apples. Some plants, such as *M. transitoria,* have three seasons of interest, with fall leaf color to add to its charms.

Malus **'Adirondack' is a good choice** for a deep container, and bears star-shaped white flowers and orange-red fruit.

Cherry *Prunus*

Plant used
Prunus 'Kiku-shidare-zakura' (syn.'Cheals Weeping')

Height and spread
H & S: up to 10ft (3m)

Exposure
Full sun

Temperature needs
Hardy to 5°F (-15°C)

Suitable pot size
18in (45cm)

Suitable container material
Stone, glazed terra-cotta, plastic

Compost type
Soil-based compost, e.g., John Innes No. 3

Flowering cherries sparkle with spring blooms, lighting up patios and gardens with their seasonal bouquets. The Cheal's Weeping cherry or *Prunus* 'Kiku-shidare-zakura' is one of the best, its pink buds opening to reveal double flowers held in dense clusters among the bronze-flushed, glossy new foliage. Easy to care for, this small tree needs pruning just occasionally to remove dead or diseased stems, and to tidy any wayward branches. Other flowering cherries suitable for growing in pots include 'Pink Perfection,' 'Fukubana' and 'Beni-yutaka'.

WATERING NEEDS

Cherry trees grown in containers must be watered regularly to ensure the compost never dries out completely, especially in the summer and in late winter when flower buds are forming. If you lead a busy life, consider installing an automatic irrigation system to ensure trees are kept moist. In the spring, remove the top layer of soil and apply a slow-release granular fertilizer mixed with fresh compost.

Prunus **'Kiku-shidare-zakura'**

Early-season flower displays

Cheer up your spring garden with a basket filled with dainty flowers and lush grasses, and display it on a table or windowsill. Alternatively, keep things simple and plant colorful low-growing alpines in troughs or small pots grouped together to create a miniature spectacle. All of these flowering beauties are easy to grow and require very little care.

Colorful basket of blooms

Plants used
Erysimum 'Poem Lavender;' Viola 'Etain;' Aubrieta 'Silberrand;' Alopecurus pratensis 'Aureus'

Height and spread
Erysimum: H 12in (30cm) S 16in (40cm); Viola: H & S 6in (15cm); Aubrieta: H 3in (8cm) S 12in (30cm); Alopecurus: H & S 12in (30cm)

Exposure
Sun or partial shade

Temperature needs
Hardy to 5°F (-15°C)

Suitable pot size
18in- (45cm-) long windowbox or basket

Suitable container material
Terra-cotta, stone, ceramic, wood, basket

Compost type
Multi-purpose compost with added soil-based compost, e.g., John Innes No. 3

Water your spring basket during dry spells, and when the plants become too congested, repot into a larger container.

When creating a flower display, start with the tallest plant for your centerpiece, such as the scented wallflower, *Erysimum* 'Poem Lavender.' Small, nodding violas and the tumbling tiny mauve blooms of *Aubrieta* add to the picture, while grasses, such as the foxtail grass, *Alopecurus*, complete the display.

Ensure your basket or pot has drainage holes at the bottom and fill with a mix of soil-based and multi-purpose compost. Plant densely, but ensure the top of the compost is 2in (5cm) below the basket rim to allow space for watering.

TOP TIP: DEADHEADING VIOLAS

For a long-lasting display, spend a few minutes every day or two removing fading flowers. This not only ensures that the basket looks its best, but deadheading also encourages the plants to put all of their energy into making showy flowers rather than seeds.

Spring alpines

Plant used
Saxifraga stribrnyi

Height and spread
H 4in (10cm)
S 8in (20cm)

Exposure
Full sun

Temperature needs
Hardy to 5°F (-15°C)

Suitable pot size
8in (20cm) shallow
or pan-shaped pots

Suitable container material
Terra-cotta, stone

Compost type
Soil-based compost,
e.g., John Innes No.
2, with added sand

They may be small, but alpines are charming plants blessed with attractive foliage and pretty flowers. Among the most popular alpines are saxifrages, a diverse group of evergreen plants that includes *Saxifraga stribrnyi*, whose small silvery rosettes will spread readily across the surface of a pot filled with well-drained compost. Many saxifrages flower in the summer or autumn, so check labels before you buy. Other good choices for spring color include *S.* Southside Seedling Group, with its tight leaf rosettes and white flowers spotted with red, and *S. sancta,* which has bright green spiky leaves paired with cup-shaped yellow flowers.

Although alpines come from mountainous terrains and are incredibly tough, most need protection from excessive winter rain to prevent rotting, and a site in full sun. Plant them in gritty compost to improve drainage, and top with a gravel mulch to keep the foliage dry. Feed annually in the spring with a granular fertilizer.

GROUPING PLANTS

To make a more dramatic statement with these diminutive plants, group several pots filled with different alpines. Alternatively, combine a few plants in a trough or antique ceramic sink. You can also group them with bulbs, such as species tulips and late-flowering daffodils.

Spring-flowering saxifrages make a low mound of textured foliage that erupts with stems of dainty flowers.

SPRING SPECTACLES

CHOOSING SPRING ALPINES

Aubrieta *species* form a carpet of soft gray-green leaves, and generally produce pink or purple, single or double flowers, although other shades are available.

Gentiana acaulis *is an evergreen perennial that forms a carpet of dark green leaves masked in spring by trumpet-shaped blue flowers. A good choice for dappled shade.*

Leontopodium alpinum, *commonly known as edelweiss, produces gray leaves topped by dainty white spring flowers. It needs well-drained soil and sun.*

Androsace villosa *var.* jacquemontii *produces a low cushion of silky, hairy leaf rosettes, and deep pinky-purple flowers with yellow or green eyes.*

Dramatic spring finale
Rhododendron and *azalea*

See out spring in style by growing rhododendron and azaleas in containers. Available in a wide range of colors and sizes, most need a large pot and space to show off their stems of glossy leaves and oversized flowers, although some dwarf forms are more compact and suit small patios, balconies, and decks.

Plants used
Rhododendron
'Gunborg;'
Tiarella 'Snow
Blanket;'
Viola 'Etain';
*Lysimachia
nummularia*
'Goldilocks'

Height and spread
Rhododendron:
H 3ft (1m) S 24in
(60cm); *Tiarella*:
H 6in (15cm)
S 12in (30cm);
Viola: H & S 6in
(15cm); *Lysimachia*
H 4in (10cm)
S 36in (90cm)

Exposure
Sun or partial shade

Temperature needs
Most are hardy to
5°F (-15°C)

Suitable pot size
18in (45cm)

**Suitable container
material**
Stone, glazed
terra-cotta, ceramic

Compost type
Soil-based
ericaceous compost,
e.g., John Innes
Ericaceous Compost

*Center **A tall standard
rhododendron**
creates a sparkling
flower display above
a carpet of bedding
and trailing plants.*

Many admire the vibrant flowers of rhododendrons and azaleas, but not everyone has the acid soil they need to thrive. The solution is to grow these attractive bushes in containers filled with ericaceous compost, a formulation devised to suit the specific needs of acid-loving plants.

Growing standards with a clear stem allows space for underplanting to broaden the interest. For example, the rose-pink flowers of *Rhododendron* 'Gunborg' look stunning above a frill of *Tiarella*, with its pretty lobed foliage and delicate flower spires. Trailing *Lysimachia* is a good choice for softening the edges of the containers, while duotone violas provide an additional splash of spring color. 'Gunborg' is a yakushimanum rhododendron, a group known for their slow growth and compact form. A type that has been grafted on to a straight stem makes a tall plant, but in a smaller area, use an ungrafted specimen. Other yakushimanum to choose from include 'Dreamland,' 'Dopey,' and 'Lemon Dream.'

PRUNING AND TRAINING

To keep shrubs in shape, remove faded flowers to prevent seeds from forming; use your thumb and forefinger, and avoid damage to the new buds beneath. Most plants need just a light clean up after flowering by cutting back or removing wayward stems, and rub off any buds that appear along the clear stems of standards.

TOP TIP: PLANTS WITH SIMILAR NEEDS

Rhododendrons and azaleas are not the only acid-loving plants that you can grow in pots. *Pieris*, camellias (*right*), magnolias, and *Skimmia* all require similar soil conditions. Feed all these plants in spring with granular fertilizer formulated for acid-lovers worked into the top layer of compost.

Choosing acid-loving bushes

Rhododendron *'Palestrina'* *is a dwarf evergreen azalea with white flowers. Protect with fabric in the winter.*

Rhododendron *'Temple Belle'* *has evergreen rounded leaves accompanied by bell-shaped, pink spring flowers.*

Rhododendron augustinii *is a bushy evergreen and produces large violet-blue flowers in mid-spring.*

Rhododendron *'Fragrantissimum'* *has highly scented, large white flowers. It is tender and needs protection from frost.*

Rhododendron *'Louise Dowdle'* *is a compact, spreading, evergreen azalea with large, brilliant pink flowers.*

Rhododendron luteum *is a very highly scented deciduous azalea with glorious canary yellow, late-spring flowers.*

Rhododendron *'Yellow Hammer'* *is an upright evergreen with tubular flowers that often bloom again in the fall.*

Rhododendron yakushimanum *is a compact, domed species with rose-pink flowers that fade to white or pale pink.*

SPRING SPECTACLES

Spring bouquets

When spring bulbs start to bloom outside in the garden, match their vibrant displays with color indoors by growing flowering houseplants. Azaleas, cyclamen, and cinerarias are traditional favorites, but you can give them a modern makeover by teaming them with funky or elegant containers to match your home.

SPRING SPECTACLES

Indian azalea *Rhododendron simsii*

Plant used
Rhododendron simsii
white hybrid

Height and spread
H & S 14in (35cm)

Exposure
Bright, but not
in direct sunlight

Temperature needs
54–59°F (12–15°C)

Suitable pot size
6in (15cm)

**Suitable container
material**
Plastic, inside a
decorative pot

Compost type
Ericaceous compost

Indian azaleas are compact, evergreen houseplants that produce masses of flowers in a wide range of colors, including white, pink, purple, and red, as well as bicolors. Although they are related to hardy rhododendrons, these tender types need winter protection, requiring a minimum temperature of 54°F (12°C) to thrive. However, they also suffer in a hot environment, so try to keep temperatures below 75°F (24°C). In the winter, buy plants with a profusion of tight buds; avoid those with lots of open flowers; the display will be short lived.

GROWING AZALEAS

Place Indian azaleas in a cool, brightly lit area, but not in direct sunlight. Keep the compost moist while plants are in bud and flowering, ideally using rainwater because they do not like hard tap water. Dry compost at this time can cause both buds and blooms to fall prematurely. Feed azaleas every two weeks with fertilizer formulated for acid-loving plants and remove faded blooms to extend the flower display.

TOP TIP: SUMMER CARE

After plants have finished flowering, do not feed, and water less frequently, allowing the compost to almost dry out before watering more.

In summer, repot plants in ericaceous compost, and after all danger of frost has passed, place your azaleas in a sheltered, shaded area outside. Increase watering and start feeding again as the plant comes back into growth. Bring plants back indoors in early fall before frost threatens.

Plant Indian azaleas *in plastic pots and set these inside more decorative containers in a cool room indoors.*

Cyclamen *Cyclamen persicum*

Plant used
Cyclamen persicum

Height and spread
H 8in (20cm)
S 6in (15cm)

Exposure
Bright, but not
in direct sunlight

Temperature needs
Min. 55–61°F
(13–16°C) in winter

Suitable pot size
6in (15cm)

Suitable container material
Plastic, inside a
decorative pot

Compost type
Soil-based compost,
e.g., John Innes No. 2

The swept-back petals and nest of marbled leaves can look old-fashioned when a cyclamen is grown in a dowdy container, but give it a sleek glazed pot, and this traditional houseplant won't look out of place in a modern home. Slow to raise from seed, it's best to buy ready-grown plants. When flowering, keep the compost moist, and feed every two weeks with a high-potash liquid feed. After the blooms have faded, stop watering and place the pot on its side until midsummer. Then repot into a slightly bigger pot, ensuring the tuber is just above the compost surface.

POSITIONING PLANTS

Cyclamen wilt, foliage turns yellow, and plants perform poorly if they are in the wrong spot. They dislike warm dry air and too much light, and thrive on a cool, north-facing windowsill away from radiators. They also enjoy being misted occasionally to raise humidity levels.

Cyclamen persicum

Cineraria *Pericallis x hybrida*

Plant used
Pericallis x *hybrida*
Senetti Series

Height and spread
H 18in (45cm)
S 10in (25cm)

Exposure
Bright, but not
in direct sunlight

Temperature needs
Min. 45°F (7°C)

Suitable pot size
6in (15cm)

Suitable container material
Plastic, inside a
decorative pot

Compost type
Multi-purpose
compost

The bold flowers of *Pericallis* x *hybrida* Senetti Series

Popular winter and spring houseplants that will brighten up your indoor space, cinerarias come in a wide range of colors. The large, daisylike flowers that rise above clumps of triangular-shaped leaves are available in pink, white, blue, purple, coppery orange, and red, often sporting a contrasting white center. Technically perennials, cinerarias are best added to the compost heap after flowering because they are difficult to maintain and rarely perform well the following year. Keep plants healthy by never allowing the compost to dry out, and feed every two weeks with a balanced liquid fertilizer.

GROWING PLANTS FROM SEED

Although plants are readily available, it's easy to grow cinerarias from seed. At any time from spring to midsummer, fill a small pot with seed compost, and sow on the surface. Cover pots with a plastic bag sealed with a rubber band, and put in a light place to germinate. Remove the bag when seedlings appear.

Roses for containers

The classic choice for a country garden design, roses tend to need plenty of elbow room to produce their romantic, often scented, flowers. However, breeders have developed many equally beautiful compact forms, perfect for container growing. Most rose nurseries offer a good selection, and they are all easy to care for.

SUMMER BLOOMS

Plants used
Rosa Regensberg
Bacopa 'Snowflake'
(syn. *Sutera cordata*
'Snowflake')

Height and spread
Rosa: H & S 30in
(75cm);
Bacopa: H 4in (10cm)
S 12in (30cm)

Exposure
Full sun

Temperature needs
Rosa is hardy to
-10°F (-23°C); *Bacopa*
is not hardy below
32°F (0°C)

Suitable pot size
18in (45cm)

**Suitable container
material**
Stone, terra-cotta,
glazed ceramic,
plastic

Compost type
Soil-based compost,
e.g., John Innes No. 3

When selecting a rose for a container, look for patio roses, or miniatures, which are ideal for small pots. Many compact ground cover shrubs, standards, and patio climbers are also suitable, but need larger containers. *Rosa* Regensberg (syn. 'Macyoumis') is a floriferous patio rose, with large sweetly scented blooms that look as if they have been hand painted. Roses like plenty of air and light, and don't take kindly to tall plant partners that will steal many of the nutrients in the compost. However, a low growing carpet of *Bacopa* is perfect, softening the sides of a container with its dainty foliage and small white flowers.

When planting a rose in a container, make sure that the graft union (knobby joint between the roots and stem) is just beneath the surface of the compost. If you're planting a rose from late fall to late winter, trim back stems to 4in (10cm) in length to encourage lots of new growth in the spring. Place the pots in a sunny location and water plants freely in the spring and summer.

PRUNING ROSES

Remove faded blooms regularly; this promotes the production of more flowers and will extend the display. Prune plants annually in the early spring to retain an attractive shape and to remove dead, diseased, or spindly growth. To rejuvenate roses, in late winter or early spring cut back all the stems halfway to healthy buds, or to within 3in (8cm) of the previous year's growth.

*Center: **Choose pots
in contrasting colors**
to bring out the hues
of your patio roses,
such as these blue
containers and pale
pink* Rosa Regensberg.

TOP TIP: FEEDING ROSES

Roses are thirsty and hungry plants. As well as watering regularly, feed them every two weeks with a fertilizer high in potash to encourage flowering—you can buy products formulated specifically for roses. Also, get plants off to a good start in the spring by mixing slow-release fertilizer granules into the compost surface.

Rose choices

Rosa *Sweet Dream* *is a bushy patio rose with sweetly scented, fully double, apricot-colored blooms.*

Rosa *Stacey Sue* *is a continuous flowering miniature rose with fully double, soft pink blooms.*

Rosa *Queen Mother*, *a floriferous patio rose, produces clusters of beautiful pink flowers and glossy mid-green foliage.*

Rosa *Drummer Boy* *is a dwarf bush that bears clusters of double, lipstick-red flowers throughout the summer.*

Rosa *Anna Ford* *has lightly fragrant, semi-double flowers that start off bright orange and turn red as they age.*

Rosa *Baby Masquerade* *is a miniature rose ideal for a small pot, with yellowish flowers edged with pink.*

Rosa *Chatsworth* *bears a succession of deep pink flowers from summer until early winter that fade as they mature.*

Rosa *Baby Love* *is a patio rose that produces canary-yellow summer flowers followed by orange hips.*

Shrubbery staples

Shrubbery provides great background color and structure for more showy perennial flowers, but some also become a star themselves with summer blooms and other decorative features. Hebes offer pretty evergreen foliage, hydrangeas produce beautiful flowers and attractive seedheads, and hibiscus have large blooms and a graceful shape and form.

Hydrangeas

Hydrangea *Endless Summer* blooms all summer on old and new stems, and should be pruned like a mophead.

Plants used
Hydrangea macrophylla
Endless Summer
Twist-n-Shout

Height and spread
H & S: 3ft (1m)

Exposure
Dappled shade

Temperature needs
Hardy to 5°F (-15°C)

Suitable pot size
18in (45cm)

Suitable container material
Stone, terra-cotta, glazed ceramic, plastic

Compost type
Soil-based compost, e.g., John Innes No. 3 (some need ericaceous compost)

Offering large heads of summer flowers in a wide range of colors, hydrangeas also sport decorative seedheads in the fall and winter. Forms of *H. macrophylla*, known as mopheads, have rounded domes of flowers, while *H. paniculata* produces conelike flowerheads. New mophead cultivars provide even greater value with extended flowering seasons. The Endless Summer range is a good example, with long-lasting flowers that look like scattered confetti, and red-tinted fall foliage.

Hydrangeas like moist soil conditions, and plants should be covered with fabric in the spring to protect them from late frosts. Most also benefit from annual pruning, but the method you use depends on the species (*see Top Tip box below*).

COLOR OPTIONS
Hydrangeas come in shades of pink, red, purple, blue, white, and near-green. The color of the flowers is determined by the compost. Pink types need alkaline soil, while ericaceous compost is required for blue and purple forms.

TOP TIP: PRUNING HYDRANGEAS
Allow the spent flowers of *H. macrophylla* to remain on the plant over the winter to protect the new growth below. In mid-spring, use shears to cut stems down to the first strong pair of buds. To prune forms of *H. paniculata*, which flower on stems made in the current year, prune back all the stems in early spring to a pair of healthy buds about 10in (25cm) from the base. If either hydrangea becomes overcrowded, remove a quarter of the older branches in spring.

SUMMER BLOOMS

Hebes

Plant used
Hebe 'Johnny Day'

Height and spread
H & S 24in (60cm)

Exposure
Sun, sheltered

Temperature needs
Hardy to 23°F (-5°C)

Suitable pot size
8in (20cm)

Suitable container material
Terra-cotta, stone, glazed ceramic

Compost type
Soil-based compost, e.g., John Innes No. 3

Grown for their handsome evergreen leaves and spikes of blue, purple, white, or pink flowers, hebes make excellent container specimens. Some are large, so check labels before you buy, and select those that are naturally compact, such as 'Johnny Day,' 'Silver Queen,' 'Watson's Pink,' 'Rosie,' and Hebe topiaria. All are magnets for butterflies and bees and require little maintenance apart from regular watering in the growing season and some slow-release general fertilizer in spring.

OVERWINTERING TENDER TYPES

Few hebes do well when whipped by cold winds and some are very tender, so unless your yard is very sheltered, protect their foliage during windy, wintry weather with garden fabric. If you have a tender type, move it to a cool, light, frost-free place indoors for the winter.

The young foliage of Hebe 'Johny Day' is deep purple.

Hibiscus *Hibiscus syriacus*

Plant used
Hibiscus syriacus Blue Bird (syn. 'Oiseau Bleu')

Height and spread
H 6ft (2m)
S 4ft (1.2m)

Exposure
Full sun

Temperature needs
Hardy to 5°F (-15°C)

Suitable pot size
12–18in (30–45cm)

Suitable container material
Stone, terra-cotta, metal, glazed ceramic

Compost type
Well-drained, soil-based compost, e.g., John Innes No. 2

If you want to add a Mediterranean touch to your patio, deck, or garden, you can't beat a hibiscus shrub for pure flower power. The blooms come in many different colors and sizes, but Blue Bird is one of the best, with large purple-blue flowers with cream centers set against a foil of dark-green lobed leaves. Perfect for a sunny, sheltered area, this deciduous shrub will put on a head-turning spectacle from midsummer to early autumn. Plant in a large container of soil-based compost, such as John Innes No. 2, and water plants regularly in summer. Add some slow-release granular fertilizer to the compost in the spring.

WHEN TO PRUNE

For the best show of flowers, prune plants in the spring. Start by shortening last year's shoots to maintain an attractive shape and bushy look. Then remove any dead, diseased, or crossing branches that may rub each other and cause a wound. Finally, take out some older stems to prevent congested growth.

Hibiscus *Blue Bird* *is covered with purple-blue flowers in the late summer.*

Versatile dahlias

Flamboyant, glamorous, and alluring, dahlias are the divas of the horticultural world. Emerging on slender stems above decorative foliage, their head-turning blooms draw the crowds from mid- to late summer until the first frost in the fall. Provide simple containers that do not distract from your star performers.

Plants used
Dahlia 'Gallery Art Deco;' *Thymus* 'Silver Posie'

Height and spread
Dahlia: H & S 18in (45cm); *Thymus*: H 12in (30cm) S 18in (45cm)

Exposure
Full sun

Temperature needs
Not reliably hardy below 32°F (0°C)

Suitable pot size
12in (30cm)

Suitable container material
Glazed ceramic, stone, terra-cotta

Compost type
Soil-based compost, e.g., John Innes No. 3

Perfect for illuminating a sun-baked patio or border, dahlias comprise a large group of tuberous perennials ranging in height from 12in (30cm) to 11ft (3.5m) whoppers. Natives of Mexico, dahlia blooms are incredibly diverse and include plain, striped, and speckled types. You can also choose from flowers resembling little pompoms, waterlilies, or spiky balls of narrow, pointed petals, known as cactus dahlias, and leaves range from bright green to smoldering dark purple. While many are too large to squeeze into a container, plenty more have been bred for patio pots, including the Gallery Series, which are compact and floriferous, and available in a range of colors. Dahlias make striking centerpieces in large summer arrangements, alongside petunias and foliage plants, such as variegated thyme.

GROWING DAHLIAS FROM TUBERS

Dormant tubers can be planted indoors in mid-spring. Half-fill a 4in (10cm) pot with multi-purpose compost, place the tuber on top and cover with compost. Set pots on a light windowsill or in a greenhouse but do not water. When shoots appear, water lightly—you can increase the amount of water you give them as they grow. The dahlias will be ready for planting into larger containers outdoors when all danger of frost has passed in the late spring. Water plants regularly in the growing season, and apply a liquid tomato fertilizer every couple of weeks in summer.

*Center: **The dazzling orange and red flowers** of* Dahlia *'Gallery Art Deco' explode from a cool frill of scented thyme.*

TOP TIP: OVERWINTERING TUBERS

When frost blackens the foliage, pull the tubers from the compost and remove as much of the soil as you can. Cut back the stems to about 6in (15cm) and allow the tubers to dry for a few weeks. Place in seed trays filled with dry compost, and store in a frost-free place until spring. Then pot them up as described above.

Choosing dahlias

Dahlia 'Tally Ho' *produces fire-engine red flowers that show very well against dark greeny-black foliage.*

Dahlia 'Pink Giraffe' *is a knee-high variety with pink and white variegated flowers with swept-back petals.*

Dahlia Gallery Series *comprises a range of compact dahlias named after painters and art movements.*

Dahlia 'Small World' *has long stems of pure white pompom flowers held above neat clumps of green foliage.*

Dahlia 'Yellow Hammer' *is a dwarf dahlia with clear yellow flowers and contrasting near-black foliage.*

Dahlia 'Purple Gem' *is ideal for a large container and produces hand-sized, deep purple, cactus-style flowers.*

Dahlia 'Roxy' *is a popular form, with a striking combination of dark purple foliage and magenta-pink flowers.*

Dahlia 'David Howard' *produces smoky-orange flowers held in sharp relief against a foil of dark leaves.*

SUMMER BLOOMS

Dazzling highlights

Dull corners of a patio, bare walls, or an empty window ledge can be quickly transformed into an exuberant area with a few prized summer flowers. Gerberas, scented geraniums, and blanket flowers are among the best for injecting intense color with their long-lasting blooms. All are drought resistant and make excellent container plants.

Gerbera

Plant used
Gerbera (Landscape Series) 'Mount Rushmore'

Height and spread
H & S 14in (35cm)

Exposure
Sun or partial shade

Temperature needs
Min. 41°F (5°C)

Suitable pot size
8in (20cm)

Suitable container material
Terra-cotta, plastic, stone, glazed ceramic

Compost type
Multi-purpose compost

A striking group of perennials, gerberas have daisylike flowers that sit like saucers on top of stout stems and bloom all summer long. There are many suitable for containers, including the Landscape Series, a group of herbaceous perennials that have been bred for their compact growth and long season of large flowers. Among the showy varieties in this series is the pinky-red 'Mount Rushmore,' pink bicolored 'Everglades,' and 'Klondike,' which has orange flowers. Apart from adding a splash of color to gardens, the flowers can also be cut for indoor displays.

PLANT CARE
Ready-grown plants are available from garden centers and nurseries and can be placed outside in pots of multi-purpose compost after the last frost in early summer. Keep the compost damp and feed plants every four weeks with a balanced liquid fertilizer. Remove faded flowers to prolong the floral display, and bring plants back indoors before frost threatens in the fall.

Gerbera *'Mount Rushmore' needs no competition from planting partners to make an impact on a patio or terrace.*

TOP TIP: PLANT HARDY GERBERAS

Most gerberas are frost tender and cannot be left outside all year, but a new breed of hardy gerberas is now available, such as the Everlast and Garvineas Series. Perfect for growing in pots in summer, they can then winter in a sunny area in a border, or be given a sheltered site by the house.

Scented geraniums

Plant used
Pelargonium 'Trend Scarlet Red'

Height and spread
H 10in (25cm)
S 6in (15cm)

Exposure
Full sun

Temperature needs
Not reliably hardy
below 32°F (0°C)

Suitable pot size
6in (15cm) or larger

Suitable container material
Terra-cotta, glazed ceramic, stone

Compost type
Soil-based compost, e.g., John Innes No. 2

Scarlet pelargoniums make a good partner for lobelia.

Evocative of Spanish courtyard gardens, scented geraniums, or pelargoniums, lend a Mediterranean tone to patios and are prized for their long-lasting flowers. Countless different varieties are available in shades of red, white, pink, purple, and orange. Blooms are held on stout stems above rounded foliage, which is often scented, variegated, marked, or veined.

ANNUAL CARE
Feed plants every month while in flower with a high potash fertilizer, and water regularly—once a week should suffice for most containers. Remove fading flowerheads to encourage more to form. Scented geraniums can survive year after year if you cut the stems back by about two-thirds before frost threatens in the fall. Stow pots in a frost-free place in winter, keeping the compost slightly damp, but not too wet.

Blanket flower *Gaillardia*

Plant used
Gaillardia x *grandiflora*

Height and spread
H 3ft (90cm)
S 18in (45cm)

Exposure
Full sun

Temperature needs
Fully hardy

Suitable pot size
12in (30cm)

Suitable container material
Terra-cotta, glazed ceramic, stone

Compost type
Soil-based compost, e.g., John Innes No. 3

With daisylike blooms that can measure up to 5½in (14cm) in diameter, blanket flowers are eye-catching, bushy perennials that perform continuously from early summer to fall. The compact cultivars of *Gaillardia* x *grandiflora* are most suitable for pots. Try 'Kobold,' with yellow-tipped red petals; 'Goldkobold,' which has golden blooms; or 'Dazzler,' with its yellow-edged orange blooms.

Plant in pots of soil-based compost and set plants in a sunny spot. Keep the pots well watered, feed with a balanced liquid fertilizer every month after flower buds appear, and deadhead regularly to prolong blooming.

GROWING PLANTS FROM SEED
Although many varieties of blanket flower are readily available as plugs or young plants, there are some that will flower in their first year if grown from seed. In late winter, fill small pots with compost, sow seeds, and cover with a thin layer of vermiculite. Keep at 55–64°F (13-18°C), and when seedlings are large enough to handle, separate the roots carefully and repot in individual pots.

Gaillardia x *grandiflora* has long-lasting blooms.

Alpine collection

As the saying goes, the best gifts come in small packages, and this is certainly true of alpines. Tiny but tough, many provide a year-round show of textured evergreen foliage, together with a dazzling array of colorful blooms from spring until fall. Collect together a few with different characteristics in a pot for a dynamic display.

SUMMER BLOOMS

Plants used
Mixed alpines

Height and spread
H up to 6in (15cm)
S up to 12in (30cm)

Exposure
Full sun

Temperature needs
Fully hardy

Suitable pot size
6–8in (15cm–20cm)

Suitable container material
Terra-cotta, stone

Compost type
Soil-based compost, e.g., John Innes No. 3, with extra sand

Alpines are a diverse group of miniature beauties that include bulbs, perennials, and conifers, as well as diminutive trees and shrubs. Some form ground-hugging mats, just ½in (1cm) tall, while the largest will slowly grow to reach a modest 24in (60cm). Many of the varieties within this Lilliputian tribe are evergreen, with beautiful foliage for 12 months of the year, but it's the flowers that provide the razzle dazzle. Blooms come in a wide variety of colors, shapes, and sizes, and by choosing plants carefully you can have a succession from spring until early autumn. One of the most attractive ways to show them off is to plant a collection in a stone trough or old ceramic sink to create a miniature alpine landscape. Smaller groups also look good in pots, together with succulents, but check plant labels and bring containers under cover in the winter if you choose tender succulent varieties, such as *Pachyphytum* and *Oscularia*.

PLANTING AND CARING FOR ALPINES
Alpines hate wet roots and require well-drained compost to thrive. Use soil-based John Innes No. 3 mixed with some extra horticultural sand, which should be washed first to remove any residues. Ensure plants are not set too deeply in the soil, because this may rot their foliage, and cover the surface of the compost with decorative gravel to keep the lower leaves dry. Also set your containers on pot feet or pebbles to maintain good drainage.

To keep plants healthy and thriving, place them in a sunny hot spot, and water once or twice a week in the growing season. Remove any dead or frayed foliage when you see it.

Sempervivum arachnoideum *is known as the cobweb houseleek due to the fine white hairs that cover the foliage.*

TOP TIP: UNUSUAL CONTAINERS

Alpines grow in thin, dry soils in their natural habitats, and their drought tolerance makes them easy to grow in tiny pots and unusual containers. Be really creative and try growing them in recycled food cans, large shells, hollowed-out gourds, colanders, or even old boots. There's no limit to what you can use; the only requirement is that your receptacle has a big enough gap for you to push in some gritty compost, and that it has drainage holes in the bottom.

Alpine plant options

Helianthemum *'Rhodanthe Carneum'* *is a low-growing, spreading shrub with masses of pink flowers in the summer.*

Sedum rupestre *is an evergreen with succulent leaves and short, spiky bright yellow summer flowers.*

Phlox subulata *'Lilacina,'* *known as moss phlox due to its hairy leaves, has lavender blue flowers in late spring.*

Sempervivum tectorum *is a dramatic houseleek that produces dense mats of robust, burgundy-red leaf rosettes.*

Mix together alpines and succulents *with varied appearances, shapes, and foliage to create an eye-catching summer display. Those here include* Delosperma, Sedum sedoides, Sedum rupestre, *and the tender* Oscularia deltoides *and* Pachyphytum.

Outdoor aquatics

If you would like a pond but think your garden is too small, make a container water feature. Many aquatic plants grown for their attractive foliage or beautiful flowers will thrive in the shallow water, allowing even the most space-strapped gardeners to enjoy dwarf water lilies and a wealth of other colorful aquatics.

Water lilies *Nymphaea*

Plant used
Nymphaea odorata
var. *minor*

Height and spread
S 18in (45cm);
planting depth
10–12in (25–30cm)

Exposure
Partial shade, with
sun for some of
the day

Temperature needs
Hardy to 23°F (-5°C)

Suitable pot size
Min. 18in (45cm)
wide and 12in
(30cm) deep

**Suitable container
material**
Aquatic baskets
inside watertight
glazed terra-cotta,
half-barrel, or plastic
containers

Compost type
Aquatic compost

The undisputed stars of the garden aquatics, water lilies are elegant plants grown for their cup-shaped or starlike flowers, which appear from late spring until the first frosts. Although most need a large pool, many diminutive types are happy in a 12–18in- (30–45cm-) deep container.

Plant water lilies in aquatic baskets filled with aquatic compost, and place them in a watertight container, such as a glazed ceramic pot or half-barrel. Put containers in a partially shaded spot. Top off the water level in hot weather and remove dying leaves and flowers as you see them. Place lilies in a sheltered area close to the house, or a frost-free place for the winter.

TOP TIP: CHOOSING TINY LILIES

There are many dwarf water lilies to choose from, but the following are among the best. *N. tetragona* has small white flowers; *N.* 'Pygmaea Rubra' bears rosy-red blooms; *N.* 'René Gérard' has delicate pink flowers (*right*); and *N.* 'Pygmaea Helvola' has tiny star-shaped yellow blooms.

Nymphaea odorata
var. **minor** *produces
small, fragrant, star-
shaped blooms that
look stunning in a
glazed blue container.*

Beautiful buckets

Plants used
*Equisetum hyemale;
Zantedeschia hybrid;
Lobelia siphilitica*

Height and spread
Equisetum hyemale:
H 30in (75cm) S 12in
(30cm);
Zantedeschia hybrid:
H & S 12in (30cm);
Lobelia siphilitica:
H 24in (60cm) S 12in
(30cm)

Exposure
Partial shade

Temperature needs
Fully hardy, except
Zantedeschia, which
is not hardy below
32°F (0°C);

Suitable pot size
Min. 12in (30cm)

**Suitable container
material**
Aquatic baskets
inside any
watertight container

Compost type
Aquatic compost

A colorful plastic or metal bucket makes an effective container for a group of compact aquatics. Not only will it accommodate several of these fascinating plants, but it is small enough to squeeze onto the tiniest patio, deck, or balcony. Good choices include the cardinal flower, *Lobelia siphilitica*; *Equisetum hyemale,* with its striped, bamboolike stems; and *Zantedeschia,* the tender forms of which come in many colors and are ideal for containers; they can be easily brought under cover in the winter.

Plant in one or two aquatic baskets filled with aquatic compost, adding a layer of gravel on top to help stabilize the soil surface, and set these in the bucket. If possible, fill with rainwater from a barrel, leaving a 2in (5cm) gap between the water surface and lip of the container, and place in a partially shaded spot. Ensure that the plants are at the correct depth of water, raising them up on large pebbles if necessary.

CARING FOR AQUATIC PLANTS
Regularly remove dead and dying leaves, and any flowers as they start to fade. When the baskets become congested with growth, remove the plants, divide, and replant them in new baskets. Any tender plants must be moved to a light, frost-free place for the winter.

Equisetum hyemale and Zantedeschia *are best planted with their root balls 4in (10cm) below the water; the blue* Lobelia siphilitica *is happier with its root ball at water level.*

CHOOSING AQUATICS FOR CONTAINERS

Lobelia cardinalis *produces tall spires clad with red flowers, which make it stand out. Set the top of the root ball at water level and protect plants in the winter.*

Juncus ensifolius *is a shallow water lover best planted with its root ball at the surface. It has a clump of grassy leaves topped by tiny brown pompom flowerheads.*

Iris laevigata, *commonly known as the Japanese water iris, likes its roots 4in (10cm) below the surface. Its blue flowers are held on tall stems, and it's best in a large pot.*

Caltha palustris *has beautiful buttercuplike spring flowers, held on 24in (60cm) stems that contrast well with the round leaves. Set the top of the root ball at water level.*

Star performers

There are many tender plants that put on great flower displays in the garden in the summer, but perhaps none are as spectacular as these three. Hibiscus, lantana, and flowering maples perform their starring roles at this time of year, bearing exotic blooms over a long period. Before frost threatens in the autumn, bring them back inside to wait out the winter in the warmth of your home.

Hibiscus *Hibiscus rosa-sinensis*

SUMMER BLOOMS

Plant used
Hibiscus rosa-sinensis 'Athene'

Height and spread
H 4ft (1.2m)
S 24in (60cm)

Exposure
Bright, but out of midday sun in summer

Temperature
Min. 50°F (10°C)

Suitable pot size
12in (30cm)

Suitable container material
Stone, glazed ceramic, terra-cotta, plastic

Compost type
Soil-based compost, e.g., John Innes No. 3

The large flowers of the hibiscus possess exotic good looks, and its many cultivars come in vibrant shades, ranging from dark red to yellow and white. The bold flowers often measure 4in (10cm) in diameter, and feature a cluster of elegant stamens in the center. Most have glossy, dark, evergreen leaves, but 'Cooperi' has showy pink, white, and green variegated foliage. Available as standards or as bushy shrubs, hibiscus needs protection from frost, but thrives in a sunny site outdoors during the summer.

WATERING AND FEEDING
Pot plants in soil-based compost in a large pot. Water regularly in the summer, and feed monthly with a balanced liquid fertilizer to encourage a great show of color. In early spring, apply a slow-release granular fertilizer. Before frosts threaten, move plants to a bright room indoors and reduce watering, allowing the compost to almost dry out between applications.

TOP TIP: DEADHEADING AND PRUNING

For a long-lasting floral spectacle, remove faded flowers regularly to ensure plants do not waste energy on producing seeds. Plants do not require much pruning; just reduce the length of stems in late winter to keep plants within bounds and maintain an attractive shape. This will also encourage bushy growth.

Hibiscus rosa-sinensis **'Athene'** *produces breathtaking golden blooms with red eyes.*

Lantana *Lantana camara*

Plant used
Lantana camara
'Sunkiss'

Height and spread
H & S 4ft (1.2m)

Exposure
Full sun

Temperature
Min. 50°F (10°C)

Suitable pot size
12in (30cm)

Suitable container material
Terra-cotta, stone, glazed ceramic, plastic

Compost type
Soil-based compost, e.g., John Innes No. 3

Butterflies love the nectar-rich flowers of this evergreen shrub from South Africa and South and Central America. The flowerheads comprise tiny flowers that open in succession from the outer edges to the center. Plants are often sold as standards with a bushy, lollipop-shaped head.

Grow *Lantana* in a bright place indoors and in the summer place pots outside in a sheltered, sunny area. Water plants regularly, and feed monthly with a balanced liquid fertilizer after flower buds appear. Also apply a slow-release granular fertilizer in the spring.

COLOR CHOICES

Available in white, yellow, orange, pink, and red, the flowers often appear two-tone as they open from buds of different hues. 'Sunkiss' has orange and red flowers, 'Feston Rose' is pink and yellow, and 'Mine d'Or' has golden yellow blooms.

Lantana with *Abelia* x *grandiflora* 'Kaleidoscope'.

Flowering maple *Abutilon* x *hybridum*

Plant used
Abutilon x *hybridum*

Height and spread
H 4ft (1.2m)
S 24in (60cm)

Exposure
Light, bright location

Temperature
Not hardy below
32°F (0°C)

Suitable pot size
12in (30cm)

Suitable container material
Terra-cotta, stone, glazed ceramic, plastic

Compost type
Soil-based compost, e.g., John Innes No. 3

Part of a large plant group, flowering maples are named after the shape of their leaves, not because they are related to maple trees. Plants are available in many colors, including white, yellow, orange, and pink, as well as red. Choose a large container for your *Abutilon,* as plants can grow up to 4ft (1.2m) in height, and create a memorable design by teaming a scarlet-flowered plant with a simple, white, glazed pot with a cracked antique finish.

YEAR-ROUND CARE

Flowering maples are tender, and best grown in a sunroom or a light room indoors; move them to a sunny location in the garden when the threat of frost has passed. Ensure the compost does not dry out in summer and feed monthly with a balanced liquid fertilizer to prolong the flower display. In winter, when the plant is under cover, reduce watering, and apply a slow-release granular fertilizer in early spring. Prune plants in the fall to maintain a good shape.

Flowering maples produce vibrant blooms.

Small stars

They may be small, but these houseplants make up for their size with a long floral display of delicate blooms. Available in a rainbow of colors, Cape primroses will flower on and off all year, while African violets brighten the home from late spring and throughout summer. Both plants are very easy to care for, and thrive on east- or west-facing windowsills.

Cape primroses *Streptocarpus*

SUMMER BLOOMS

Plants used
Streptocarpus 'Gwen,' *Streptocarpus* 'Katie'

Height and spread
H & S 12in (30cm)

Exposure
Bright, but avoid direct sunlight

Temperature
Min. 55°F (13°C) in the winter

Suitable pot size
8in (20cm)

Suitable container material
Any

Compost type
Multi-purpose compost

Cape primroses form a compact, bushy rosette of heavily textured, strappy leaves beneath a bouquet of dainty flowers held on slender stalks. They come in many vibrant single colors, or produce two-toned, striped, or veined blooms in striking hues. The plants are most floriferous in the summer months, but the Crystal Series of *Streptocarpus* flower on and off all year round.

Place Cape primroses in a bright location, but ensure they are not in direct sunlight or the flower colors will start to fade and the leaves may scorch. An east- or west-facing windowsill is ideal. Plants can be moved outside in the summer, but ensure they are in dappled shade.

Streptocarpus 'Gwen' and 'Katie'
make a beautiful pair, with their medley of white and purple shades. The glass-bead mulch lends a hint of glamour to the display.

WATERING AND FEEDING

Water plants regularly, allowing the compost to dry out completely between applications, and feed monthly while they are in flower with a half-strength liquid fertilizer that is high in potash. Most plants need a rest over the winter, but some, including the Crystal Series or winter-flowering forms, require feeding and watering as usual.

TOP TIP: WINTER CARE

For most *Streptocarpus*, reduce watering in the winter and do not feed plants. Cape primroses can remain on an east- or west-facing windowsill, but they will need to be protected from very cold conditions, so bring them into the room at night if your windows are single-glazed. Remove dead flowers and leaves, and watch for mealy bugs, taking action to control the pest if necessary (see p. 243). Increase watering again in the spring.

African violets *Saintpaulia*

Plant used
Saintpaulia
Spectra-Color Series

Height and spread
H & S 10in (25cm)

Exposure
Bright location, not
in direct sunlight

Temperature
64–77°F (18–25°C)

Suitable pot size
6in (15cm)

**Suitable container
material**
Plastic pots placed
inside a decorative
container

Compost type
Multi-purpose
compost

Considered unfashionable by many, today's
African violets are a world apart from the single
colors and sparsely flowering varieties of old.
Modern breeding has led to a floriferous tribe
of plants that put on a great display for much
of the year if you give them the care they need.
The single, semi-double, or double flowers are
available in a wide range of shades, with petals
that often have margins or centers of a different
color. Plants also range in size, from micro-
miniatures, with leafy rosettes only 3in (8cm) in
width and height, to large varieties measuring
more than 16in (40cm).

Looking after African violets is easy. Water
from below by standing pots in a tray of water
until the top of the compost is moist. Allow the
compost to dry out between waterings and feed
every six weeks with a half-strength dose of
liquid fertilizer that is high in potash. Place in a
bright area in the summer, out of direct sunlight.

*Like all African
violets, the Spectra-
Color hybrids, grown
here with mind-your-
own-business, need a
site by a south-facing
window in the winter.*

CHOOSING AFRICAN VIOLET VARIETIES

S. 'Fancy Pants' *is a beautiful type,
with a rosette of dark leaves
beneath a mass of sophisticated,
single, white flowers with frilly
petals edged in pinkish-red.*

S. 'Delft' *is a real head-turner`,
with its wavy-edged blooms above
dark leaves. The large, semi-double
cornflower-blue flowers have
contrasting yellow centers.*

S. 'Kristi Marie' *is a relatively large
plant, spreading up to 16in (40cm).
It has dark green leaves that
provide the perfect foil for its
white-edged, bright red flowers.*

S. 'Rococo Anna' *is grown for its
large, double, deep-pink flowers,
which are borne in profusion above
a rosette of mid-green leaves with
lighter undersides.*

Topiary designs

The sharp outline of closely clipped topiary makes a compelling statement, adding structure and color to a winter garden. So, whether you want a cone, spiral, dome, or a menagerie of animals, grab your shears and start clipping; or if you are wary of making your own, buy an already formed plant from a nursery.

Plant used
Buxus sempervirens,
(box) spiral

Height and spread
H 4ft (1.2m)
S 18in (45cm)

Exposure
Sun or partial shade

Temperature needs
Hardy to 5°F (-15°C)

Suitable pot size
18in (45cm)

Suitable container material
Terra-cotta, stone, wood, metal

Compost type
Soil-based compost, e.g., John Innes No. 3

Whether they are grown in a pair of sleek galvanized steel containers outside your front door or in terra-cotta pots on a patio, topiary shapes are guaranteed to catch the eye. Balls, cones, cubes, lollipops, spirals, or cloud-pruned trees add a dash of formal elegance whatever the weather, but they are most treasured in the winter when there's little of interest in the garden, providing much-needed structure, texture, and lush color.

Holly, privet, shrubby honeysuckle (*Lonicera nitida*), viburnum, laurel, phillyrea, yew, bay, and many other evergreen plants respond well to close clipping, but the most popular topiary plant is box. If you're adventurous, you could start a piece of topiary off from scratch, but it's far easier to buy an already trained shape that you can maintain with a pair of sharp secateurs, clippers, or topiary shears. Ensure that pots of topiary are kept well watered and work some slow-release fertilizer granules into the compost in the spring. Also feed with a liquid fertilizer after clipping.

WHEN TO PRUNE

Most topiary should be pruned in early summer and again in late summer to give it a crisp outline over the winter. However, yew only needs pruning once in midsummer, while fast-growing shrubs, such as box, may need cutting up to four times a year. It's possible to trim simple shapes, like cones and balls, by eye, but for more accurate straight edges use a pole as a guide.

TOP TIP: TRIMMING SPIRALS

Topiary spirals may look like they would be tricky to keep in shape, but they are easy to maintain. Working from top to bottom, shape the upper surface of the spiral, removing the foliage as far back as the main stem. Work your way down the spiral, maintaining its curved edges and standing back now and then to check the shape.

*Center: **Box spirals provide a vertical accent** in a winter border, flanked by lollipop topiaries and the rich bronze seedheads of sedums.*

Plants for topiary

Ilex crenata *'Mariesii'* *is a very slow-growing form of Japanese holly with tiny leaves ideal for shaping.*

Lonicera nitida *'Baggesen's Gold,'* *or shrubby honeysuckle, has golden foliage that grows densely if clipped.*

Hedera helix *is common ivy. Its fast-growing, leafy stems can be easily manipulated over topiary frames.*

Viburnum tinus *'Variegatum'* *is a bushy shrub with gold-edged green leaves, perfect for simple shapes.*

Taxus baccata, *or yew, responds well to close clipping and is ideal for geometric or intricate topiary shapes.*

Laurus nobilis *is the herb, bay. Its bushy form is often used for lollipop shapes and pyramids in a herb garden.*

Autumnal effects

If your displays start to fade as autumn approaches, give them a boost with dainty blooms, dramatic foliage, and bright, cheerful berries. Michaelmas daisies come in many colors and are ideal for late floral displays, while many shrubs grown for their fiery leaves or beadlike fruits grow well in containers, boosting drab patios and borders.

Bedding asters *Callistephus* species

Plant used
Bedding asters;
Bacopa

Height and spread
Asters: H & S 10in
(25cm); Bacopa:
S 12in (30cm)

Exposure
Full sun

Temperature needs
Not hardy below
32°F (0°C)

Suitable pot size
12in (30cm)

Suitable container material
Basket, terra-cotta,
stone

Compost type
Multi-purpose
compost

Use a wicker basket *for a cottage garden-style plan of bedding asters and late-flowering trailing plants. Set your basket on a bench or pebbles to help with drainage.*

Don't despair if your garden looks a little flat following a spectacular show of summer color. Plant some bedding asters, and you'll be rewarded with a stunning display of flowers that will last well into autumn. These compact annual bedding plants are *Callistephus*, and are not to be confused with the genus *Aster*.

To make a rustic container, line a basket with a plastic sheet punctured with drainage holes. Add multi-purpose compost, and plant a mix of large- and small-flowered bedding asters, together with trailing bacopa. Place in the sun, and keep plants well watered for a long display.

TOP TIP: CHOOSING ASTERS FOR POTS

Annual bedding asters provide a season of color, but for a show year after year grow perennial species. The New York Michaelmas daisy or *Aster novi-belgii* has the brightest colors, while *Aster amellus* (right) is compact and floriferous. Both are great for pots.

Autumn leaves

Plant used
Hydrangea
quercifolia

Height and spread
H & S 4ft (1.2m)

Exposure
Sun or partial shade

Temperature needs
Fully hardy

Suitable pot size
18in (45cm)

**Suitable container
material**
Terra-cotta, glazed
ceramic, stone

Compost type
Soil-based compost,
e.g., John Innes No. 3

Hydrangea quercifolia makes a mound of fiery foliage.

Many shrubs earn their keep in containers by providing gardens with breathtaking autumn color. Commonly known as oak leaf hydrangea, *Hydrangea quercifolia* is among the best and produces an attractive mound of deeply lobed green leaves that in autumn take a dramatic turn as they fire up in shades of red and purple before falling. Other gems with superb autumn color include the Japanese maples (*see pp. 68–69*); a slow-growing form of smoke bush, *Cotinus coggygria* 'Young Lady;' the winged spindle bush *Euonymus alatus* 'Compactus;' the Eastern redbud *Cercis canadensis* 'Forest Pansy;' and *Liquidambar styraciflua* 'Gumball,' a compact sweet gum with burnt orange foliage.

All are sizable bushes and require large pots or half barrels and soil-based compost. Keep plants well watered, and feed annually in early spring with an all-purpose granular fertilizer.

Berry choices

Plant used
Dwarf *Hypericum*
hybrid

Height and spread
H 3ft (1m)
S 5ft (1.5m)

Exposure
Full sun

Temperature needs
Fully hardy

Suitable pot size
12in (30cm)

**Suitable container
material**
Terra-cotta, glazed
ceramic, stone

Compost type
Soil based compost,
e.g., John Innes No. 3

Berried plants add colour and form to an autumn patio display. Good choices include dwarf hybrids of *Hypericum*, such as *H*. 'Magical Red', which bear colourful red or pink fruits following sunshine-yellow summer flowers, and *Cotoneaster salicifolius* 'Gnom', which is a low-growing form that does well in a pot if clipped to keep it neat. Although its evergreen leaves make it welcome all year, the main season of interest is autumn when the branches drip with masses of bright red berries.

COLOR CHOICE
For a blaze of berries, match a *Hypericum* or *Cotoneaster* with other fruit-bearing plants in showy colors. Make a statement with *Callicarpa bodinieri* var. *giraldii* 'Profusion,' whose amazing metallic violet berries cling to the bare branches in the fall and winter, and *Viburnum opulus* 'Xanthocarpum' with its plump yellow berries. Plant in large pots of soil-based compost, and feed in the spring with an all-purpose granular fertilizer.

Many *Hypericum* species bear striking pink-red berries.

Evergreen grasses

If you're looking for an exciting way to create a fantastic spectacle during the cold months of the year, plant pots of evergreen grasses and sedges. Tough, graceful, and easy to care for, they provide a shot of color to brighten the bleakest day, and are often topped with long-lasting seedheads that catch the light and rustle in the breeze.

COLD-SEASON DISPLAYS

Plants used
Stipa tenuissima;
Carex comans
'Bronze Perfection;'
Eragrostis elliottii

Height and spread
Stipa: H & S 24in (60cm); *Carex:* H 12in (30cm) S 16in (40cm); *Eragrostis* H 32in (80cm) S 24in (60cm)

Exposure
Sun or partial shade

Temperature needs
Hardy to 5°F (-15°C)
Eragrostis hardy to 23°F (-5°C)

Suitable pot size
8–12in (20–30cm)

Suitable container material
Stone, terra-cotta, glazed ceramic, metal

Suitable compost
Soil-based compost, e.g., John Innes No. 3

Evergreen grasses really earn their keep. They look good all year, but are prized in the winter for their colors, shapes, and textures. They also boast several other attributes, such as the gentle rustle of the leaves as they sway in the wind, and their dancing seedheads. There is a wide selection of grasses, sedges, and grasslike plants to choose from, including *Carex*, *Festuca*, *Acorus*, *Stipa*, and *Ophiopogon*. Some have upright appearances, while others produce a fountain of arching leaves. Perfect alongside other plants in a container, you can also group several grasses together, combining a selection of different colors and shapes.

Place pots in sun or partial shade, and water regularly, especially in the summer. However, do not overwater, and place containers on "feet" or large pebbles to allow excess moisture to drain away. Feed monthly with a liquid fertilizer during the growing season.

GROOMING PLANTS

Evergreen grasses can become choked with dead leaves and debris over time, which inhibits their growth. To clean up soft-leaf types, put on gardening gloves and comb your hands through the foliage from top to bottom. Use shears to remove dead or damaged foliage from wide-leaf grasses.

TOP TIP: DIVIDING

When healthy, evergreen grasses will grow vigorously, eventually filling their original containers. In the spring, either move them into larger pots or divide them in two. To do this, remove the plant from its pot and pull apart the root ball carefully by hand or, if the roots are very compacted, use a sharp knife to cut it down the middle. Before repotting the sections in fresh compost, use a pair of shears to remove any dead or damaged growth.

Steel-blue **Festuca glauca** *forms a compact head of spiky foliage, ideal for windowboxes and small pots.*

Choosing grasses for winter

Carex *'Ice Dance'* *is a clump-forming sedge with variegated strap-like leaves and brown flowers.*

Acorus gramineus *'Ōgon'* *makes a cascading clump of yellow, green, and cream variegated leaves; it prefers sun.*

Carex flagellifera *produces a large, low waterfall of bronze leaves. It is happy in sun or partial shade.*

Ophiopogon planiscapus *'Nigrescens'* *is not a true grass, but its dramatic black, grasslike leaves are invaluable.*

Combine grass and container colors *and shapes to make an exciting garden display. Stipa tenuissima and Carex comans are evergreen, while the deciduous Eragrostis retains its leaves until late fall.*

Winter at home

If cold gloomy days get you down, bring some cheer into your home with a range of colorful houseplants. Amaryllis provide big, bold blooms in the depths of winter, while bush lilies, with their beefy, straplike leaves and vibrant orange flowers, make a dramatic statement. The bright fruits of Christmas cherries complete the picture.

COLD-SEASON DISPLAYS

Amaryllis *Hippeastrum*

Plants used
Hippeastrum
varieties;
*Synonium
podophyllum;* ferns

Height and spread
Hippeastrum:
H 30in (75cm)
S 12in (30cm);
Synonium:
H & S 16in (40cm)

Exposure
Light with some
direct sun

Temperature
64–75°F (18–24°C);
cooler when
in bloom

Suitable pot size
6in (15cm) or larger

**Suitable container
material**
Metal, glazed
terra-cotta, plastic

Compost type
Soil-based compost,
e.g., John Innes No. 2

With bold, flamboyant flowers on top of sturdy stems that don't need staking, amaryllis cannot fail to impress. This bulbous plant often receives undivided attention, since it has very little competition when it bursts into flower in the depths of winter. Choose from deep red, pink, pale green, white, and striped forms. Packing a few bulbs together in a wide, shallow, container and underplanting with foliage helps to disguise the stems and plain leaves, producing a dazzling indoor design with the blooms performing the starring role.

SURVIVAL STRATEGY

Provide plants with plenty of light, including some direct sun. Keep the compost moist when in active growth, and feed fortnightly with liquid fertilizer. After flowering, stop watering, and allow the bulbs to dry off and the leaves to wither. Start watering again in the fall to stimulate plants back into growth. In the second year, repot in fresh compost after the summer dormancy, and then feed and water regularly.

TOP TIP: PLANTING DRY BULBS

In early fall, buy dry bulbs and soak them in a bucket of lukewarm water for a few hours to soften them. Choose a pot just larger than the bulb and fill the base with compost. Place the bulb on top, and fill in with more compost, leaving the top third of the bulb protruding. Water and leave in a warm spot.

Create an exotic winter display with amaryllis grouped together with leafy goosefoot plants (Syngonium) and ferns.

Bush lily *Clivia*

Plant used
Clivia miniata

Height and spread
H 28in (70cm)
S 24in (60cm)

Exposure
Bright, light location
out of midday sun

Temperature
64°F (18°C);
min 45°F (7°C)

Suitable pot size
6–8in (15–20cm)

Suitable container material
Glazed terra-cotta,
metal, plastic

Compost type
Houseplant compost

A combination of long, straplike, glossy leaves and dense heads of large dramatic flowers make *Clivia* a much-prized houseplant. The flowers are produced on top of a sturdy stems in late winter or early spring, and color options include red, orange, yellow, or apricot flowers. Plant these lilylike plants in a small pot in houseplant compost; they enjoy cramped conditions, so do not worry if you see the roots pushing out of the top of the pot.

WATERING AND FEEDING
It is difficult to water root-bound plants from above, so place containers in a bucket of water, leave until the top of the compost is moist, then remove and allow to drain. Water plants regularly during the growing season, keeping the compost moist but not too wet. Feed plants regularly during this time with a liquid fertilizer.

Clivia miniata **produces bright vase-shaped flowers.**

Christmas cherry *Solanum*

Plant used
Solanum pseudocapsicum

Height and spread
H & S 12in (30cm)

Exposure
Full light but away
from midday sun

Temperature
64–75°F (18–24°C);
min 50°F (10°C)

Suitable pot size
6–8in (15–20cm)

Suitable container material
Glazed terra-cotta,
metal, plastic

Compost type
Houseplant compost

Christmas cherries are usually grown as annuals, and the bright red berries of this pretty little plant bring a ray of sunshine to gloomy winter days. Unripe berries are green, and then turn yellow, orange, and finally red, but they are often all displayed at the same time, giving the plant a multicolored effect. Dwarf varieties are ideal for small, decorative pots. A word of warning: the berries may look edible, but they are poisonous, and plants must be kept out of the reach of children and pets.

PLANTING NEEDS
Plant in pots of houseplant compost, keep them well watered, and feed regularly with a liquid fertilizer. Reduce watering and stop feeding when the berries wither at the end of winter; resume regular care after a few weeks.

Solanum pseudocapsicum

COLD-SEASON DISPLAYS

Forced bulbs

Narcissus and *Hyacinthus*

When it's too cold to step out of your back door, cheer yourself up by bringing the garden inside. Pots of colorful bulbs will instantly brighten up a dreary winter's day and fill your home with a combination of beautiful blooms and heady scent.

COLD-SEASON DISPLAYS

Plants used
Narcissus and *Hyacinthus* species

Height
Narcissus: H 8in (20cm); *Hyacinthus:* H 8in (20cm)

Exposure
Bright and sunny, away from direct heat

Temperature needs
Fully hardy outside; happy indoors at 68°F (20°C)

Suitable pot size
6–8in (15–20cm)

Suitable container material
Terra-cotta, ceramic, glazed terra-cotta, glass

Compost type
Bulb fiber

Daffodils and hyacinths naturally flower in the spring, but it's possible to produce a display in the winter if you carry out a technique called "forcing." To do this, buy bulbs in early autumn that are labeled "Prepared," "For Forcing," or "Heat-treated." These have been grown especially for indoor displays.

Either plant single bulbs in small pots, or try groups of three or five in shallow bowls filled with bulb fiber. Hyacinths should be planted with the top half of the bulb showing above the compost, while the pointed tips of narcissus bulbs should be just below the surface. Water the pots lightly after planting, then place them in a box and store in an unheated shed or garage. Check them after about ten weeks, and when bulbs have shoots 1in (2.5cm) long, move the pots to a cool windowsill indoors. When flower buds appear, bring them into a warmer room to bloom, and keep the compost damp at all times.

PLACING BULBS IN THE HOME
For long-lasting blooms, display plants in a cool, sunny place, such as a tabletop near a south-facing window. Avoid putting pots near a direct heat source, such as a radiator; this will cause them to fade quickly. Don't overdo the hyacinths; a single pot will have ample flowers to fill a room with scent. After flowering, discard bulbs or allow the foliage to fade and plant in the garden.

TOP TIP: CHOOSING HEALTHY BULBS

Healthy bulbs should be plump, firm, and unblemished, so before buying, inspect them carefully. Reject any that are moldy, bruised, shriveled, or show premature signs of growth, and also leave those that have lost their outer skins. Give the remaining bulbs a squeeze; if they are soft, they are probably rotten.

Forced daffodils and hyacinths will flower in the depths of winter, and are very easy to grow from prepared bulbs.

Bulb choices

Hyacinthus orientalis *'Blue Jacket'* *produces dense spikes of sweetly scented blue flowers and dark leaves.*

Hyacinthus orientalis *'City of Haarlem'* *is an old favorite, with spikes of highly perfumed yellow flowers.*

Hyacinthus orientalis *'Ostara'* *has heavily scented, violet-blue, bell-shaped flowers, marked white at the edges.*

Hyacinthus *'Pink Pearl'* *produces fat spikes packed with bright pink flowers that emit a wonderful fragrance.*

Narcissus *'Avalanche'* *produces short stems, each carrying over a dozen scented white flowers with yellow cups.*

Narcissus *'Cheerfulness'* *has double, creamy-white flowers with egg-yolk yellow centers and a knock-out scent.*

Narcissus *'Ice Follies'* *has large, pale yellow cups that stand proud on white petals on knee-high flower stalks.*

Narcissus *'Salome'* *bears creamy-white petals and yellow cups that age gracefully to a peachy color.*

FRUIT AND VEGETABLES

Many delicious edibles thrive in containers on a patio, balcony, or deck, bringing community gardening closer to home. Use the advice in this chapter to select a range of crops that suit smaller spaces and discover which plants will best suit your garden exposure. Also try new varieties of fruit and vegetables that are not available in the grocery to broaden your culinary experience.

Plant strawberries in large baskets to produce bumper summer crops, and use wooden crates to grow your own onions. Thornless blackberries have been bred for large pots, while chard grows easily from seed.

Planning your crops in pots

With so many grow-your-own fruit and vegetables to choose from, it's worth taking a little time to explore your options. Some varieties of fruit, for example, have been bred especially for containers, while many unusual vegetables are only available as seed, and well worth growing. Use the seasonal sowing and planting guide opposite to help plan your gardening year.

Choosing crops for containers

When planning your container collection of fruit and vegetables, choose those that are easy to grow and produce abundant crops, or select unusual varieties that are not available to buy in stores. All the edibles in this chapter will grow well in a container or growing bag and produce a good harvest. You can also obtain more advice about specific cultivars and how well they will cope with cramped growing conditions from specialty seed companies and nurseries.

In addition, choose your containers and compost carefully, ensuring that they will suit your chosen crops. Details of both are in the boxes adjacent to the plant entries in this chapter.

Choose compact plants, such as herbs, chilis, and tomatoes for small pots on a sunny patio, roof terrace, or balcony. Set pots on crates to improve drainage.

Placing your pots

Most vegetables and fruits require sun to thrive, so if your site is shady, your choices will be limited to leafy crops, rhubarb, mint, parsley, and chives, among others; few crops tolerate deep shade.

Find a sheltered area away from strong winds, which can blow over pots and reduce insect numbers and pollination rates. Protect crops in exposed sites with a semi-permeable windbreak that allows some air to pass through.

Tomatoes demand a warm, sunny spot, which ensures their fruits will ripen well before the frost in the fall. Grow plants under cover in early spring to lengthen the growing season.

Rhubarb is happy in a slightly shaded site but will suffer if grown in deep shade. To thrive, plants must be watered well.

VEGETABLE AND HERB SOWING AND PLANTING GUIDE

LATE WINTER/EARLY SPRING
Sow seeds of these crops under cover from late winter to early spring, and transplant outside after the final frost.

MID- TO LATE SPRING
Sow seeds directly into pots outside, and transplant crops sown inside into larger pots outdoors after the last frost.

EARLY TO MIDSUMMER
Sow directly into pots outside. Sow small quantities of fast-maturing crops over a few weeks for a long harvest.

LATE SUMMER TO AUTUMN
Sow spring-maturing crops directly into pots outside from late summer to early fall. Some may need cloches.

LATE WINTER/EARLY SPRING	MID- TO LATE SPRING	EARLY TO MIDSUMMER	LATE SUMMER TO AUTUMN
Asian leaves *pp. 158–9*	Asian leaves *pp. 158–9*	Asian leaves *pp. 158–9*	Asian leaves *pp. 158–9*
Basil *p. 198*	Basil *p. 198*	Beets *p. 185*	Chicory *p. 160*
Bay *p. 196*	Beets *p. 185*	Bok choy *p. 173*	Chives *p. 163*
Bok choy *p. 173*	Bok choy *p. 173*	Carrots *pp. 186–7*	Garlic *p. 171*
Carrots *pp. 186–7*	Carrots *pp. 186–7*	Chicory *p. 160*	Lettuces *pp. 156–7*
Chamomile *p. 195*	Chicory *p. 160*	Cilantro *p. 203*	Mint *pp. 192–3*
Chicory *p. 160*	Chives *p. 163*	Endive *p. 191*	Peas *pp. 180–1*
Chives *p. 163*	Coriander *p. 203*	Fennel *p. 194*	Radishes *p. 162*
Eggplant *p. 166*	Endive *p. 191*	Kale *p. 174*	
Ginger *p. 203*	Fennel *p. 194*	Kohlrabi *p. 173*	
Green beans *pp. 176–7*	Green beans *pp. 176–7*	Leeks *p. 190*	
Green onions *p. 163*	Green onions *p. 163*	Lettuces *pp. 156–7*	
Horseradish *p. 184*	Horseradish *p. 184*	Parsley *p. 200*	
Kohlrabi *p. 173*	Kale *p. 174*	Peas *pp. 180–1*	
Leeks *p. 190*	Kohlrabi *p. 173*	Peppers *pp. 168–9*	
Lemongrass *p. 202*	Lemon balm *p. 195*	Pumpkins and winter squashes *pp. 188–9*	
Lettuces *pp. 156–7*	Lettuces *pp. 156–7*	Spinach *p. 175*	
Onions and shallots *p. 170*	Mint *pp. 192–3*	Thyme *p. 198*	
Orach *p. 161*	Orach *p. 161*	Winter cabbage *p. 191*	
Oregano *p. 201*	Peas *pp. 180–1*	Zucchini and summer squash *p. 167*	
Parsley *p. 200*	Potatoes *pp. 182–3*		
Peas *pp. 180–1*	Pumpkins and winter squashes *pp. 188–9*		
Peppers *pp. 168–9*	Radishes *p. 162*		
Potatoes *pp. 182–3*	Rosemary *p. 201*		
Radishes *p. 162*	Runner beans *pp. 178–9*		
Sage *p. 197*	Sorrel *p. 161*		
Spinach *p. 175*	Spinach *p. 175*		
Swiss chard *p. 172*	Swiss chard *p. 172*		
Tomatoes *pp. 164–5*	Thyme *p. 198*		
Zucchini and summer squash *p. 167*	Winter cabbage *p. 191*		

WEATHER WATCH

Although this seasonal advice is accurate for most areas, if you live in a warmer climate by the coast, for example, you may be able to plant your crops outside a little earlier. Conversely, in colder locales, delay planting vulnerable seeds and plants outside until the last frost has passed, which may be in early summer. Cover pots with fabric if unexpected late frosts are forecast.

For autumn-sown plants, protect from severe frosts by placing a cloche or a few sheets of garden fabric over your containers. Alternatively, bring them close to the house or into an unheated greenhouse.

Fresh lettuce

Among the easiest vegetables to grow, lettuces are ideal for pots, where they can be more easily protected from marauding slugs and snails. The widest selection is available in seed form, and the cut-and-come-again types are ready to pick just a few weeks after sowing. Try a mix of lettuces for different textures and tastes.

SALADS

Plants used
Dazzle and Green
Frills lettuces

Height and spread
H up to 8in (20cm)
S up to 12in (30cm)

Exposure
Sun or partial shade

Temperature
Fully hardy

Harvesting period
Summer to winter

Suitable pot size
6in (15cm) or larger

Container material
Metal, terra-cotta,
plastic, baskets

Compost type
Multi-purpose
compost

Lettuces are not only delicious when picked fresh from the garden, but they also make decorative features in pots. Fill a container, large or small, with some multi-purpose compost and sow your seed thinly on the surface. In small containers, try to sow about three or four seeds of butter, Romaine, and iceberg, which form a heart, or just sprinkle cut-and-come-again varieties more densely; you will not need to thin these out. Sow a few pots each week for a continuous supply of leaves throughout the summer, but remember that seeds will not germinate if the temperature is above 77°F (25°C). When heart-forming varieties reach an inch or so in height, thin them out to appropriate spacings, which will be given on the packet of seeds, or leave them a little closer.

CARING FOR LETTUCES

Keep your lettuces well watered at all times, especially in hot weather when you will have to water daily, and move pots to a slightly shaded spot in the height of the summer. Lack of water or too much heat will cause the plants to "bolt" and produce long flowering stems—the leaves then become bitter. However, do not allow the compost to become waterlogged or the lettuces will rot. Most multi-purpose composts contain enough nutrients to sustain lettuces for a few weeks, but after that, give them a boost with a nitrogen-rich fertilizer formulated for leafy crops. The main pests to look out for are slugs and snails. Inspect plants every few days and pick off any culprits.

An old tin bathtub
makes a good home
for a collection of
Green Frills and dark
red Dazzle cut-and-
come-again lettuces.

TOP TIP: HARVESTING LEAVES

Allow the butter, Romaine, and iceberg varieties to mature into solid heads of leaves, and then slice the main stem off at the base with a sharp knife. Cut-and-come-again types can be harvested once by cutting all the leaves off an inch above the base.

New leaves should then regrow, giving you a second crop. Alternatively, just pick off a few leaves as and when you need them; more will then grow to replace them. Growing some of each type gives you the best of both worlds.

Choosing lettuce varieties

'Nymans' *is a two-tone lettuce with burgundy leaves and bright green bases. Slow to bolt and mildew-resistant.*

'Winter Density' *is a compact variety with dark green hearts that offer fresh greens in the winter from fall sowings.*

'Bubbles' *has distinctive crumpled leaves with a very sweet flavor. Its compact form makes it perfect for pots.*

'Lollo rosso' *has crisp frilly leaves that add color and texture to salads and are a feature in pots in the garden.*

'Pandero' *is a delicious mini red Romaine lettuce with crisp leaves that develop a good color and are mildew-resistant.*

'Tintin' *is slightly larger than a 'Little Gem'; it has a great flavor and bubbly leaves with a crisp heart.*

'Salad Bowl' *has wavy-edged leaves that can be left to produce a loose head, or treat it as a cut-and-come-again.*

'Little Gem' *is a popular variety that produces upright, dark green, crunchy hearts with an excellent sweet flavor.*

SALADS

Asian leaves

They may be small, but these salad leaves are big on flavor, and when combined with flowers, they make a pretty ornamental display. Easy to grow, the tasty crops are ready to harvest within weeks of sowing— micro greens are even quicker—and all require little care, apart from watering and picking the leaves regularly to keep the plants productive.

Mustard and mizuna

Plants used
Mustard 'Red Giant;' mizuna; *Calendula* (pot marigold)

Exposure
Sun or partial shade

Temperature
Not hardy below 0°C (32°F)

Harvesting period
Spring to fall

Suitable pot size
Min. 8in (20cm)

Suitable container material
Any

Compost type
Multi-purpose compost

A wicker basket makes a decorative container for a vibrant mix of tasty oriental leaves and orange pot marigolds. The mizuna's serrated leaves contrast well with the rounded, purple foliage of mustard 'Red Giant,' and both will add a peppery kick to salads. The pot marigold doesn't just help to brighten up the basket, its edible petals can also be tossed into salads.

To grow the leaves, mix together a pinch of mustard and mizuna seed, then sow across the surface of a container filled with multi-purpose compost. Raise your marigolds separately, sowing seed in pots and transferring a few seedlings into the container when they reach 6in (15cm). Alternatively, buy young plants.

CARING FOR CROPS
Water regularly, especially during hot weather, to ensure the compost is always moist; dry soil will cause the salad leaves to turn bitter and the plants to bolt. To ensure a regular supply of fresh leaves, cut them as you need them from the outside edge of the plants.

TOP TIP: SOWING SALAD LEAF SEEDS

Sow seeds of mustard, mizuna, arugula, or salad leaf mixes in pots filled with multi-purpose compost. Sow seeds thinly across the surface of your container and cover with ½in (1cm) of compost. Firm gently, then water. Thin out overcrowded seedlings when they are large enough to handle; eat the thinnings.

Leafy mustard and mizuna should be cropped little and often to keep plants productive and prevent them bolting.

SALADS

Arugula

Plant used
Arugula

Exposure
Sun or partial shade

Temperature
Frost tender

Harvesting period
Late spring to early autumn

Suitable pot size
8in (20cm)

Suitable container material
Any

Compost type
Multi-purpose compost

The peppery leaves of arugula are ideal for adding heat to salads or blending together with olive oil to make a fiery version of pesto sauce. Seeds will germinate readily at any time between early spring and early fall, and a single container will provide tasty pickings for several weeks if you harvest leaves regularly, which also prevents plants from flowering and going to seed. Although a large pot will provide you with plenty of leaves, this is a great crop for sowing in small containers, such as windowboxes. Water plants regularly to ensure the compost doesn't dry out.

PEST PROTECTION
Cover up your leaves with fine mesh to prevent cabbage white butterflies from laying their eggs. These will later hatch into ravenous caterpillars that will munch their way through your crops.

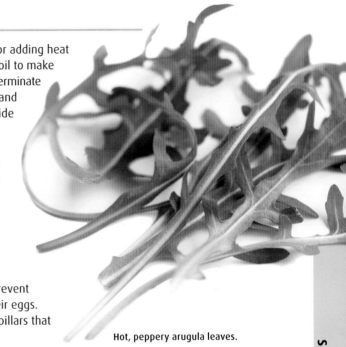
Hot, peppery arugula leaves.

Micro greens

Plants used
Micro greens

Exposure
Full sun

Temperature
Grow indoors

Harvesting period
Spring to late autumn

Suitable pot size
A seed tray or recycled shallow container

Suitable container material
Plastic

Compost type
Vermiculite

Micro greens are ready to harvest in just a few days.

Prized by top chefs, micro greens are tiny vegetable seedlings that are harvested between six and 21 days after germination. They may be small but their flavor is intense. Micro crops grow well in seed trays, plastic berry baskets, or other shallow containers with good drainage. Add a 1in (2cm) layer of vermiculite to your container, then scatter seeds liberally over the surface, and do not cover them. Stand the container in a tray filled with water, and leave until the surface of the vermiculite is wet, then drain. Place the container on a sunny windowsill in a warm room to germinate, and don't let the vermiculite dry out. Harvest crops with scissors when they have formed their first leaves.

WHAT TO GROW
Lots of vegetables make tasty micro leaves. Try pea pod, sugar pea, sunflower, broccoli, arugula, radish, beet, celery, Swiss chard, and red mustard. Herbs, such as basil, fennel, coriander, and chervil, are also options.

Spicy salad mix

If you can't face another boring green salad, these three fantastic leaves will perk up your palate and your plate with their distinctive flavors and colorful leaves. Chicory is famously bitter; orach tastes a little like salty spinach; and sorrel has a mild citrus flavor. You'd be hard pressed to find the last two in a supermarket, but luckily they are easy to grow.

Chicory

SALADS

Plant used
Chicory 'Treviso Precoce Mesola'

Exposure
Full sun

Temperature needs
Fully hardy

Harvesting period
Summer to winter

Suitable pot size
18in (45cm)

Suitable container material
Terra-cotta, plastic, glazed ceramic

Compost type
Multi-purpose compost

Chicory is famed for its bitter leaves, and there are three types available. Sugarloaf and red chicory, which is better known as radicchio, are grown for their leaves, while Belgian or Witloof forcing chicory produces tender white hearts, known as "chicons", when deprived of light.

All seeds are started the same way. Sow them thinly across the surface of a pot filled with seed compost and cover with ½in (1cm) of sieved compost. Water and place in a sunny site. When seedlings have a few leaves, transplant three into an 18in (45cm) pot. Spring sowings provide summer leaves, while seeds sown in the summer will be ready from fall through winter.

TOP TIP: BLANCHING CHICORY

Once forcing chicory has developed a good head of leaves in late autumn, cut the tops off, leaving a 2in (5cm) stump. Water plants well, then cover the stumps with an upturned bucket to exclude any light, and stand in a frost-free place. Your blanched chicons will be ready to harvest after a month.

'Treviso Precoce Mesola' is a really colorful radicchio with white-ribbed, red-flushed leaves.

Sorrel

Plant used
Red-veined sorrel

Exposure
Sun or partial shade

Temperature needs
Fully hardy

Harvesting period
Spring to early autumn

Suitable pot size
12in (30cm)

Suitable container material
Plastic, terra-cotta, glazed ceramic

Compost type
Soil-based compost, e.g., John Innes No. 2

Difficult to find in stores, sorrel is a perennial herb grown for its tangy, slightly citrusy leaves. It's perfect for adding flavor to green salads or perking up soups. Most sorrels are not pretty plants, but the red-veined variety (*Rumex sanguineus*) has attractive bright green leaves with distinctive red markings. Buckler-leaf or French sorrel (*Rumex scutatus*) is also worth growing for its green, shield-shaped leaves, which have a slight green-apple flavor.

GROWING SORREL
Sow seeds in the spring ½in (1.5cm) deep, thinning out seedlings to a final spacing of 12in (30cm). Young plants are also available. Plant in a container filled with John Innes No. 2 compost and keep well watered. Pick leaves when needed, and pinch off flowers as soon as they develop, to prevent plants from running to seed.

Red-veined sorrel is grown for its mild citrus flavor.

Orach

Plant used
Red orach

Height
H 3ft (1m)

Exposure
Partial shade

Temperature needs
Hardy to 5°F (-15°C)

Harvesting period
Early spring to summer

Suitable pot size
12in (30cm)

Suitable container material
Plastic, terra-cotta, glazed ceramic

Compost type
Soil-based compost, e.g., John Innes No. 2

Orach is an extremely attractive annual herb that is grown for its spinachlike leaves. It's fast growing and will quickly shoot up to an imposing 3ft (1m).

Sow seeds in small pots of moist compost in late winter or early spring, cover them with a layer of vermiculite, and keep moist. Stand pots on a warm windowsill to germinate but avoid direct sun. When seedlings are large enough to handle, transplant them into individual pots to continue on. In mid-spring, plant into large containers filled with John Innes No. 2 compost. Water regularly; if plants become lanky, pinch off the growing tips to encourage bushy growth. To prevent leaf scorch, place containers in partial shade.

WHAT TO GROW
Red orach (*Atriplex hortensis* var. *rubra*) is a showy plant with reddish-purple triangular leaves. Gold orach has golden foliage, and 'Scarlet Emperor' produces dusky purple and pink, two-tone leaves.

Red orach is a beautiful plant.

Tangy salad boosters

If your salads are a little on the bland side, spice them up by sowing some fast-growing crops with loads of flavor. Perfect in pots on their own or dotted in gaps around the base of larger plants, radishes, chives, and spring onions are incredibly easy to grow and will shoot up quickly from seeds sown in succession from spring to late summer.

Radishes

Plant used
Radish 'French Breakfast'

Exposure
Sun or partial shade

Temperature needs
Not hardy below 32°F (0°C)

Harvesting period
From spring to fall

Suitable pot size
8in (20cm)

Suitable container material
Terra-cotta, metal, plastic, baskets

Compost type
Multi-purpose compost

Perfect for adding a peppery crunch to salads, radishes are a cinch to grow, and often produce mature crops within four weeks of sowing. There are many different types to choose from, in different colors, shapes, and sizes. Short-rooted radishes can be grown in shallow containers, such as windowboxes, while those with longer roots need deeper pots to develop properly.

SOWING SEEDS
Seeds can be sown at any time from late winter to early autumn, but early and late sowings need protecting from frost and heavy rain. Either place pots in a greenhouse or cool light room, or cover them with a bell cloche. Sow seeds thinly across the surface of a pot and cover with a ½in (1.5cm) layer of compost. If seedlings are too crowded, thin out to appropriate spacing. Keep plants well watered, especially during hot, dry spells.

Easy to grow, *radishes are a good choice for children to try since they are ready to eat within weeks of sowing.*

SALADS

CHOOSING RADISH VARIETIES

'Scarlet Globe' *is a fast-growing variety with round, scarlet roots and crisp, white flesh. It is a great choice for a windowbox or shallow pot, or for dotting around other plants.*

'French Breakfast' *is a popular radish with slender roots that have a sweet, mild taste. It requires a fairly deep pot to accommodate the long, pinkish-red roots.*

'China Rose', *known as the Chinese or winter radish, has long, peppery roots that need a very deep pot. It is favored because it stores well and can be used in the winter.*

'Cherry Belle' *radishes have bright red skins and white flesh, and a sweet, mild flavor. This variety is exceptionally fast-maturing and perfect for small pots on a patio.*

Chives

Plant used
Chives

Height and spread
H 12in (30cm)
S Indefinite

Exposure
Sun or partial shade

Temperature needs
Fully hardy

Harvesting period
From spring
to fall

Suitable pot size
8in (20cm)

Suitable container material
Terra-cotta, metal, plastic

Compost type
Soil-based compost, e.g., John Innes No. 3

The pungent, mild onion taste of chives gives a boost to salads and other dishes. You can either buy a young plant or grow your own from seeds sown in the spring. Sow seeds about ¼in (0.5cm) deep in a small 3in (7.5cm) pot of seed compost, and place in a heated propagator to germinate. You can then pot the seedlings outside into larger containers of soil-based compost, such as John Innes No. 3, in late spring when the weather has warmed up. To harvest, simply cut the leaves as needed just above the compost.

REJUVENATING CLUMPS

Chives spread fairly quickly and will eventually fill their containers. At this stage, either move plants into larger pots, or lift them out and divide them in two with a sharp knife. Replant healthy sections in new pots of fresh compost.

Chives are ideal for small pots.

Green onions

Plant used
Red spring onions

Exposure
Sun or partial shade

Temperature needs
Fully hardy

Harvesting period
Summer to
mid-autumn

Suitable pot size
18in (45cm)

Suitable container material
Terra-cotta, metal, plastic, deep baskets

Compost type
Multi-purpose compost

Red spring onions add color to a mixed salad.

Grown for their tangy bulbs and stems, green onions, or spring onions, are easy to raise from seed and should be ready for harvesting within 12 weeks of sowing. Seeds can be sown in the spring and summer into pots filled with multi-purpose compost; either make shallow rows across the surface and sprinkle the seeds into the grooves, or scatter them thinly on top of the compost and cover with a ½in (1cm) layer of compost. Thin seedlings if necessary. The disease downy mildew can present a problem. If you spot a white fungal growth, remove affected plants immediately.

CHOOSING VARIETIES

There are many varieties of green onions to choose from. 'White Lisbon' is popular for its mild, white bulbs and stems with green tops, while 'Vigour King' has a hotter onion taste. 'North Holland Blood Red' has striking dark red bulbs and lower stems with green tops, and adds color as well as flavor to mixed salads and stir-fries.

Sweet tomato treats

Homegrown tomatoes are a world apart from those you buy at the supermarket. Whether you grow young plants bought from a garden center, or sow your own from seed, you will be picking fresh fruits from midsummer until the beginning of fall. Most tomatoes require large pots or deep baskets to thrive.

MEDITERRANEAN MIXES

Plant used
Tomato 'Tumbling Tom Red'

Exposure
Full sun

Temperature needs
Not hardy below 32°F (0°C)

Harvesting periods
Summer to early autumn

Suitable pot size
12in (30cm) or larger

Suitable container material
Terra-cotta, baskets, plastic

Compost type
Multi-purpose compost

The taste of tomatoes that have ripened naturally over a long season in the sun is unrivaled and makes growing them yourself well worth the effort. Most are happy in pots, as long as the containers can hold sufficient compost and water. Trailing varieties are perfect in deep hanging baskets or large tubs, while cordon types, which are grown as a single stem against a pole, can be planted in big containers or growing bags (*see p.241*).

A good range of young plants is available from garden centers in the spring, but for a wider selection, sow seeds indoors in the late winter. Fill a 3in (7.5cm) pot with seed compost, scatter seeds thinly over the surface, and cover them with a layer of vermiculite. Then water the pots and place in a heated propagator until the seeds have germinated. When seedlings are almost 1in (2.5cm) tall, carefully lift them out of the pot, separate the root balls, and plant each one in a 3in (7.5cm) pot. Keep plants in a light, frost-free place, and when roots show at the bottom of the pots, move them into 5in 12.5cm) pots filled with multi-purpose compost. At the end of spring, most tomatoes can be planted outside.

FEEDING REGIME
Tomatoes are greedy crops and need to be fed every week with a tomato fertilizer once the flowers appear. This regime should be increased to two doses a week when the fruit has set, and continued until the last tomato has been picked.

TOP TIP: WATERING NEEDS

It's important that tomatoes are never allowed to dry out or all of your hard work raising the plants will be wasted. Irregular watering can cause the tomatoes to split or hard black patches to form on the bottom of the fruits. This is known as blossom end rot, and is caused by a lack of calcium, which is found in water.

*Center: **Red 'Tumbling Toms'** produce bumper crops in large hanging baskets, given a sunny site and lots of water and fertilizer.*

Choosing tomato varieties

'Tumbling Tom Yellow' is perfect for a large hanging basket that will hold plenty of compost and water. The large trusses of sweet, cherry-sized fruit look great cascading over the sides and can be picked all summer long.

'Totem' is a short and compact variety, making it ideal for a large hanging basket or even a deep windowbox. Its stocky branches carry a heavy crop of bright red fruits. The sideshoots must be removed to ensure a good crop.

'Sungold' produces an abundance of small, sweet, and juicy, bright orange to yellow fruits with very thin skins. Plants are best grown as cordons, with a pole to support the stems, in large pots or growing bags.

'Moneymaker' is a long-time favorite, popular for its ease of growth and dependable crops of medium-sized, red fruits that are borne in large trusses. It should be grown as a cordon in a large container or growing bag.

'Sweet Olive' produces trusses of olive-shaped fruits that hang down from the stems of this cordon variety. It is easy to grow, and will produce a heavy crop in a pot or growing bag, even if you don't remove all of the sideshoots.

'Tigerella' is a decorative variety with orange fruit emblazoned with bright green stripes that looks good in the garden and on the plate. It is a cordon type and produces heavy crops when grown in a large pot in a greenhouse.

MEDITERRANEAN MIXES

Fruits of the Med

Their plump, juicy fruit and showy blooms make eggplant, zucchini, and squash a great choice for a decorative patio display, set among pots of summer flowers and other fruiting crops. Plant them in large containers in a warm sheltered spot, water them well, and let these Mediterranean delights swell to perfection in the heat of the sun.

MEDITERANNEAN MIXES

Eggplant

Plant used
Eggplant 'Pinstripe'

Height and spread
H 24in (60cm)
S 12in (30cm)

Exposure
Full sun

Temperature needs
Not hardy below
32°F (0°C)

Harvesting period
From summer
to early autumn

Suitable pot size
8in (20cm)

Suitable container material
Plastic, terra-cotta

Compost type
Multi-purpose
compost

Even before the plump fruits start to form, eggplants make beautiful patio plants, with pretty pink flowers and scallop-edged foliage. Although you can buy young plants, the choice of seed is much greater, and the best option if you want more unusual varieties. To grow plants from seed, fill a small pot with seed compost and scatter a few seeds over the surface. Then cover with a layer of vermiculite and put the pot in a heated propagator. When shoots appear, move the pot from the propagator to a light windowsill. Transfer each seedling into a separate pot when they are about 2in (5cm) tall.

TEMPERATURE REQUIREMENTS

Eggplants will not fruit well during wet summers since they need a long growing season and plenty of warmth. To help overcome this problem, sow seed in late winter. This gives plants more time to establish, resulting in robust growth and a better crop. You can also extend the growing season further by raising them in a warm greenhouse or a sunroom.

'Pinstripe' is a beautiful eggplant variety, with white-striped, mauve fruits and a compact form ideal for pots.

TOP TIP: INCREASING YIELDS

Plants grown outside produce about five fruits. For a good harvest, feed eggplants every couple of weeks with a tomato fertilizer as the fruits start to swell. After five fruits have formed, cut off any sideshoots and remove the remaining flowers. Fruits are ready when they are full sized and the skin is shiny.

Zucchini and Summer Squash

Plant used
Summer Squash
'Golden Delight'

Height and spread
H & S 24in (60cm)

Exposure
Full sun

Temperature needs
Not hardy below
32°F (0°C)

Harvesting period
From summer
to early autumn

Suitable pot size
12–18in (30–45cm)

Suitable container material
Plastic, growing
bags, vegetable
bags

Compost type
Multi-purpose
compost

Easy to grow from seed, squashes are among the most productive vegetables you can grow on a patio; a single plant will keep you in fruit all summer. Bearing this in mind, don't get carried away and pot up lots of plants or you will be sick of the sight of the fruits before long.

Start seeds off in early spring by filling a 3in (7.5cm) pot with seed compost. Plant two seeds on their sides, 1in (2.5cm) deep, and cover with more compost. Water, and put the pot in a propagator or on a sunny windowsill. Keep moist and when the roots of your seedlings show through the drainage holes at the bottom, move individual plants into 5in (12.5cm) pots. When there is no risk from frost, place a single plant in a large pot or colorful growing bag. Water regularly and harvest fruits with a sharp knife when they are about 3in (10cm) long.

'Golden Delight'
makes a great patio
focal point when grown
in a pretty vegetable
bag. Pick three
squashes a week to
keep plants productive.

MEDITERANNEAN MIXES

CHOOSING ZUCCHINI AND SQUASH VARIETIES

'Parador' produces large clusters of head-turning golden yellow fruit, which lend a decorative touch to the garden or patio. They have a great taste and mature early.

'De Nice A Fruit Rond' is perfect if you're looking for something a little different. These spherical green fruits are best picked when they are the size of a golf ball.

'Defender' is a tried and trusted favorite, due to its resistance to cucumber mosaic virus. It produces a bumper crop of large, tasty fruits over a long season.

'Venus' is a compact zucchini, ideal for container growing, with uniform, dark green cylindrical fruits that are produced from midsummer through early autumn.

Fiery peppers

If you like spicy food with a bite, turn up the heat in your garden by growing some hot peppers. An essential ingredient of many fiery dishes, peppers come in a range of shapes, colors, and sizes, and will grow well in containers. Not all peppers are hot, so if you prefer a mild flavor, try the sweet ones.

MEDITERRANEAN MIXES

Plant used
'Cheyenne' chili pepper;
Petunia Million Bells;
Viola; *Lotus berthelotii*;
Greek basil

Height and spread
Pepper H 18in (45cm) S 12in (30cm); *Petunia* H & S 12in (30cm); *Viola* H & S 8in (20cm); *Lotus* H 22in (50cm) S 3ft (1m); Basil H & S 6in (15cm)

Exposure
Full sun

Temperature needs
Not hardy below 32°F (0°C)

Harvesting period
From late summer to early autumn

Suitable pot size
12in (30cm)

Suitable container material
Terra-cotta, metal, baskets

Compost type
Multi-purpose compost

*Center: **Match orange chilis** with small violas and contrasting purple petunas. A cascading* Lotus berthelotii *and tangy Greek basil complete this delicious display.*

Peppers are grown for their jewel-like, glistening fruits, which come in a range of colors, including red, green, yellow, orange, brown, and purple. Although they can be grown in a pot on their own, peppers don't attract attention until the fruit develops, so create early interest by planting them in a basket or pot with flowers and herbs. Good companions include purple trailing petunias, violas, silver-leaved *Lotus berthelotii,* and basil.

Buy young pepper plants in the spring, or grow them from seed sown indoors in the late winter. Seeds germinate easily and will need to be moved into increasingly larger pots several times before they are ready to go outside in late spring, when all danger of frost has passed. When plants are about 8in (20cm) tall, or before if they start to lean, support them with a small stake. Pinch off the tops of the shoots when they are about 12in (30cm) tall to encourage lots of fruiting stems to form. The peppers will be ready to harvest from midsummer on and can be removed with a sharp knife or shears. Picking the fruit regularly helps to ensure the plant puts its energy into producing more crops.

WATERING AND FEEDING

For a good harvest water plants regularly, especially in hot weather, and feed every two weeks with a liquid tomato fertilizer. Start feeding your peppers when the flowers first appear, often while plants are still indoors before the frosts are over, and continue until all the fruits have been picked.

TOP TIP: SOWING SEEDS

Fill a 3in (7.5cm) pot with good-quality seed compost and sow a few seeds on top. Cover with a fine layer of vermiculite and place the pot in a heated propagator. After the seeds have germinated, move the pot to a windowsill. When plants are about 1in (2.5cm) tall, move to a 4in (10cm) pot.

Hot and mild pepper options

'California Wonder' is a very sweet, mild pepper with brick-red fruit, produced on compact plants.

'Gourmet' is a sweet pepper with eye-catching, bright orange fruits that appear on small plants, ideal for pots.

'Pepper Gypsy' produces tasty, wide, tapering sweet peppers that start green, and then turn orange and red.

'Alma Paprika' is a hot pepper with fruits that start yellow and turn red. They have a sweet, mildly hot flavor.

'Cherry Bomb' is a chili with round red fruits. They are very hot, and the plant makes an ornamental patio display.

'Prairie Fire' produces hundreds of tiny fruits that make up for their size with an explosive fiery taste.

'Numex Twilight' is a compact chili that produces a large crop of small purple, yellow, orange, and red fruits.

'Aji Amarillo' is a compact plant, laden with long, hot chilis that turn from green to yellow, then orange.

MEDITERRANEAN MIXES

Potted onions and garlic

Onions, shallots, and garlic are staple ingredients in many kitchens. Growing your own in containers allows you to sample a wide variety of shapes, sizes, and colors, and to enjoy the freshest flavors. All members of the onion family take up very little space and require the minimum of care.

MEDITERRANEAN MIXES

Plants used
Garlic, onions, shallots

Exposure
Full sun

Temperature requirement
Hardy to 14°F (-10°C)

Harvesting period
Summer

Suitable pot size
Shallots and onions: 24in (60cm)
Garlic: 12in (30cm) or larger

Suitable container material
Any

Suitable compost
Soil-based compost, eg, John Innes No 3

GROWING ONIONS AND SHALLOTS
Onions and shallots are best grown from sets (small, immature bulbs) planted in the spring. Choose a large container, such as a wooden storage crate, that's at least 10in (24cm) deep and 24in (60cm) wide. Fill with soil-based compost and make holes 4in (10cm) apart for onions and 6in (15cm) apart for shallots. Drop a bulb in, ensuring the pointy end is facing upward, then cover with compost, firm with your fingers, and water well. The nose of the bulb should be just visible. Sprinkle on a handful of blood, fish, and bone fertilizer; and keep well watered. In summer, when the leaves turn brown, crops are ready to harvest. Leave them to dry on a wire rack for three weeks before storing.

GROWING GARLIC
Best planted in fall or early winter, garlic is divided into two groups: soft-neck garlic, which forms a mass of strappy leaves and stores well; and the hard-neck, stiff-stalked types, which are best used fresh. Split open the bulb and separate the cloves—plant only the largest, healthy ones. Fill a 12in (30cm) container with soil-based compost, then make shallow holes, 4in (10cm) apart, around the outside. Place a clove in each, making sure the flat base is facing downward. Cover with compost; sprinkle on a handful of blood, fish, and bone; water well; and place in a sunny spot. Garlic is ready to harvest in the summer when the leaves start to turn yellow.

Braid the stems *of your garlic bulbs and store them in a cool, dark place.*

TOP TIP: DRYING AND BRAIDING GARLIC BULBS

Dried, soft-neck garlic will keep for a long time if stored correctly. The easiest way is to arrange a single layer of bulbs on a slatted wooden tray, keeping them in a cool, dry, dark place, such as a shed. Those with more patience could take a tip from the traditional French garlic sellers and try braiding the leaves together to create a decorative garlic rope. Simply twist off a bulb when you want to use it.

Choosing varieties

Elephant garlic produces huge bulbs of up to 4in (10cm). Enjoy the mild flavor when bulbs are roasted whole.

Shallot 'Mikor' is perfect for storing. This French shallot has reddish skin and white flesh with a pink tinge.

Shallot 'Red Sun' is a neat, spherical bulb with red skin and white flesh. It is delicious chopped into salads.

Onion 'Red Baron' is a red variety that keeps well after harvesting and has a strong, intense flavor.

Plant onions in a wooden box to lend a rustic note to a patio or balcony. Keep bulbs well watered, and you will be enjoying fresh crops all summer.

Leaves and stems

Leafy chard, bok choy, and kohlrabi, which also produces delicious swollen stems, form a trio of ornamental edibles that are easy to grow and ready to harvest within a few weeks of sowing. Highly nutritious, use them in the kitchen and to dress up dreary patios or balconies with their vibrant stems and designer good looks.

TASTY GREENS

Chard

Plant used
Mixed chard

Exposure
Sun or partial shade

Temperature
Needs protection in the winter

Harvesting period
Spring to fall

Suitable pot size
Min. 12in (30cm)

Suitable container material
Any

Compost type
Multi-purpose compost

Many vegetables look rather utilitarian in pots, but leafy chard's brightly colored stems sit comfortably among more decorative displays. Ruby chard has green leaves with red stems and veins, while 'Lucullus' has green leaves with white stems, but for striking looks, nothing beats the eye-popping red, white, orange, yellow, pink, and purple stems of 'Bright Lights.'

Young plants are available in the spring, but chard is easy to raise from seed sown from early to late spring. Sow seeds 1in (2.5cm) deep in a small pot of compost. When seedlings have a few leaves, transplant them into their own pots; repot them again when you see roots growing through the drainage holes. Water regularly, and protect plants with fabric or cloches in winter.

HARVESTING STEMS AND LEAVES
Spring sowings of chard are ready to pick after 12 weeks. Harvest what you need by cutting leaves from the outside of the plant. Picking the leaves frequently prompts the plants to produce more, and extends the harvest period.

TOP TIP: PLANT A COLORFUL MIX

Rather than growing a single plant in a small pot, create an eye-catching display by planting a large container with several different-colored chards. Check that the container you choose has adequate drainage. Fill with multi-purpose compost and space plants 4in (10cm) apart.

Feed chard in containers once a month with a nitrogen-rich fertilizer to keep foliage and stems healthy.

Kohlrabi

Plant used
Kohlrabi

Exposure
Full sun

Temperature
Fully hardy

Harvesting period
Summer to winter,
depending on
sowing time

Suitable pot size
8in (20cm)

**Suitable container
material**
Terra-cotta, plastic
inside decorative pot

Compost type
Multi-purpose
compost

You either love or hate the mild turnip taste of kohlrabi, but there's no denying that it makes a fascinating plant for a pot. Pick the young leaves for a salad, or steam as a spinach substitute. Grate the crunchy round stems raw into salads (like celeriac), or steam or boil. 'Olivia' is a pretty, pale green-skinned variety, while 'Violetta' has white flesh and a violet-blue skin.

STARTING FROM SEED
Sow seeds indoors in spring by planting three seeds ¾in (2cm) deep in a small pot of compost. After germination, remove the two weakest seedlings. When they have a few leaves, pot seedlings into a larger container, and move plants to their final pot outside in the summer. Water plants frequently, and harvest six weeks after sowing, when no bigger than a tennis ball; much larger and they start getting woody.

'Purple Vienna' is a stunning crop for a container.

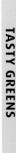

TASTY GREENS

Bok choy

Plant used
Bok choy

Exposure
Full sun

Temperature
Fully hardy

Harvesting period
Summer to autumn

Suitable pot size
8in (20cm)

**Suitable container
material**
Plastic

Compost type
Multi-purpose
compost

An Asian vegetable related to the cabbage, bok choy (or pak choi) is steadily increasing in popularity. The leaves can be chopped into salads, or toss both leaves and stems into a stir fry or lightly steam. Plants can be started from seed, but there's a tendency for them to bolt, so you may find it easier to buy young plants. After a month or so, you can start picking the young leaves from around the outside of the plant. Alternatively, allow the plant to mature fully and harvest the entire head by cutting it off at the base.

WATERING NEEDS
Bok choy has short roots that run close to the surface of the compost, and plants bolt if the compost is allowed to dry out. Apply a mulch of shredded bark, slate chippings, or gravel to help retain moisture, and water daily in hot weather and in the summer.

Leafy bok choy needs plenty of water.

Pots of dark greens

If you're looking for a nutritious vegetable that's tough, attractive and can be picked in the winter, then look no further than leafy kale. After a heavy frost, the flavor will even sweeten up. Spinach, too, can be grown to provide rich pickings when there's little else to harvest, but for a real show-stopper, try Mexican tree spinach.

Kale

Plant used
Kale 'Black Tuscany' and 'Dwarf Green Curled'

Exposure
Sun or partial shade

Temperature
Fully hardy

Harvesting period
Winter

Suitable pot size
18in (45cm)

Suitable container material
Plastic

Compost type
Multi-purpose compost

Some members of the brassica or cabbage family look rather utilitarian, but kale is queen of the crops. Many cultivars are blessed with great looks and provide color, interest, and food through the winter. Perhaps the most attractive one of all is 'Black Tuscany' (often called cavolo nero or black cabbage), with its upright "fronds" of near-black, textured leaves.

In the spring, sow seeds indoors into small pots of multi-purpose compost, then cover with ¾in (2cm) of compost and water. When seedlings are big enough to handle, move into individual small pots. In late spring, plant into larger containers outside. If the leaves start to yellow or growth slows, apply a balanced fertilizer.

LOOKING AFTER PLANTS
Keep plants well watered and cover with netting to deter pigeons and cabbage white butterflies. Harvest leaves as required from around the plants, or cut off entire heads. In winter, check plants regularly for wind-rock, firming the soil around the base of the stems to secure the roots.

Kale 'Black Tuscany' and 'Dwarf Green Curled' provide tasty and colorful leaves over the winter months.

TOP TIP: CHOOSING KALE VARIETIES

'Black Tuscany' has crimped, near-black leaves with a peppery flavor. The green leaves of 'Redbor' turn a deep red, while 'Red Curled' has tightly curled red leaves. 'Red Russian' boasts frilly red and green leaves (left), and the compact 'Dwarf Green Curled' will grow well in open, exposed areas.

Spinach

Plant used
Mexican tree spinach (*Chenopodium giganteum*)

Exposure
Full sun

Temperature
Fully hardy

Harvesting period
Summer, fall, and winter

Suitable pot size
12in (30cm)

Suitable container material
Plastic

Compost type
Multi-purpose compost

There's no point pretending that spinach will stop you in your tracks when you lay eyes on it. It may be highly nutritious, but it's green and pretty dull. Not so Mexican tree spinach (not related to true spinach), which is a stunning plant, with triangular leaves and magenta shoots that will add height and color to a patio display. When young, the leaves are delicious in salads, and mature leaves can be steamed like conventional spinach. The more you pick the foliage, the longer it will continue to crop.

GROWING SPINACH

Sow conventional spinach seeds 1in (2.5cm) deep in pots of multi-purpose compost; Mexican tree spinach is sown on the surface. Thin seedlings when they are large enough to handle, allowing about 3in (7cm) between plants. Keep pots well watered, especially during dry spells, because plants will bolt if stressed. If growth slows, feed with a nitrogen-rich fertilizer.

Spinach can be sown throughout the year to provide leaves at different times. For a summer crop, sow from early spring to early summer; for winter pickings, sow seed from late summer to early fall. Plants grown in the winter will need protecting from the worst of the weather with cloches or fabric. Harvest by snipping leaves from around the outside of the plants.

Lofty Mexican tree spinach may need staking.

CHOOSING SPINACH FOR CUT-AND-COME-AGAIN LEAVES

Perpetual spinach *is also known as beet spinach. It's a good autumn/winter crop with tender, tasty leaves. Plants can last up to two years if picked regularly.*

New Zealand spinach *is unrelated to spinach, but it can be harvested and used in the same way. It is a bushy plant and can be picked until cut down by the first frost.*

'Galaxy' *has dark green, glossy leaves with a better flavor than the ones that come in those expensive supermarket bags. For baby leaves, don't thin out your seedlings.*

'Medania' *has a mild, sweet flavor. It will keep producing succulent leaves as long as you keep it well watered. It also has good mildew resistance.*

Towers of beans

Choose from the old-fashioned varieties of green beans with loads of flavor or modern hybrids that promise succulent stringless pods, and you will never want to eat store-bought again. Not only do those grown in the garden taste better, but they can be picked and enjoyed when they are young and tender.

PERFECT PODS

Plant used
Green bean;
Thunbergia elata
(black-eyed Susan)

Height and spread
Green bean:
H 5ft (1.5m);
Thunbergia:
H 5ft (1.5m)

Exposure
Full sun

Temperature needs
Not hardy below
32°F (0°C)

Harvesting period
From late spring
to early autumn

Suitable pot size
18in (45cm)

Suitable container material
Terra-cotta, plastic, stone

Compost type
Multi-purpose compost

Many people with small gardens understandably give beans a wide berth, but climbing green beans are perfect for tiny gardens since they can be grown in a large pot up an ornamental obelisk or a cane wigwam. While some beans are naturally decorative with brightly colored pods, others are less ornamental and can be teamed with flowering climbers to create a striking combination. For example, you can jazz up a plain green bean by planting it with a yellow-flowered black-eyed Susan or some sweet peas.

Sow bean seeds indoors in early spring or plant them directly into a large pot of multi-purpose compost outdoors after all danger of frost has passed. Alternatively, buy young plants from the garden center. These climbing beans naturally grip their supports, but it's best to give them a helping hand until they're established by tying them to their supports with soft twine. Dwarf varieties of green beans do not need any supports.

CARING FOR GREEN BEANS

Water plants frugally until they are established, increasing the amount you give them after the first flowers appear and until the last pods are picked. Also feed plants with a tomato fertilizer every two weeks after the flowers form. Beans will be ready to harvest 8-12 weeks after sowing. Picking pods regularly when they're small and tender encourages the plant to produce more.

TOP TIP: SOWING BEAN SEEDS

Place one seed in a 3in (7.5cm) pot of seed compost and put it in a light, bright, frost-free place until it has germinated. Seedlings will be ready to plant outdoors in late spring. Or sow two seeds, 2in (5cm) deep, in the compost at the base of each leg of your support. When the seedlings have germinated, remove the weakest.

*Center: **Grow green beans with a black-eyed Susan** in a large pot for a blaze of color and fresh summer vegetables.*

Choosing bean varieties

'Blue Lake' is an old favorite that produces good-sized pods that are tender and stringless.

'The Prince' is a dwarf green bean that doesn't need staking. It's renowned for its heavy crops of long, flat pods.

'Delinel' produces tasty, slender, stringless beans with a good texture on dwarf plants that don't need staking.

'Purple Tepee' is a dwarf bean that looks and tastes great. Pods are deep purple, turning green when cooked.

'French Rocquencourt' is a very showy dwarf bean that will draw attention with its long golden pods.

'Cobra' is a vigorous variety and requires a large pot. It is valued for its heavy yields of long, tasty pods.

PERFECT PODS

Runner bean feast

A traditional favorite, runner beans are incredibly rewarding to grow. Not only will you enjoy a bumper harvest with the minimum of effort, their flowers are beautiful, too, and there are many tasty seed varieties to choose from, with pods in an assortment of sizes and flavors. Beans will do well in a large pot if given a sturdy support of bamboo sticks or hazel twigs to climb.

PERFECT PODS

Plant used
Runner bean 'Red Rum'

Exposure
Full sun

Temperature needs
Not hardy below 32°F (0°C)

Harvesting period
Summer to autumn

Suitable pot size
18in (45cm)

Suitable container material
Plastic, stone, terra-cotta

Compost type
Multi-purpose compost

Runner beans are a top-heavy crop, so choose a heavy pot for stability. Depending on the variety, they can grow to 6ft (2m) and will need a support for their long, twining stems, mass of leaves, and crop of pods. A bamboo wigwam is simple to make: space four to eight canes 6–9in (15–22cm) apart in a circle and bind the tops together with twine. Dwarf runner beans, which won't grow higher than 24in (60cm), will grow well in a deep window box or patio pot with only a few pea sticks for support.

SOWING, FEEDING, AND WATERING

Start seeds off in small pots indoors in mid-spring for planting outdoors about six weeks later, after the last frost. Alternatively, sow directly into a pot outdoors in late spring or early summer. Sow two seeds 2in (5cm) deep at the base of each cane. Water in well. After germination, leave the most vigorous seedling to climb up the cane and remove the other. Runner beans are self-supporting climbers and won't need tying in.

Water plants regularly after the first flower buds appear. If the compost is allowed to dry out, the flowers will fall. During dry weather, mist occasionally with a handheld sprayer to raise humidity levels. When the beans reach the top of their supports, pinch off the growing tips to encourage more stems with pods to form. Runner beans are hungry crops: use a kelp-based fertilizer weekly, switching to a high-potash feed when flowers form.

TOP TIP: HARVESTING

You can expect to be picking beans about three months after sowing. To ensure a constant supply, harvest them every few days while they are young and tender. The time you leave them to grow before picking depends on the variety. In general, if you leave runner beans too long on the plant, they will become tough and stringy, and if you can feel the beans inside the pods, they will be too old and not worth eating.

Picked when young and tender, runner beans need little more than lightly steaming and a drizzle of butter for a delicious dish.

Choosing runner bean varieties

'White Lady' produces pretty white flowers followed by thick, tender pods. The flowers are a favorite with bees.

'Painted Lady' bears such pretty red and white flowers that the long, tasty beans are almost an added bonus.

'Polestar' produces masses of tender, stringless beans with smooth pods and bright scarlet flowers.

'Lady Di' has vibrant red flowers with heavy crops of long, slender, tasty beans with no hint of stringiness.

The runner bean 'Red Rum' needs a large pot and bamboo cane supports for its mass of scrambling stems. Its beautiful red flowers ensure it doesn't look out of place on the patio.

Peas and pods

You don't need loads of space to grow peas, snow peas, or sugar snaps. These crops climb vertically up supports in large containers, squeezing onto tiny patios and balconies. Plants will reward you with baskets of tender pods to add to traditional fare and Asian dishes, while young crops are delicious when eaten fresh off the plant.

Peas

Plant used
Peas

Exposure
Full sun

Temperature
Not hardy below 32°F (0°C)

Harvesting period
Summer

Suitable pot size
32°F (30cm) or larger

Suitable container material
Plastic, terra-cotta, fabric or planting bags

Compost type
Multi-purpose compost

Freshly shelled peas eaten within seconds of being picked are a melt-in-the-mouth sensation. As well as tasting delicious, some peas also make decorative patio plants and really earn their keep in the garden. 'Purple Podded' is a heritage variety with dusky purple pods, while 'Blauwschokker' has red and violet flowers, followed by purple pods.

SOWING FROM SEED

Sow pea seeds 2in (5cm) deep in large pots of multi-purpose compost between spring and midsummer. Water well, and when seedlings appear, add supports for the plants to climb up. For an earlier crop, start a few seeds off in small pots indoors in early spring, and plant out the seedlings when the frosts have passed.

Water plants frequently, making certain the compost does not dry out, but ensure pots have good drainage by standing them on "feet;" or place bags on pebbles. Feed with a tomato fertilizer when flowers appear, and harvest pods regularly to encourage more to form.

TOP TIP: STAKING PLANTS

When seedlings are about 2in (5cm) in height, add some supports to prevent plants from collapsing as they grow. Either make a rustic wigwam with twigs, use bamboo canes tied together at the top, or, for an ornamental display, use a decorative tripod. Once they get going, peas will grip the supports with their tendrils, but give young plants a helping hand by securing the stems with soft twine.

White flowers and ripening peas make an ornamental display in a planting bag. Set bags on pebbles to aid drainage.

Snow peas

Plant used
Snow peas

Exposure
Full sun

Temperature
Not hardy below
32°F (0°C)

Harvesting period
Summer

Suitable pot size
12in (30cm) or larger

Suitable container material
Plastic, terra-cotta, fabric or planting bags

Compost type
Multi-purpose compost

Snow peas ripen throughout the summer.

Grown for their flattened tender pods that are eaten whole, snow peas can be steamed or boiled, or added to stir fries. There are many tasty varieties: 'Carouby de Maussanne' has long wide pods that follow attractive purple flowers, or try 'Oregon Sugar Pod', which has broad pods with a intensely sweet flavor.

Sow seeds, water, and feed snow peas as you would peas (*see opposite*). Also provide sturdy supports for the stems, which can grow up to 3–5ft (1–1.5m) in height.

PICKING PODS
Snow peas are best picked and eaten young before they become tough and stringy. As a rule of thumb, pick crops when the pods are about 2in (5cm) long. Harvest frequently to encourage a long-lasting supply of pods to form.

Sugar snaps

Plant used
Sugar snap peas

Exposure
Full sun

Temperature
Not hardy below
32°F (0°C)

Harvesting period
Summer

Suitable pot size
12in (30cm) or larger

Suitable container material
Plastic, terra-cotta, fabric or planting bags

Compost type
Multi-purpose compost

The fat pods of sugar snaps are eaten whole when the peas inside are fully developed. Sweet, crisp, and tasty, they are the perfect ingredient for stir-fries, or you can steam them for a few minutes so that they still retain their crunch. Sow seeds directly into large pots of multi-purpose compost outside from late spring to midsummer, and add supports before plants fall over.

Sugar snaps require the same growing conditions and watering and feeding regime as peas (*see opposite*). The main pests for all three pod plants are slugs, snails, and birds. Protect containers from slugs and snails with copper bands (*see p. 243*) and net plants to keep birds at bay.

WHAT TO GROW
There is a limited selection of sugar snaps to choose from, but it is worth selecting varieties carefully, as some are extremely vigorous and can scale heights of 6ft (1.8m). Among the best for large containers are 'Sugar Ann,' which grows to a compact 30in (75cm), and 'Cascadia,' which reaches 3ft (90cm).

Sugar snaps are ideal for frying.

PERFECT PODS

Perfect potatoes

Roasted, mashed, sautéed, boiled, or baked, potatoes are an essential ingredient in many favorite dishes. Despite being a root vegetable with a sizable root system, potatoes are relatively easy to grow in pots. Plant in early or mid-spring, and they'll be ready to harvest in just a few months.

DELICIOUS ROOTS

Plant used
Potatoes

Exposure
Full sun

Temperature needs
Hardy to 5°F (-15°C)

Harvesting period
From late spring to early fall, depending on type of potato

Suitable pot size
At least 12in (30cm) wide and 12in (30cm) deep

Suitable container material
Plastic; fabric bags

Compost type
Multi-purpose compost

Although there are a great array of different potato varieties available to grow in just as many different colors, shapes, and sizes, relatively few of them make it onto the supermarket shelves. If you want to sample some of these more unusual, and often delicious, types you will have to grow your own.

PLANTING POTATOES IN CONTAINERS

Before planting, potato tubers need "chitting" to encourage them to produce shoots. In late winter, place the tubers in a shallow tray, an egg carton, or on sheets of newspaper and leave in a cool, light place. When shoots are about 1in (2.5cm) long, which can take up to six weeks, the potatoes are ready to plant.

Potatoes need a deep and wide container—a plastic bin, bucket, or fabric potato bag are ideal. Just make sure it has plenty of drainage holes in the base or the tubers will rot. Put a 6in (15cm) layer of compost in the bottom of your container, then place two tubers on top, making sure the sprouts are facing upward. Cover with another 6in (15cm) layer of compost and water well. When the shoots are about 8in (20cm) tall, add a second layer of compost, leaving just the growing tips poking above the surface. As the stems continue to grow, keep adding more compost until the container is almost full. Keep your potatoes well watered, especially during hot, dry spells, and feed weekly with a kelp-based fertilizer.

*Centre **The stems of potato plants** are easily snapped. When growing in containers, push in a few peasticks for support.*

TOP TIP: HARVESTING CROPS

Potatoes are ready to harvest from early summer to early autumn. Salad and early potatoes should be dug up while the plants are flowering; maincrop types are ready when the foliage dies back. To harvest, tip the container on its side and loosen the compost with your fingers, "combing" through it to scoop up all the tubers.

Choosing potato varieties

'Foremost' produces neat, round tubers with yellow skins and firm, white flesh. Use as a new and salad potato.

'Red Duke of York' has oval-shaped tubers with eye-catching red skins and creamy-white flesh. Good for baking.

'Accent' is great for boiling. This early potato has oval tubers with pale yellow skins and flesh. Good slug resistance.

'Belle de Fontenay' produces small, yellow, kidney-shaped tubers with waxy flesh. A salad potato that stores well.

'Yukon Gold' is a large, yellow-skinned potato that is perfect for baking or frying. It has a rich buttery flavor.

'Pink Fir Apple' has knobby tubers that are impossible to peel, so just scrub them. Delicious served cold in salads.

'Ratte' is an old French variety with nutty-tasting, smooth-textured, waxy tubers that can be eaten hot or cold.

'Charlotte' is a great tasting, high-yielding salad potato with slender tubers and firm, creamy-yellow flesh.

DELICIOUS ROOTS

Health-promoting roots

You may not have considered growing root vegetables in containers, but as long as you give them a good depth of compost and keep them well watered, they should do well. Beets are a virtually maintenance-free crop, while perennial horseradish requires a little more hands-on attention, but if you're a fan of the spicy sauce, it's well worth the effort.

DELICIOUS ROOTS

Horseradish

Plant used
Horseradish

Height and spread
H 30in (75cm)
S Indefinite

Exposure
Sun or partial shade

Temperature needs
Fully hardy

Harvesting period
Autumn

Suitable pot size
Min. 12in (30cm)

Suitable container material
Plastic

Compost type
Multi-purpose compost

When planted in the ground, perennial horseradish is an invasive thug, but it can be tamed by growing it in a large container. Bare root plants, known as "thongs," are sold in the spring; young plants are available later in the season. To plant thongs, fill a pot with multi-purpose compost, make deep vertical holes with a dibber, then drop in a thong so thatthe top sits 2in (5cm) beneath the surface of the compost. You'll fit three thongs in a 12in (30cm) pot. Cover with compost and keep well watered. With its white-splashed foliage, *Amoracia rusticana* 'Variegata' is much showier than the commonly grown green species.

REJUVENATING PLANTS
Horseradish is a vigorous plant that will quickly fill a pot. When you harvest it in the fall, rejuvenate your plants at the same time. Turn the pot over and remove about half the slender white roots, then replant the remaining portion in fresh compost. These will stir into life in the spring, producing a flush of new leaves.

Variegated horseradish makes an attractive foliage plant, and produces the same hot roots as the plain, green species.

TOP TIP: STORING ROOTS

Horseradish is best used fresh, but if you have too much, bundle roots together and place them in a wooden box or tray covered with damp sand. Put the box in a cool, dark, frost-free place. Alternatively, peel and grate roots and dry them in a low oven for a few hours. Store in an airtight container for 2–3 months.

Beets

Plant used
Beets

Height and spread
H 6ft (1.8m)
S 3ft (1m)

Exposure
Full sun

Temperature needs
Fully hardy

Harvesting period
Summer into early fall

Suitable pot size
12in (30cm)

Suitable container material
Plastic, terra-cotta

Compost type
Multi-purpose compost

If you have never eaten fresh beets before, you're in for a real treat. They have a warm, earthy taste that is so much sweeter than anything you will find pickled in vinegar. Tender baby beets are delicious grated raw in salads, while mature roots are best boiled or roasted. Harvest them before they have a chance to develop a woody core—ideally when they are no bigger than 2½in (6cm) in diameter. You can also eat the colorful leaves; harvest them when they are young to add to salads, or steam them like spinach.

If you want something different, there is a huge range of variously shaped and colored roots to try, and all have one thing in common— they are easy to grow.

SOWING SEEDS

Sow seed from mid-spring to early summer. Fill a container with compost, leaving a 2in (5cm) gap between the surface and the rim to allow space for watering. Sow seeds thinly across the surface and cover over with a 1in (2cm) layer of compost that has been sifted to remove any lumps. Keep well watered. When seedlings are large enough to handle, thin them out so that plants are about 5in (12cm) apart, to give the roots plenty of space to develop. Use the thinnings in a salad.

Colorful beets are easy to grow from seed; just keep them well watered and you're guaranteed a good crop.

CHOOSING BEET VARIETIES

'Red Ace' grows strongly and is tolerant of dry conditions. It produces dark red roots that are round and uniform in size with a fine, sweet flavor.

'Chioggia Pink' beets are rosy pink on the outside, but when cut open they reveal pretty pink and white concentric circles. Keep well watered to prevent bolting.

'Boltardy' is a very popular variety due to its resistance to bolting. It also matures quickly from an early sowing. Tender spherical roots have a smooth skin.

'Forono' is perfect for slicing due to its long cylindrical roots. Young crops taste particularly good. Delay sowing the seed until mid-spring to prevent bolting.

Crunchy carrots

While we're used to seeing carrots growing in neat rows in the vegetable patch, they do well in large pots, too. You just need to match the type of carrot you grow to the depth of compost: long and tapering varieties will need a deep container, while short, stumpy types are fine in shallow pots and growing bags.

DELICIOUS ROOTS

Plant used
Carrot 'Mini Finger'

Exposure
Full sun

Temperature needs
Hardy, although young plants may be damaged by frost

Harvesting period
Late summer to fall

Suitable pot size
8in (20cm)

Suitable container material
Plastic, terra-cotta, window box

Compost type
Soil-based compost, e.g., John Innes No. 3

Rounded, stump-rooted carrots are the obvious choice for growing in pots, but if you have a deep enough container you can grow the traditional long-rooted varieties. Ideally, harvest these carrots when young, before there's any hint of woodiness. Wait for them to color up—in most cases, they will turn orange—and pick them when they are about the width of a finger. Alternatively, grow a Lilliputian patio carrot, such as 'Mini Finger,' which has quick-maturing, slender roots.

Early varieties can be sown in early spring, but will need covering with cloches or fabric to protect them from the worst of the weather. From mid-spring to midsummer, carrots can be sown outdoors without any protection.

To make growing carrots worth your while, have several pots in process; sow seeds in each at two-week intervals. Alternatively, divide up a large container or growing bag and stagger the sowing times in different sections. To sow, scatter seeds thinly across the surface of damp compost—space them about ¾–1¼in (2-3cm) apart—and cover with a ½in (1cm) layer of compost.

WATERING AND FEEDING
The compost should remain damp at all times, but be careful to avoid overwatering as this will result in lots of leafy top growth at the expense of root development. Watering after the compost has remained dry for several days will cause the roots to split. Fresh soil-based compost contains sufficient nutrients to ensure a good crop without supplementary feeding.

*Center: **Carrot 'Mini Finger'** produces cylindrical-shaped carrots that will be at their most tender when finger width.*

TOP TIP: PROTECTION FROM CARROT FLY

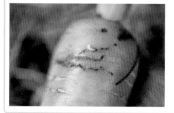

When seedlings are thinned out, carrot fly are attracted by the smell and lay their eggs. After hatching the larvae burrow into the carrot. As a precaution, avoid thinning by sowing seed thinly, and cover pots with a fine mesh to prevent flies from landing.

Choosing carrot varieties

'Bangor' *is best grown in a deep container. This maincrop variety boasts tasty, smooth, cylindrical roots.*

'Carson' *is a tapering carrot with a sweet taste and a crunchy texture. The crops also store well.*

'Chantenay Red Cored 2' *is a delicious, sweet-tasting carrot. The stump-shaped roots are a deep orange color.*

'Infinity' *has long, slender, roots that are very sweet and crunchy. Can be picked three months after sowing.*

'Amsterdam Forcing 3' *is an old and popular variety with bright orange, sweet-flavored roots. Delicious raw.*

'Autumn King 2' *produces tasty, red-cored roots that have good resistance to splitting. Needs a deep container.*

'Volcano' *is a very tasty carrot that is frost resistant (good for early sowing) with long, slender, orange roots.*

'Parmex' *is a quick-to-mature, round-rooted carrot with a great taste; roots can be eaten whole.*

DELICIOUS ROOTS

Colorful squash

Whether tumbling down the sides of a container or climbing up supports, squashes and pumpkins produce colorful fruits to brighten up the garden in early fall. They can be stored for up to six months, providing you with tasty treats that can be roasted, steamed, or boiled in winter dishes. Small fruits also make ornamental table decorations for the home.

Plant used
'Harlequin' and pattypan squashes; small pumpkin

Exposure
Full sun

Temperature
Not hardy below 32°F (0°C)

Harvesting period
Autumn

Suitable pot size
Min. 12in (30cm)

Suitable container material
Plastic, raised beds, growing bags

Compost type
Multi-purpose compost

With their wildly colorful fruits in all sorts of shapes and sizes, the choice in winter squashes and pumpkins is vast. As well as tasting delicious, the fruits also look great in containers, raised beds, or growing bags on a sunny, sheltered patio.

Either buy young plants in late spring or start your own off from seeds sown indoors. Sow two seeds on their sides, 1in (2.5cm) deep in small pots from early to late spring, and place in a heated propagator. After germination, remove the weaker of the two seedlings. When roots appear at the base of the pots, move seedlings into larger containers, and plant outside after the last frost. If you don't have room to allow the plants to trail across the ground, train them up supports. Not all are self-supporting, so you will need to tie stems in, and make sure the supports are sturdy enough to take the weight of your plants when they are laden with fruit. Water pots regularly, especially in hot weather.

RIPENING PUMPKINS
To encourage fruits to develop and ripen, they need lots of light and air, so snip off any leaves that are shading them. Harvesting time depends on the variety you grow, but all need picking before the first fall frost.

TOP TIP: STORING WINTER SQUASH

After harvesting your pumpkins and squashes, spread them out on a clean surface in a light, sunny spot, such as a shelf in a cool room or a greenhouse bench, for about a week until the skins harden. This process prevents the flesh from drying out during the long winter storage. Your fruits will keep until spring if stored in a cool, frost-free place on a dry layer of cardboard or clean straw.

'Harlequin' and pattypan squashes, and small pumpkins require feeding weekly with a high potash formula, such as tomato fertilizer. Your rewards will be these highly decorative fruits.

Choosing squash varieties

'Turk's Turban' is one of the most colorful squashes available. The pale-lemon flesh tastes a little like turnip.

'Jack Be Little' produces up to eight tiny fruits per plant—just the right size for an individual portion.

'Sweet Dumpling' has up to 10 striped fruits per plant. Either roast them whole or use for soups and stews.

'Crown Prince' has ribbed, blue-gray skin and orange flesh, which is delicious roasted. Flowers are a magnet for bees.

Small pumpkins may not need extra support, but place heavier fruits in net bags (use those sold holding citrus fruit) and tie these to sturdy canes to prevent the stems from snapping.

Winter staples

If you enjoy growing your own food, there's no reason for pickings to come to an end in the fall. Extend the growing season with these hardy crops to add fresh flavors to your dishes throughout the winter months. All can be grown in large pots and are easy to raise from seed or young plants bought from the garden center.

Leeks

Plant used
Leeks

Exposure
Full sun

Temperature
Fully hardy

Harvesting period
Late autumn to winter

Suitable pot size
12in (30cm) or larger

Suitable container material
Stone, growing bags, plastic, wooden crates

Compost type
Soil-based compost, e.g., John Innes No. 3

This staple of the vegetable garden is a handsome plant for a pot thanks to its upright stems and cascading, bluish-gray leaves. For a good show and decent harvest, plant enough leeks to make several meals. Grow them in a few inexpensive plastic pots or large containers, such as wooden packing crates, that are at least 14in (35cm) deep.

Plants prefer a sunny, sheltered spot and well-drained, soil-based compost. Sow seeds in pots indoors in mid-spring, and plant seedlings in their final containers in late spring or early summer. Keep crops well watered and harvest in late autumn and throughout the winter.

TOP TIP: PLANTING SEEDLINGS

Plant leek seedlings in large pots outside in late spring or early summer. First, make holes with a dibber, 8in (20cm) deep and 6in (15cm) apart, and drop a seedling into each. Pour water into the holes and leave to soak. This draws enough soil over the plants to cover the roots and produce blanched stems.

Feed leeks in pots with a high-nitrogen fertilizer in midsummer to sustain growth until plants are ready to harvest.

Winter cabbage and endive

Plant used
Endive

Exposure
Full sun

Temperature
Fully hardy

Harvesting period
Late autumn to winter

Suitable pot size
Large rectangular trough or 18in (45cm) pot

Suitable container material
Stone, growing bags, plastic

Compost type
Soil-based compost, e.g., John Innes No. 3

There aren't many vegetables you can pick in the winter, but growing cabbages in pots is an ideal way to ensure you have some fresh crops at this time of year. They also make attractive plants that will happily put up with the worst of the weather. There's a good choice of varieties available, from smooth-skinned types to the Savoy cabbages, famed for their highly textured, corrugated leaves.

Sow seeds in late spring, and plant out the seedlings in midsummer. Use a trough or rectangular container that will fit several cabbage plants and produce a decent-sized crop. Cover pots with netting to keep out cabbage white butterflies; their caterpillars will gobble up your crops in no time. Water the plants well, and feed with a balanced granular fertilizer when planting outside.

GROWING ENDIVE

The frilly leaves of endive are highly decorative, but the bitter flavor is an acquired taste. Sow seeds into large troughs in midsummer, then thin out to space plants 8in (20cm) apart. Pick the outer leaves as required, or allow the whole head to mature and cut it off, leaving a short stump. This may resprout with new growth. Cover with a cloche or fabric in the winter to extend the harvest.

Endive looks decorative in pots and has a bitter taste that adds a kick to winter dishes.

COOL-SEASON CROPS

SELECTING CABBAGE VARIETIES

'January King 3' is a Savoy-style cabbage and a traditional winter favorite, with large, tasty heads concealed between bluish-gray, frilled outer leaves.

'Jewel' is resistant to bolting and will happily endure tough winter weather to form a loose head of very tasty, smooth, dark green leaves ideal for winter stews.

'Siberia' lives up to its name and will shrug off frost, snow, and any other winter weather conditions without discoloring. It is a Savoy cabbage with a sweet flavor.

'Tarvoy' has been bred to survive the toughest of winter weather. A Savoy cabbage, it produces an attractive, dense, wrinkly head of dark green, nutritious leaves.

Fresh mint

A favorite garnish for iced tea, tangy spearmint is also used to make classic mint sauce, while peppermint makes a wonderfully soothing tea itself. But why limit yourself to just "minty" mints when you could also be growing spicy ginger, apple, and even chocolate-flavored types? With leaf shapes as excitingly varied as their flavors, plant a selection in individual pots.

HERBS

Plants used
Mentha suaveolens 'Variegata'; *Viola; Bacopa* (syn. *Sutera cordata*)

Height and spread
Mentha H & S 12in (30cm); *Viola* H 6in (15cm); *Bacopa* S 12in (30cm)

Exposure
Sun or partial shade

Temperature needs
Fully hardy

Harvesting period
Spring to fall

Suitable pot size
12in (30cm)

Suitable container material
Terra-cotta, stone

Compost type
Mix of multi-purpose and soil-based composts

If mint is planted straight into the ground, you run the risk of it spreading everywhere. To avoid this problem, keep it safely confined in a container, which you can either stand by the back door within easy reach of the kitchen, or plunge into a gap in the border—just make sure the lip of the container remains above the surface to prevent shoots from escaping over the top.

There are dozens of different mints to try. Tashkent mint, *Mentha spicata* 'Tashkent,' is an upright plant with heavily textured leaves, while chocolate peppermint, *M.* x *piperita* f. *citrata* 'Chocolate,' has dark brown leaves that taste like chocolate creams. *M.* 'Berries and Cream' has a fruity kick, and *M. arvensis* 'Banana,' as its name suggests, smells of bananas. If you want to grow several different mints, don't plant them side by side or they will lose their individual scent and flavor.

Looking after mint is easy. Grow in a sunny or partly shaded spot and keep plants well watered, especially during hot, dry weather. Sprinkle twice a year with a handful of bonemeal.

Picking leaves regularly keeps plants compact and encourages them to produce lots of new shoots. When your plants have finished blooming in the summer, cut back any flowered shoots to 2in (5cm) above the surface of the compost.

PRESERVING MINT
Mint is best used fresh, but you can preserve leaves for use in the winter when the plant dies back. Pick shoots, wash well, shake dry, then chop into small pieces and put in an ice-cube tray. Fill with water and freeze. Whenever you need some mint for cooking, simply remove an ice cube and add it to your recipe.

Lemon mint, Mentha x piperita f. citrata 'Lemon,' combines peppermint and citrus flavors and works well in both green and fruit salads.

TOP TIP: NEW PLANTS

When pots of mint become congested, you will need to rejuvenate the plant. To do this, overturn the container and ease out the root ball. Split it in half, teasing the roots apart, and repot a portion in the same container in fresh compost.

Mint is also easy to propagate from stem cuttings—push 4in (10cm) lengths of stem into small pots of damp compost or stand in water until rooted.

Choosing mints

Apple mint, Mentha suaveolens, *has oval leaves and mauve flowers that appear in summer. Good in mint sauce.*

Horse mint, Mentha longifolia, *is a wild plant with gray leaves and spires of purple flowers. Used in aromatherapy.*

Ginger mint, Mentha x gracilis, *has oval leaves with a spicy mint scent that goes well with vegetables and fruit.*

Eau de cologne mint, Mentha x piperita f. citrata, *is highly aromatic. Infuse leaves in vinegar.*

Pineapple mint underplanted with violas and bacopa *makes a cottage-style combination for a large rustic container, such as an old chimney pot.*

HERBS

Calming herbs

Herbs aren't just for flavoring foods; many are also renowned for their calming properties and have foliage or flowers that can be used to make delicately flavored, soothing teas. Fennel, lemon balm, and chamomile are three such herbs. They thrive in sunny spots and are welcome additions to any container garden.

Fennel *Foeniculum vulgare*

Plants used
Florence fennel
(*Foeniculum vulgare* var. *azoricum*) and herb fennel
(*F. vulgare*)

Height and spread
Both: H 6ft (2m)
S 18in (45cm)

Exposure
Full sun

Temperature
Fully hardy

Harvesting period
Leaves from spring to fall; seeds in fall; harvest Florence fennel roots in fall

Suitable pot size
12in (30cm) or larger

Suitable container material
Plastic, metal

Compost type
Soil-based compost, e.g., John Innes No. 3

There are two types of fennel: Florence and the herb. Florence fennel is a biennial grown for its aniseed-flavored root, which is delicious grated raw into salads or braised, while the feathery leaves of the perennial herb fennel, *F. vulgare*, add an aniseed tang to salads. The pungent seeds of the herb, which follow the yellow flowers, are also used for cooking or to make tea (*see below*). As well as the green-leaf species, try the cultivar 'Smokey' with its bronze leaves and sweet, licorice flavor.

SOWING AND GROWING
In spring, sow Florence fennel seeds indoors into small pots. After the last frost, transfer seedlings outdoors, spacing them 12in (30cm) apart, and cover plants with fabric until the weather warms up. Grow herb fennel from seed or buy young plants. Both types need a free-draining, soil-based compost with a little slow-release, balanced granular fertilizer mixed into the top layer. Keep plants well watered, and mulch the surface with garden compost.

Florence (center) and herb fennel *make the perfect combination if you love the taste of aniseed.*

TOP TIP: MAKING FENNEL TEA

Fennel seeds have long been used to make a subtly flavored tea that is said to aid digestion and relieve stomach cramps. To make a brew, boil 1 pint (500ml) of water, then add one teaspoon of fresh fennel seeds and leave to steep for 10 minutes. Strain and pour into cups. Serve with fresh orange rind.

Chamomile *Chamaemelum nobile*

Plant used
Chamomile
(*Chamaemelum nobile*)

Height and spread
H & S 12in (30cm)

Exposure
Full sun

Temperature
Fully hardy

Harvesting period
Summer

Suitable pot size
12in (30cm)

Suitable container material
Terra-cotta, stone, plastic

Compost type
Soil-based compost, e.g., John Innes No. 3

Chamomile tea is made by adding the fresh or dried flowers of this mat-forming perennial to boiling water. The white, daisylike flowers appear in summer on long stems above green, feathery foliage, which is highly fragrant when crushed. Roman chamomile (*Chamaemelum nobile*) is the best for flowers— try the form 'Flore Pleno,' which reaches 6in (15cm) and produces double flowers. Low-growing types, such as 'Treneague,' are used for lawns, but they don't produce the flowers needed for tea.

GROWING GUIDE

Grow from seed, or buy young plants in the spring. Plant in 12in (30cm) pots filled with soil-based compost and stand in full sun. Raise pots up on "feet" to prevent plants from rotting in the winter, and feed every six weeks in the summer with a liquid organic fertilizer. Trim occasionally to prevent stems becoming leggy.

Chamomile soothes frayed nerves.

Lemon balm *Melissa officinalis*

Plant used
Lemon balm
(*Melissa officinalis* 'All Gold')

Height and spread
H 30in (75cm)
S indefinite

Exposure
Full sun

Temperature
Fully hardy

Harvesting period
Late spring to autumn

Suitable container size
8in (20cm)

Suitable container material
Terra-cotta, stone, plastic

Compost type
Soil-based compost, eg, John Innes No. 3

Lemon balm 'All Gold' is ideal for tea.

The essential oil from the leaves of this highly scented perennial herb are widely used in aromatherapy, while lemon balm tea is thought to help relieve tension, aid digestion, and improve memory. The plain green species, *Melissa officinalis*, is rather dull to look at, but the cultivar 'All Gold' is a striking yellow, while variegated 'Aurea' has dazzling green- and yellow-splashed leaves. All three have aromatic leaves that will release their volatile oils at the lightest touch and make soothing teas.

For the best scent, position plants in full sun, and raise containers so they are within easy reach. Trim plants regularly to encourage bushy growth, and remove flower spikes.

WINTER CARE

Lemon balm is a hardy, deciduous, perennial plant, but it may suffer during wet winters. Raise containers on pot "feet" and place them in a sheltered location, such as a spot adjacent to the wall of a house or a fence.

HERBS

Permanent herb displays

Evergreen herbs are valuable plants to grow in the garden. They not only provide color, structure, and beauty all year round, but during the winter months they're a mainstay when there's very little else to harvest in the herb garden. Bay is an essential ingredient in the classic bouquet garni, together with parsley and thyme, while sage makes the perfect stuffing for roast meats.

Bay *Laurus nobilis*

Plant used
Standard bay
(*Laurus nobilis*)

Height and spread
H 6ft (1.8m)
S 20in (50cm)

Exposure
Full sun

Temperature needs
Hardy, but should
be protected in
hard winters

Harvesting period
All year round

Suitable pot size
12in (30cm) or larger

Suitable container material
Any

Compost type
Soil-based compost,
eg, John Innes No 2

A pair of standard bay lollipops in attractive containers is one of the most elegant ways to frame a front door or entrance. A single plant would also make the perfect centerpiece for a group of pots on the patio, or an accent of green in a colorful annual flower border.

Originally from the Mediterranean, bay needs lots of sun and good drainage. Raise containers on pot "feet" to improve drainage and prevent roots rotting in soggy compost. If possible, move plants to a frost-free place for the winter, or, at the very least, wrap the top in fabric to protect the leaves from wind scorch.

PRUNING BAY
An evergreen shrub with dense-growing leaves, bay is perfect for simple topiary—a cone or pyramid shape is easy to achieve. If left unpruned, plants will soon become messy, so clip them in the summer. Clear shoots from standard stems by cutting or twisting them off.

TOP TIP: PRESERVING LEAVES

Bay leaves are best used fresh, but stems or individual leaves can be dried in a furnace room. Store the leaves whole in airtight bags or containers for up to a year.

Together with parsley and thyme, bay leaves make up the classic flavor of bouquet garni. Gather a handful of herbs and tie them tightly together with string. Use to flavor soups and casseroles.

Feed bay trees in the spring and again in midsummer with a balanced organic fertilizer.

Sage *Salvia officinalis*

Plants used
Variegated sage
(*Salvia officinalis*
'Tricolor');
Strawberries

Height and spread
H 16in (40cm)
S 1m (3ft)

Exposure
Full sun

Temperature needs
Hardy to frost-
hardy, depending
on variety

Harvesting period
All year round

Suitable pot size
10in (24cm)

Suitable container material
Any

Compost type
Soil-based compost

Sage is a strong-tasting, aromatic herb that combines perfectly with onions in the popular stuffing mix for pork roasts or turkey. Common sage (*Salvia officinalis*) has the best taste, but its gray-green leaves make it a nondescript plant for a patio pot. Fortunately, there are many varieties of culinary sage that not only taste good but also have attractive ornamental foliage. Try growing variegated sage, *Salvia officinalis* 'Tricolor,' purple sage, *S. officinalis* 'Purpurascens,' and *S. officinalis* 'Variegata.'

A native of North Africa and the Mediterranean region, this rough-leaf herb needs a sunny, sheltered spot to set its volatile aromatic oils sizzling. Although it's a bushy perennial, sage tends to be short-lived, so expect to replace plants every four to five years. Like many perennials, it takes a long time to grow from seed, so either buy young plants from a nursery or take softwood cuttings in the spring.

ANNUAL CARE

Common sage is an undemanding plant. Water regularly over the summer and keep plants compact by pruning in late spring. Sage doesn't like cold and wet, so place pots in a sheltered spot and raise up on pot "feet." Feed annually in the spring with an all-purpose granular fertilizer.

Sage and strawberries *are combined here to create an attractive and aromatic fruit and herb container.*

CHOOSING VARIETIES OF SAGE

S. elegans *'Scarlet Pineapple' is not a culinary herb, but is worth growing for its pineapple-scented foliage and, in autumn, spires of scarlet flowers.*

S. officinalis *'Tricolor' is an attractive form of common sage that looks and tastes good, with cream, green, and pink variegated leaves. Needs winter protection.*

S. officinalis *'Purpurascens' is a hardy form, with tactile, deeply textured, pungent leaves. In the summer, it is topped by tall spires of pretty mauve flowers.*

S. officinalis, *or the common sage, has aromatic gray-green leaves that are wonderfully useful for cooking. It is fully hardy and will survive outside in winter without any fuss.*

Rich flavors

The aromatic foliage of these flavorful herbs is at its best on warm, sunny days when the volatile oils they contain fill the air with their pungent scent. Grow thyme and basil in a sunny spot in containers on their own or in combination with other Mediterranean herbs or edible plants for a display that will look as good as it tastes.

Thyme *Thymus vulgaris*

Plants used
Golden thyme; tarragon; chives

Height and spread
H & S 10in (25cm)

Exposure
Full sun

Temperature requirement
Hardy, but protect from winter wet

Harvesting period
All year round

Suitable pot size
6in (15cm) or larger

Suitable container material
Any

Suitable compost
Soil-based compost, e.g., John Innes No. 3

Position pots or hanging baskets of thyme close to the kitchen door or near to your outdoor eating area, so that you can pick fresh leaves to sprinkle over salads or barbecued meats.

Thyme is a resilient evergreen bush, and very drought tolerant. It thrives in a sunny site in well-drained compost, and you can prevent plants from becoming leggy by keeping the compost on the dry side. In the winter, improve drainage by raising pots on "feet." Feed plants every two weeks in summer with a kelp-based fertilizer, and trim to shape after flowering.

BEST FOR POTS

There are many fabulous ground cover or spreading thymes, but choose upright types for containers. Among the best for scent, flavor, and good looks are the golden lemon thyme (*Thymus* 'Golden Lemon'), orange-scented thyme (*T.* 'Fragrantissimus'), and *T. pulegioides* 'Archer's Gold.'

TOP TIP: PLANTING PARTNERS

Thyme combines well with other herbs and edible plants. Try growing it alongside red lettuces, chives, and sage for an attractive display in a large container. Apart from culinary uses, thyme makes an excellent companion plant because its pungent smell helps to ward off pests that could damage other crops. Bees also love its pollen- and nectar-rich flowers.

Golden thyme, tarragon, and chives all love the free-draining conditions of a hanging basket.

HERBS

Basil *Ocimum basilicum*

Plants used
Basil; French
marigolds (*Tagetes*);
thyme; tomatoes

Height and spread
H & S 18in (45cm)

Exposure
Full sun

**Temperature
requirement**
Not hardy below
32°F (0°C)

Harvesting period
Spring to early
autumn

Suitable pot size
6in (15cm) or larger

**Suitable container
material**
Plastic, terra-cotta,
stone

Suitable compost
Multi-purpose
compost

Homegrown basil tastes and looks far superior to those leggy seedlings sold in plastic boxes in supermarkets. Start these half-hardy annuals off from seed sown in late winter or early spring. Fill a 3in (7.5cm) pot with seed compost, firm down, and sow a few seeds of your favorite variety over the top. Cover with a thin layer of vermiculite, water carefully, and pop it into a propagator. If you don't have one, cover the pot with a small, clear plastic bag and secure with a rubber band. After germination, remove from the propagator or plastic bag. Keep the compost moist, and when the seedlings have four or five leaves, transfer to 3in (7.5cm) pots, placing two or three seedlings in each. Move to larger pots when roots show through the drainage holes at the bottom. Wait until the temperature warms to 50°F (10°C) before moving plants outside.

KEEPING PLANTS PRODUCTIVE

Basil will continue to produce fresh leaves until the end of the summer if you transfer plants into larger containers when you see roots through the holes at the bottom of their current pot. Keep plants bushy and productive by pinching off the stem tips regularly, and remove flowers. Feed plants once a month with a balanced liquid fertilizer, and water in the morning.

Basil mixes well with tomatoes, marigolds, and thyme.

HERBS

CHOOSING BASIL VARIETIES

Ocimum basilicum var. purpurascens 'Dark Opal' *has purple, oval-shaped, spicy-scented leaves. In the summer it produces clusters of small pink flowers.*

O. basilicum 'Horapha Nanum,' *or Thai basil, is a compact plant with narrow, deeply veined, aniseed-scented leaves that are widely used in Thai cooking.*

O. basilicum 'Well Sweep Purple Miniature' *is a diminutive type of purple basil that forms a low mound. It has great tasting, green-edged, tapering leaves.*

O. basilicum 'Minette' *is a compact basil that forms an attractive rounded mound in a small container. The leaves have a deliciously spicy flavor.*

Cooking essentials

Parsley, rosemary, and oregano are three of the most useful and commonly used herbs in the kitchen, but these culinary delights are not just for eating. All possess handsome foliage, and rosemary and oregano produce pretty flowers that attract beneficial wildlife. Place pots near the kitchen door so they are always close at hand.

Parsley *Petroselinum crispum*

Plant used
Petroselinum crispum

Height and spread
H 12in (30cm)
S 10in (25cm)

Exposure
Partial shade

Temperature needs
Fully hardy

Havesting period
All year round

Suitable pot size
10in (25cm)

Suitable container material
Plastic, stone, terra-cotta

Compost type
Multi-purpose compost

If you want an herb to add to winter dishes, sow some parsley seeds in the fall, and you'll have plenty of tasty leaves to pick in the chilly months ahead. Alternatively, sow in the spring for leaves that can be snipped all year. Technically a biennial, parsley is usually grown as an annual, and performs well in pots of multi-purpose compost in a partially shaded site. Water plants regularly and pick leaves frequently, which will encourage more to form. Although curly-leaved parsley looks great and has textured foliage, flat-leaf parsley has a stronger taste and is more useful in the kitchen.

HERBS

TOP TIP: SOWING PARSLEY SEED

Fill a clean container with compost, and sow seeds thinly on top. Cover with a ½in (1cm) layer of compost and water. Leave in a cool spot to germinate, which may take up to a month. When large enough to handle, thin the seedlings so they are ½in (2cm) apart.

Curly-leaf parsley makes an ornamental plant for a patio pot and produces fresh leaves all year round.

Rosemary *Rosmarinus officinalis*

Plant used
Rosmarinus officinalis
Prostratus Group

Height and spread
H 6in (15cm) S 12in
(30cm) or more

Exposure
Full sun

Temperature needs
Hardy, but protect
in hard winters

Havesting period
All year round

Suitable pot size
8in (20cm)

Suitable container material
Any

Compost type
Soil-based compost,
e.g., John Innes No. 3

Trailing rosemary is a good option for a stone pot.

Ideal for perking up a patio or terrace all year round, rosemary is an evergreen shrub with pungent, needlelike leaves that release their scent every time you brush past. Plants are perfect for busy gardeners because they require very little care other than watering and feeding annually in spring with a slow-release granular fertilizer. Rosemary produces pretty blue flowers in the spring and summer; cut back stems after the blooms start to fade to keep plants compact.

ROSEMARY CHOICES

There are several rosemaries that make good container plants. 'Miss Jessopp's Upright' is tall and thin, growing to 24in (60cm) in a pot, while Prostratus Group has cascading stems. 'Lady in White' has white flowers, 'Majorca Pink' offers pink blooms, and the sprawling, low-growing 'McConnell's Blue' reaches just 16in (40cm).

Oregano *Origanum vulgare*

Plant used
Origanum vulgare

Height and spread
H & S 12in (30cm)

Exposure
Full sun

Temperature needs
Fully hardy, but
protect from
winter rain

Havesting period
Late spring to fall

Suitable pot size
6in (15cm)

Suitable container material
Any

Compost type
Soil-based compost,
e.g., John Innes No. 3

An essential pizza topping, oregano is easy to grow from seed sown in the spring, or you can buy young plants from garden centers. Grow in small pots filled with well-drained, soil-based compost, and place in a sunny spot. Although green-leaf oregano is the most popular, there are several showier varieties: 'Gold Tip' has leaves with yellow tips, while 'Aureum Crispum' has yellowish-green wrinkled leaves. 'Kent Beauty' is one of the most ornamental—its small pink flowers are surrounded by deep pink bracts.

PLANT CARE

Water plants regularly, but avoid overwatering as the roots may rot in waterlogged conditions. Stand on pot "feet" to allow excess moisture to drain away, and in the winter, prevent roots from rotting by moving plants to a sheltered spot next to a house wall or into an unheated greenhouse. Trim stems after the flowers fade in the summer to keep plants compact, and then give them a boost by applying a liquid fertilizer.

Oregano makes a compact leafy display.

Thai herbs and spices

If you enjoy eating Thai food, why not try growing the flavorings for your favorite dishes? Citrussy lemongrass, fresh spicy root ginger, and the seeds and leaves of cilantro are considered to be "store cupboard" ingredients in Southeast Asian cooking, and all three will grow well in containers on a sunny, sheltered patio.

HERBS

Lemongrass *Cymbopogon citratus*

Plant used
Lemongrass

Height and spread
H 36in (90cm)
S 24in (60cm)

Exposure
Full sun

Temperature
Not hardy below
32°F (0°C)

Harvesting period
All year round

Suitable pot size
8in (20cm)

Suitable container material
Plastic, glazed ceramic

Compost type
Soil-based compost, e.g., John Innes No. 3

Largely grown for the swollen bases of its edible stems, lemongrass is an exotic grass. It makes a fountain of gently arching, strappy foliage, and can even be grown alongside exotic summer flowers and other ornamentals.

New plants are easily propagated from pieces of stem bought from the supermarket (*see below*), or you can raise them from seed sown indoors in late winter. Sow seeds thinly in pots, and germinate in a heated propagator. When seedlings are large enough to handle, transplant three into a small pot and stand on a bright, frost-free windowsill. When roots show through the bottom of the pot, move into a larger one, and continue to repot as the plants grow.

CARING FOR LEMONGRASS
In early summer, stand plants outside in a sunny location, and water frequently. Feed every two weeks with a balanced fertilizer. In late summer, move your plants to a bright area indoors, and reduce watering, allowing the compost to dry out between each application.

TOP TIP: PROPAGATING PLANTS FROM STEMS

Buy fresh lemongrass stems and stand them in a jar of water on a sunny windowsill to root. This will take a week or two. Change the water regularly. Once roots have developed, trim the top of the stalks, and plant into small pots of moist, soil-based compost. Keep compost damp in summer, but not too wet.

Harvest lemongrass when stems are about 12in (30cm). Cut at the base, leaving a 1in (2cm) stump, which will then reshoot.

Cilantro and ginger *Coriandrum sativum* and *Zingiber officinale*

HERBS

Lemongrass, root ginger, and cilantro have exotic looks and flavors, yet they are surprisingly easy to grow in containers.

Plant used
Cilantro and ginger

Height and spread
Cilantro: H 20in (50cm) S 8in (20cm); ginger: H 36in (90cm) S 16in (40cm)

Exposure
Sun or partial shade

Temperature
Not hardy below 32°F (0°C)

Harvesting period
Cilantro: summer to early fall; ginger: fall

Suitable pot size
8in (20cm)

Suitable container material
Plastic, placed inside a decorative pot

Compost type
Multi-purpose compost

Cilantro makes a pretty clump of decorative foliage in either a sunny or partially shaded location in the garden. Grow the cultivars 'Cilantro' or 'Leisure' if you want to use the leaves; for seeds, choose the species *Coriandrum sativum*. All three grow easily from seed sown in early summer. Sow thinly across the surface of a container filled with multi-purpose compost, and cover over lightly with a sprinkling of compost. If you want to harvest the leaves, thin seedlings to 1in (2.5cm) apart, and for seeds, thin to 4in (10cm). Keep the compost just damp.

GROWING GINGER

In spring, start plants off from rhizomes, moving them outside in summer (*see right*). Keep the compost moist at all times, and feed every month with a balanced fertilizer. Plants like high humidity, so occasionally mist with a handheld sprayer. Ginger needs high light levels and heat to survive winter, so it is best to allow plants to dry out in the fall, and then harvest the roots.

TOP TIP: SPROUTING GINGER

Ginger is easy to grow from rhizomes. In spring, buy fresh, plump, firm roots from the supermarket with lots of knobby "eyes." Cut roots into 2in (5cm) lengths, making sure each piece has at least one eye. Bury single lengths 2in (5cm) deep in a small pot filled with multi-purpose compost. Water and stand in a bright spot. When shoots appear, move out of direct sun and repot as needed. Feed every two weeks with a liquid fertilizer. Ginger isn't hardy and must come back indoors at the end of summer.

Lemons and limes

Sweetly fragrant flowers, followed by delicious, aromatic fruits make lemon and lime trees highly desirable plants for a cool sunroom in the winter, and a warm, sheltered patio throughout the summer. Both trees are easy to grow if you can provide the right conditions, and your rewards will be juicy fruits and elegant plants to dress up your home.

CITRUS FRUIT

Lemons

Plant used
Citrus x meyeri 'Meyer'

Height and spread
H 6ft (1.8m)
S 5ft (1.5m)

Exposure
Bright and sunny

Temperature needs
Min. 45°F (7°C)

Harvesting period
Varies, depending on type

Suitable pot size
18in (45cm)

Suitable container material
Terra-cotta, stone, glazed ceramic

Compost type
Specialty citrus compost

Growing your own lemon tree will instantly transport you to the groves of Italy or California, where the scent of these highly fragrant fruits hangs heavy in the air. There are many good varieties to choose from. *Citrus limon* 'Variegata' has two-tone green and yellow leaves and stripy fruits, while 'Meyer' is a compact variety that produces heavy crops of rounded fruit. Ideal for a light, bright, frost-free sunroom or greenhouse, lemons can be moved outside in the summer to a warm, sunny patio or deck.

OVERWINTERING LEMONS
Plant in large pots of specialty citrus compost, water regularly with rainwater, and feed monthly in summer with a fertilizer formulated for citrus fruits. Lemons, like all citrus, are frost tender plants and may suffer at temperatures below 45°F (7°C). However, they can also fail to fruit if they are too warm in the winter, so try to maintain a temperature of 50–59°F (10–15°C). Reduce watering and feed less frequently in the winter with a specialty winter citrus fertilizer.

TOP TIP: PLANTING PIPS

Although it's easier to buy a plant, it's also fun to try growing your own lemon tree from a pip. Sow seeds from ripe fruit, ½in (1cm) deep, in small pots filled with seed compost. Place in a heated propagator or germinate at 61°F (16°C). Seedlings appear quickly, but fruit-bearing trees take many years to grow.

Lemons grow well outside in the summer when given plenty of water. Ensure the root ball is completely soaked.

Limes

Plant used
Lime

Height and spread
H 6ft (1.8m)
S 5ft (1.5m)

Exposure
Bright

Temperature needs
Min. 45°F (7°C)

Harvesting period
Summer, but can be
all year round

Suitable pot size
18in (45cm)

**Suitable container
material**
Terra-cotta, stone,
glazed ceramic

Compost type
Specialty citrus
compost

If you like homegrown limes to add to your drinks or Asian dishes, you can keep a tree in a large container in a light, bright, sunny area, such as a heated greenhouse or cool sunroom. Before considering a lime, make sure that you will have space to move around the plant, because its stems are armed with vicious thorns. Grow and overwinter limes as you would lemon trees (*see opposite*), and water plants regularly, allowing the compost to almost dry out before applying more.

HARVESTING LIMES

It's difficult to know when fruits are ripe just by looking at them, because they don't change color. The fruits do turn a lighter green when they are ready. The skins also feel smooth, and fruits are slightly soft when gently squeezed. To remove, twist the limes carefully from the plant.

Lime trees are armed with sharp thorns.

Makrut limes

Plant used
Makrut lime

Height and spread
H 6ft (1.8m)
S 5ft (1.5m)

Exposure
Bright

Temperature needs
Min. 45°F (7°C)

Harvesting period
All year round for
leaves

Suitable pot size
18in (45cm)

**Suitable container
material**
Terra-cotta, plastic,
glazed ceramic

Compost type
Specialty citrus
compost

While most limes are grown for their fruit, the makrut lime (formerly known as kaffir lime) is mainly grown for its shiny green leaves, which are widely used as a flavoring in Thai cuisine. Apart from providing you with an ingredient that can be difficult to find in all but specialty food stores, the makrut lime is a handsome plant for a large pot. Young branches are a bronze color, while each leaf is elongated and comprises two segments. Watch the stems, though, as they are armed with long thorns.

GROWING LIMES

Plant pots as for lemons (*see opposite*), and keep plants in a light sunroom or greenhouse. Ensure that temperatures do not fall below 45°F (7°C) at night and that they are a little higher during the day in winter, although they will enjoy hotter conditions in summer. Limes respond to sudden changes in temperature by dropping their leaves, but can recover when acclimatized. Feed, water, and overwinter plants as for lemons.

Makrut lime leaves and fruits.

CITRUS FRUIT

Hothouse fruit

You can create your own mini orangery or grow other citrus fruits, such as mandarins, tangerines, and the weird and wonderful Buddha's hand, if you have a frost-free greenhouse or sunroom. Provide trees with sufficient light and heat, and you can produce a range of beautiful fruits.

Plant used
Calamondin orange

Height and spread
Standard tree:
H 5ft (1.5m)
S 3ft (1m)

Exposure
Bright indoors; full
sun outside

Temperature needs
Not hardy below
32°F (0°C); min. 57°F
(14°C) when fruiting

Harvesting period
Summer to fall

Suitable pot size
18in (45cm)

**Suitable container
material**
Terra-cotta, stone,
glazed ceramic,
plastic

Compost type
Special citrus
compost or
soil-based compost,
e.g., John Innes No
3, with extra sand

Living in a cool climate, it is hard to imagine picking citrus fruits from the branches of your own tree, but it is very possible in the warmth of a heated greenhouse or sunroom.

Plants are widely available from specialty nurseries, most of which offer mail-order services. The trees require large, sturdy containers filled with specialty citrus or soil-based compost, and a bright location because they will not do well in poor light. They can be placed outside during the summer months, but ensure plants are moved back indoors before night-time temperatures start to fall at the end of summer or beginning of fall.

CARING FOR CITRUS PLANTS

Plants need regular watering, especially when the fruits are developing because dry compost at this stage can cause them to drop prematurely. Citrus trees do not like hard, calcium-rich water, so try to use rainwater if possible, and feed every month in the spring and summer with a special liquid fertilizer formulated for citrus plants in active growth. Reduce watering and feeding in the winter—when you do water, add a half-strength solution of fertilizer designed for citrus plants.

To fruit well, citrus plants need a temperature of at least 57°F (14°C) for the six months after flowering, and they may become dormant if temperatures fall below this. It can also take up to 11 months for fruit to ripen after the flowers have been pollinated.

*Center **Calamondin
is a dwarf orange**
that produces sweet
fruits and can tolerate
lower temperatures
than many citruses.*

TOP TIP: PRUNING CITRUS

Citrus plants do not require any major pruning. Simply remove any dead, diseased, or damaged branches, along with any crossing stems that may rub and create wounds. Then reduce the sideshoots to maintain an attractive rounded shape. Pruning is best carried out between winter and early spring.

Citrus choices

Orange trees are widely available and some are hardy to 23°F (-5°C). They have dark green, glossy leaves and white, scented flowers, followed by fruits in late spring and early summer. Choose a compact type for a pot.

Citrus medica var. digitata, known as Buddha's hand, is one of the most surprising fruits you're ever likely to see. Plants need heat to thrive. The inedible fruits are used in the Far East for their amazing fragrance.

Mandarin trees often bear fruit from spring until autumn. There are many cultivars to choose from, with plants in a range of sizes and fruits with different flavors. The branches are very brittle and may need to be supported.

Kumquat is a slow-growing tree that produces orange, egg-shaped fruits with a sweet skin and slightly bitter flesh. Fruits are ready to harvest between late autumn and midwinter, and follow white, scented flowers.

Tangerine trees are part of the mandarin family and produce small, sweet, easy-to-peel fruits. Watch for tangelo plants, too, which are crosses between tangerines and grapefruits or oranges.

Clementine trees are often sold as standards with bushy heads of dark, evergreen leaves. Grown for their small, sweet fruits, clementines can be harvested between autumn and midwinter, depending on the variety.

CITRUS FRUIT

Currant trends

Easy to grow, packed with vitamins, and delicious in pies, puddings, sauces, and juices, currants are suitable for new and more experienced gardeners alike. The jewel-like, sharp-flavored fruits of white and red currants will add sparkle to patio pots in summer, while new varieties of black currant produce large, sweet, and juicy fruits on tough bushes.

Red currants

Plant used
Red currant 'Rovada'

Height and spread
H up to 6ft (2m)
S 24in (60cm)

Exposure
Sun or partial shade

Temperature needs
Fully hardy

Fruiting period
Summer

Suitable pot size
Min. 12in (30cm)

Suitable container material
Terra-cotta, stone, plastic

Compost type
Multi-purpose and soil-based compost

Although red currants are closely related to black currants, they are, in fact, grown more like gooseberries. These cool-climate plants do well in cooler regions and will happily tolerate partial shade, although the fruits will ripen more quickly and taste sweeter if given some direct sun. You can buy container-grown bush and ready-trained cordon plants at any time of the year, but the best time to plant them is in early fall. Choose a sheltered spot away from strong winds and avoid frost pockets.

PLANTING IN POTS
Red currants will thrive in pots of multi-purpose compost mixed with some soil-based compost. Keep plants well watered when fruiting but avoid waterlogging—place containers on pot "feet" to allow excess water to drain away.

Keep an eye out for gooseberry sawfly caterpillars, which will quickly strip the foliage. Check regularly and either pick pests off by hand or spray with a suitable pesticide. Feed and prune as for white currants (*see opposite*).

TOP TIP: CHOOSING RED CURRANTS

There are a number of new varieties of red currant that grow well in containers. Try 'Stanza,' a late-flowering variety and good choice for frost-prone areas; 'Junifer,' which fruits very early and produces a heavy crop; and 'Rovada' and 'Red Lake,' which are both disease-resistant and heavy croppers.

Red currant 'Rovada' is a heavy cropper; when fruits start to form, move plants to a sunny spot to boost their sweetness.

Black currants

Plant used
Black currant 'Ben Lomond'

Height and spread
H 4ft (1.2m)
S 3ft (1m)

Exposure
Sun or partial shade

Temperature needs
Fully hardy

Fruiting period
Summer

Suitable pot size
Min. 18in (45cm)

Suitable container material
Terra-cotta, stone, plastic

Compost type
Multi-purpose compost

Tough and resilient, black currant bushes are relatively low maintenance and will fruit with very little effort. New varieties, with 'Ben' in their names, produce large fruits that can be eaten fresh as well as cooked. Plant them in big pots of multi-purpose compost and place in a sheltered place, out of strong winds. Plant bushes a little deeper than the original soil mark on the stem; this will encourage new underground stems to form. Feed as for white currants (*see below*).

PRUNING BLACK CURRANTS
After planting in the spring, cut stems back to one bud. The new stems will then produce fruit in the coming summer. Each year in late winter, cut the old fruiting stems back to one bud. If frost is forecast, bring pots inside or cover with fabric.

Black currant 'Ben Lomond' has large fruits.

White currants

Plant used
White currant 'Blanka'

Height and spread
H 5ft (1.5m)
S 24in (60cm)

Exposure
Sun or partial shade

Temperature needs
Fully hardy

Fruiting period
Summer

Suitable pot size
Min. 12in (30cm)

Suitable container material
Terra-cotta, stone, plastic

Compost type
Multi-purpose and soil-based compost

White currant 'Blanka' produces sweet berries.

Sweeter than red currants, white currants are cool-climate plants that fruit well in northern areas. 'Blanka' and 'Versailles Blanche' are particularly good varieties. Like red currants, they are shallow-rooted and grow well in large pots. Stand containers on pot "feet" to boost drainage. In dry weather water regularly, ensuring the compost never dries out.

In late winter, scrape off the top layer of compost from the pot and replace with fresh compost mixed with a handful of slow-release fertilizer granules. After feeding, water well and apply a mulch of well-rotted manure to aid water retention and reduce weed growth.

PRUNING WHITE CURRANTS
Prune plants in late winter or early spring. Remove a quarter of the old stems, cutting them down to the base. Reduce remaining stems by half, cutting to an outward-facing bud. Prune sideshoots back to one bud.

PIE FRUIT

Tart flavors

The stems of rhubarb and the plump, juicy fruits of gooseberries make wonderful summer treats when sweetened with sugar and turned into pies, tarts, cobblers, and crisps. Both plants produce fruit year after year with very little fuss or bother, and they not only taste delicious, but make attractive patio plants as well.

Rhubarb

PIE FRUIT

Plant used
Rhubarb 'Timperley Early'

Height and spread
H & S 18in (45cm)

Exposure
Sun or partial shade

Temperature
Fully hardy

Harvesting period
Spring to summer; late winter if forced

Suitable pot size
18in (45cm) or larger

Suitable container material
Stone, terra-cotta, plastic, glazed ceramic

Compost type
Soil-based compost, e.g., John Innes No. 3

Thanks to its massive platelike leaves, rhubarb injects a dramatic note into a patio or garden display. The pink, red, or greenish leafstalks also taste great when cooked and added to pies and cobblers. Plants like full sun, although they will also tolerate partial shade, and need a big container and copious amounts of water to thrive. Buy young plants in the spring, and repot them into larger containers several times until they reach their final size. If plants start to get too big for their designated spot, snip off a leaf or two from around the outside. Rhubarb is generally harvested in the spring, although "forcing" produces an earlier crop. Remove old growth when the plant dies back in the fall.

FORCING RHUBARB
To produce an early crop of tender pink stems, put a handful of straw over dormant plants in late winter, then exclude light by covering them with a terra-cotta forcing pot or a bucket with a solid base. The stems will develop in the dark and be ready to cut after about four weeks.

Feed rhubarb plants in early spring with a slow-release granular fertilizer, and keep the compost moist at all times.

TOP TIP: HARVESTING RHUBARB

Avoid off cutting stems of rhubarb with a knife; this will leave a wound that could become diseased and infect the plant. Instead, hold the stalk at the base and ease it out of the compost or carefully twist it off; try not to snap it off. You can harvest rhubarb stems between spring and summer.

Gooseberries

Plant used
Gooseberry
'Hinnonmäki Röd'

Height and spread
H & S up to 3ft (1m)

Exposure
Sun or partial shade

Temperature
Fully hardy

Harvesting period
Summer

Suitable pot size
18in (45cm)

Suitable container material
Stone, terra-cotta, plastic, glazed ceramic

Compost type
Soil-based compost, e.g., John Innes No. 3

Forget the sour fruits you may have bought in supermarkets—homegrown gooseberries are remarkably sweet, with tender skins and melt-in-your-mouth flesh. Producing fruits in midsummer, gooseberries are usually cultivated as bushes in the ground, but you can easily grow a lollipop-shaped half-standard in a large container. As well as taking up less space, the area around the stem of a standard can be used for growing other edibles, such as herbs.

YEAR-ROUND CARE
Buy container-grown plants at any time, but you may find they get off to the best start in the fall. Pot them in soil-based compost in sturdy containers that will not topple over as the plant matures. Standards may also need staking.

Water gooseberry plants regularly, especially in hot weather, as dry conditions can result in split fruit. Also work a slow-release granular fertilizer into the top layer of compost in late winter or early spring. When in flower, cover plants with fabric if frost threatens. Half-standards often send suckers up from the base, so either pull them off or cut them back to just beneath the compost. To ensure a bumper crop, and to maintain an attractive rounded head, prune stems after picking all the fruit, cutting sideshoots back to around five leaves.

Net gooseberry plants to keep birds off the fruits.

PIE FRUIT

CHOOSING GOOSEBERRY VARIETIES

'Invicta' is a very popular and vigorous variety, producing heavy crops of large, smooth-skinned berries with a good flavor from early to midsummer.

'Hinnonmäki Gul', like its sister 'Hinnonmäki Röd' (see main picture), produces mildew-resistant fruits in early summer. The berries are large, sweet, and aromatic.

'Xenia' is laden with large, red-skinned fruits that are ready to pick in early summer and add an ornamental touch to gardens. Plants are also mildew-resistant.

'Leveller' has smooth, light green fruits with one of the sweetest flavors available. However, plants may succumb to mildew, and growth is not as vigorous as others.

Juicy fruits

Biting into a sweet, juicy peach or apricot that has ripened to perfection is a real treat. These days you don't need a heated greenhouse to enjoy such homegrown delights because there are many new cultivars that will crop well in cooler climates. Grow them as a free-standing tree or fan-train the branches against a south- or west-facing wall for speedy ripening.

Peaches

Plant used
Dwarf peach

Height and spread
H 5ft (1.5m)
S 3ft (1m)

Exposure
Full sun

Temperature
Fully hardy

Harvesting period
Summer

Suitable pot size
Min. 18in (45cm)

Suitable container material
Any

Compost type
Soil-based compost, e.g., John Innes No. 3

Choose a peach tree on dwarfing rootstock (*see below*), and grow as a free-standing tree, or buy a partially trained fan to grow against a wall or fence. You can plant bareroot trees in late autumn or early spring, while container-grown trees can be planted all year round.

For maximum flavor and quick ripening, peaches require a sunny, sheltered space. Your tree will also need regular watering and feeding. In the spring, remove the top layer of compost in the pot and replace with fresh. Add a slow-release granular fertilizer and top that with well-rotted manure. When fruiting, give trees a weekly boost with tomato fertilizer. Protect plants from rainfall in late winter and early spring to avoid problems with leaf curl, and bring blossoming trees under cover or wrap in fabric if frost threatens.

BUMPER HARVEST
When your peach tree starts to blossom, spend a few minutes pressing the bristles of a small, soft paint brush into every flower. This will improve pollination and boost your crops.

TOP TIP: DWARF ROOTSTOCKS
Trees grown on the dwarfing rootstock 'Saint Julien A' are ideal for containers; their size is naturally limited to 4–5ft (1.2–1.5m) without the need for heavy pruning. 'Duke of York' has delicious, pale juicy flesh; 'Peregrine' is an old favorite with excellent flavor; 'Garden Lady' has sweet, juicy, yellow-fleshed fruit; yellow-fleshed 'Bonanza' is a heavy cropper. Fruit trees often need other trees close by to aid pollination, but these peaches are all self-pollinating.

Pot-grown peaches often produce bumper crops; you will need to thin out the fruits to stop the branches from snapping.

MEDITERRANEAN FRUIT

Apricots

Plant used
Apricot

Height and spread
H 5ft (1.5m)
S 3ft (1m)

Exposure
Full sun

Temperature
Fully hardy

Harvesting period
Summer

Suitable container size
Min. 18in (45cm)

Suitable container material
Terra-cotta, glazed ceramic, stone

Compost type
Soil-based compost, e.g., John Innes No. 3

A warm, sunny, sheltered patio is the perfect site for this succulent, juicy fruit. Grow as a bush, or if you're tight for space, fan-train the tree on a framework of poles against a south- or west-facing wall or fence.

Apricots are hardy, but because they flower early in the year, the blossoms and young buds are vulnerable to spring frosts—lose them and you won't get any fruit. If the temperature threatens to dip to freezing, protect your tree by wrapping it in garden fabric or bringing it under cover. Some of the new varieties, bred in the US and France, flower later, reducing the risk of frost damage.

When the baby fruits are about the size of a fingernail, thin them to a spacing of 4in (10cm). Water regularly, feed, and boost pollination as for peaches (*see opposite*). Net developing fruits to protect them from birds and squirrels. Despite all your efforts, though, a bumper crop is dependent on a long, hot summer.

ROOTSTOCK CHOICE
Like peaches, apricots are available on dwarfing rootstocks, including 'Saint Julien A' (*see opposite*). Trees suitable for container growing are also available on 'Torinel' rootstock, which is termed "semi-vigorous." They are slightly taller, but still manageable, and produce heavy crops.

Apricots need heat to ripen.

CHOOSING APRICOT VARIETIES

Flavorcot ('Boyoto') is a Canadian-bred variety that is a very heavy cropper. It produces large, orange-red fruits with a firm texture and intense flavor. Self-pollinating.

'Petit Muscat' produces an abundance of walnut-sized, yellow and red fruits. The apricots are deliciously fragrant with an intense, juicy sweetness. Self-pollinating.

'Tomcot' is the earliest cropping apricot. Its red-flushed fruits, which look pretty on the tree, are ready to pick in midsummer. It is self-pollinating and a heavy cropper.

'Alfred' has large, oval-shaped fruits with attractive orange-blushed skins and juicy orange flesh. Trees are self-pollinating and have good disease resistance.

Mediterranean treats

Transport yourself to a vacation in the sun by growing a fig or olive tree on your patio. Evocative of Mediterranean landscapes, they can still produce a good crop in cooler climates, given a little care and attention, and even if yours don't bear fruit, both figs and olives are worth growing for their ornamental foliage and graceful shapes.

Figs

MEDITERRANEAN FRUIT

Plant used
Ficus carica 'Brown Turkey'

Height and spread
H 10ft (3m)
S 6ft (2m)

Exposure
Full sun

Temperature
Fully hardy

Harvesting period
Summer

Suitable pot size
18in (45cm)

Suitable container material
Terra-cotta, stone

Compost type
Soil-based compost, e.g., John Innes No. 3

Although figs are grown primarily for their fruit, their large, deeply lobed leaves make them stand out from the crowd. They grow very well in large pots, and restricting their roots helps to prevent them developing too much top growth at the expense of fruit. More compact plants are also easier to prune.

Buy fig plants in the spring and pot them in large containers filled with soil-based compost. Water them regularly and feed with a liquid tomato fertilizer while the fruits develop. Give plants a boost in early spring by mixing some slow-release fertilizer granules into the compost.

FRUITING SEASON
Figs first appear in early spring as tiny round growths, the size of peas, on the bare branches. These swell over the spring and summer, and are generally ready to pick in late summer. A second crop of small figs appears around the same time as the first are being picked. In warm countries these will grow fat and juicy, but they need care in the winter to ripen in cold countries.

TOP TIP: OVERWINTERING FIGS

Young figs that formed in the summer won't ripen outdoors in cooler climates, so move the pot to a greenhouse or cool sunroom where the fruits can continue to ripen. If you don't have space inside, strip the stems, removing all the young fruits to prevent them from rotting over the winter and infecting the plant.

The fig 'Brown Turkey' is a popular variety and will grow and fruit well in a large container on a sunny, sheltered patio.

Olives

Plant used
Olea europaea

Height and spread
Olives are available
in many sizes.
A half-standard is:
H 6ft (2m)
S 24in (60cm)

Exposure
Full sun

Temperature
Some are hardy
to 14°F (-10°C)

Harvesting period
Autumn

Suitable pot size
12in (30cm) or larger

**Suitable container
material**
Terra-cotta, stone,
wooden Versailles
planter

Compost type
Soil-based compost,
e.g., John Innes No. 3

Olives are drought-tolerant plants that love to bask in warm, sunny, sheltered sites. Grow one in a large decorative container and enjoy its shimmering silvery foliage, tiny white flowers, which are often scented, and attractive fruits. Water well in the growing season, and set pots on "feet" to ensure good drainage. Feed monthly with a balanced liquid fertilizer to encourage a good crop of olives, and maintain an attractive shape by pruning in midsummer. Remove any dead or diseased branches when you see them.

WINTER CARE
Many olives are hardy, but branches can be damaged by severe frosts. Bring plants inside, or cover the branches with several layers of garden fabric and wrap the pots in bubble plastic. Reduce watering if placed under cover.

TOP TIP: PREPARING OLIVES TO EAT

Olives are too hard and bitter to eat directly from the tree and need preparing to make them edible. There are several methods you can use. Either dry-cure them in salt for several weeks, or soak in salt water for several days. Alternatively, cover them in oil for a few months. Specialty nurseries should be able to advise you on the best method for your olives.

Prune olive trees
in the summer to
allow time for the
wounds to heal before
their winter dormancy.

Fruit medley

These three fascinating fruits will tantalize your taste buds and are guaranteed to make people talk. Pineapples and guavas are fun to grow but both are tropical fruits and need the protection of a warm, bright sunroom, while quinces make striking specimens for outdoor containers, and the fruits are prized ingredients for pickles and jellies.

Pineapple *Ananas comosus*

EXOTIC FRUITS

Plant used
Ananas comosus

Height and spread
H & S 3ft (1m)

Exposure
Full sun, in a warm, bright sunroom

Temperature
Min. 59°F (15°C)

Harvesting period
When fruit is fully ripened

Suitable pot size
8in (20cm)

Suitable container material
Plastic, place inside a decorative pot

Compost type
Soil-based compost, e.g., John Innes No. 3 with added sand

A member of the tropical bromeliad family, the pineapple is an attractive plant with strappy, spiny leaves and spiky-topped fruit. For something so exotic, pineapples are surprisingly easy to grow. Either buy ready-grown plants or start your own in the spring from store-bought fruit. Cut a thick slice off the top of the pineapple and remove the lower leaves. Scoop out any soft flesh and leave this to dry for a few days before planting, scoop-side down, in a pot of soil-based compost. A warm, bright sunroom is essential as pineapples need six hours of bright sun a day and a minimum temperature of 59°F (15°C).

TOP TIP: ENCOURAGING FRUITING

Pineapples grow slowly and won't fruit until they are at least three years old. They need a bright, sunny spot. Keep the "well" between the leaf rosettes full of water, and mist plants now and then. When in growth, feed once a month with a liquid tomato fertilizer.

Tropical pineapples make striking plants for a sunroom, where the bright light and warmth will suit their needs.

Guava *Psidium guajava*

Plant used
Psidium guajava

Height and spread
H & S 8ft (2m)

Exposure
Full sun

Temperature
Min. 37°F (3°C)

Harvesting period
Late spring

Suitable pot size
12in (30cm) or larger

Suitable container material
Terra-cotta, stone, glazed ceramic

Compost type
Soil-based compost, e.g., John Innes No. 3

Small, green guava fruit is rarely seen in markets, and plants will be the star attraction when grown in a sunroom in cooler climates. They can be grown from seed, but it's easier to start with a young plant. Guavas need plenty of space and light, so plant them in large containers filled with soil-based compost, and set in a warm, bright room. Trees can go outside in the summer in a sheltered area next to a warm, south-facing wall, but both the early blossoms and ripening fruits must be protected from frost. Plants will only fruit after a long, hot summer.

CARING FOR YOUR TREES
Ensure the compost doesn't dry out, but avoid overwatering. Give guavas a boost in spring by working a slow-release, balanced fertilizer into the top layer of compost. Keep plants bushy and within limits by pruning shoot tips in the spring.

Guavas have a sweet, pineapple-mint flavor.

Quince *Cydonia oblonga*

Plant used
Cydonia oblonga

Height and spread
Standard plants:
H 5ft (1.5m)
S 3ft (1m)

Exposure
Full sun

Temperature
Hardy, but avoid frost pockets

Harvesting period
Autumn

Suitable pot size
Min. 18in (45cm)

Suitable container material
Terra-cotta, stone

Compost type
Soil-based compost, e.g., John Innes No. 3

Quince fruits are aromatic as well as ornamental.

The aromatic, pear-shaped, yellow fruits of *Cydonia* are used to make a sweet jelly to serve with meats and cheese, and are a world away from the far less palatable fruits that appear on the ornamental Japanese quince.

Grow trees in large containers of soil-based compost, and stand in the sunniest, warmest spot possible outside to ensure the fruits ripen. Keep plants well watered and raise containers on "feet" to aid drainage. In late winter, remove the top layer of compost in the pot and replace with fresh, mixed with a slow-release, balanced granular fertilizer. Quinces can become very large, but standard plants are more compact. Pruning the shoot tips also limits their sprawl.

HARVESTING FRUIT
Fruits are ready to harvest when they turn golden in late autumn. Pick before they get hit by frost. Store quinces, unwrapped, in a cool, dry, dark place and, because they are highly scented, store them separately from other fruits.

Strawberry basket

The quintessential summer fruit, nothing compares with the taste of fresh strawberries ripened to perfection in the sun. Grow these glistening beauties in large baskets, and choose a selection of early and late-fruiting types, or those that produce a continuous supply of delicious berries all summer long.

SUMMER BERRIES

Plant used
Everbearing strawberry

Height and spread
H 6in (15cm)
S 30cm (12in)

Exposure
Full sun

Temperature needs
Hardy

Harvesting period
From summer to early fall

Suitable pot size
12in (30cm) hanging basket or container

Suitable container material
Large baskets

Compost type
Multi-purpose compost with added soil-based compost, e.g., John Innes No. 2

Growing strawberries in baskets has several advantages. Not only are fruits raised up to head height, making picking easy, but they are also out of reach of many pests and should not rot since they have no direct contact with the soil. There are many strawberry varieties to choose from, and they are split into two groups based on when they fruit. Most are classified as summer-fruiting varieties, and usually have a single, heavy flush of fruit between early and late summer, depending on the variety. The second group, known as "everbearers" or perpetual strawberries, produce berries throughout the summer and into the fall.

Strawberries are generally planted in the fall or spring. In the spring, plant them in baskets filled with a mixture of soil-based John Innes No. 2 and multi-purpose compost, then hang in a sunny, sheltered spot. In the fall, plant baskets in the same way and store in a frost-free place until spring. Strawberries need plenty of water and a weekly dose of tomato fertilizer. Protect fruits from birds by covering plants with anti-bird netting.

OVERWINTERING PLANTS
Everbearers run out of steam after harvesting and are best replaced annually, but summer-fruiting plants will reward you with crops for about four years. After harvesting, cut back frayed foliage, and in the fall place baskets in a cool, light room or a frost-free greenhouse to protect plants from cold weather.

*Center: **Plant a large hanging basket** with perpetual berries for a continuous supply of sweet berries from midsummer until the middle of autumn.*

TOP TIP: GROWING ALPINES IN WALL POTS

Alpine or wild strawberries are valued for their intensely flavored, tiny berries. Plants produce a light crop of fruit over a long period, but you can ensure a larger yield by growing several plants in a windowbox or raised trough, where they will be easy to pick. Alpine strawberries also grow well in dappled shade.

Strawberry choices

'Cambridge Favourite' produces sweet berries that can be left on the plant longer than most without rotting.

'Albion' is an everbearing disease-resistant variety with bright red, cone-shaped, sweet, tasty fruits.

'Mara de Bois' is an everbearer, with aromatic, sweetly flavored fruits borne from midsummer to autumn.

'Domanil' is a vigorous, leafy plant, and produces masses of large, dark red berries in midsummer.

'Flamenco' is a perpetual variety that produces a heavy crop of large, sweet, and juicy fruits from midsummer.

'Elsanta' is a very popular variety with large, orangey-red, tasty berries that are borne in great profusion in midsummer.

'Sonata' bears heavy crops of very sweet, light red berries with firm flesh in the middle of the summer.

Alpine strawberries may be a fraction of the size of named varieties, but they are aromatic and deliciously sweet.

SUMMER BERRIES

Juicy fruits

Grown for their large juicy fruits, blackberries, tayberries, and loganberries offer a taste of summer. Many are too vigorous for pots, but some new plants have been developed in recent years that do well in confined spaces. All plants are grown in a similar way, and it's really easy to produce a bumper crop of berries.

Blackberry

SUMMER BERRIES

Plant used
Blackberry 'Loch Maree'

Height and spread
H 6ft (1.8m)
S 3ft (1m)

Exposure
Sun or partial shade

Temperature needs
Fully hardy

Harvesting period
Summer to early fall

Suitable pot size
12in (30cm) or larger

Suitable container material
Terra-cotta, stone, plastic

Compost type
Soil-based compost, e.g. John Innes No. 3

Many blackberries are unruly thugs that need to be tamed by training against a system of horizontal wires. However, there are varieties that are perfectly well-behaved plants for pots, including 'Loch Maree', which produces double pink flowers in spring followed by sweet, juicy berries, and its sister 'Loch Ness' with its single white flowers. Both have thornless stems.

Grow blackberries in a sunny spot, although they will also tolerate partial shade, and plant in a large container. Stake the flexible stems with canes, and water plants well, especially during dry spells. Set pots on "feet" to aid drainage; blackberries dislike waterlogged soil.

PRUNING PLANTS

After planting, tie in shoots regularly to ensure the plant doesn't grow beyond its limits. In its first winter, cut back sideshoots made on the main canes to 2in (5cm) to encourage fruiting spurs to form that will carry the berries. After that, each winter cut back to the base the old stakes that carried that season's fruit.

TOP TIP: FEEDING BLACKBERRIES

Blackberries perform well if given a feed in spring when they start to come into growth. Get plants off to a flying start when planting by mixing a balanced granular fertilizer into the compost, following the application rates on the packet. In following years, apply a slow-release granular fertilizer in spring.

The blackberry 'Loch Maree' is a thornless variety, bred specifically for large containers and small gardens.

Tayberry

Plant used
Tayberry

Height and spread
H 6ft (1.8m)
S 3ft (1m)

Exposure
Full sun

Temperature needs
Fully hardy

Harvesting period
Summer

Suitable pot size
18in (45cm)

Suitable container material
Plastic, terra-cotta

Compost type
Soil-based compost,
e.g. John Innes No. 3

Although tayberries taste much like blackberries and are grown in a similar way, they actually look more like raspberries. Clustered in dense groups from mid- to late summer, the 2in- (5cm-) long red fruits are sweet and fairly aromatic. In the past it was difficult to raise tayberries in pots because of their vicious thorny canes, but the advent of thornless varieties, such as 'Buckingham,' has made it possible to grow these beautiful berries on a patio or terrace.

GROWING TAYBERRIES
Place a piece of trellis in a container or move your pot against a wired-up wall and train the stems onto the wires. Water plants well during the growing season, but provide good drainage over the winter by raising pots up on "feet." Prune canes as for blackberries.

The tayberry 'Buckingham' has thornless stems.

SUMMER BERRIES

Loganberry

Plant used
Loganberry

Height and spread
H 6ft (1.8m)
S 3ft (1m)

Exposure
Full sun

Temperature needs
Fully hardy

Harvesting period
Late summer to
early fall

Suitable pot size
18in (45cm)

Suitable container material
Plastic, terra-cotta

Compost type
Soil-based compost,
e.g. John Innes No. 3

Choose a less vigorous variety of loganberry for a pot.

Thornless loganberries bear heavy crops of fruit when grown in large containers, but remember that some forms are fast growers, so choose a slower-growing, thornless variety such as 'Ly 654'. A cross between a raspberry and a blackberry, loganberries produce long, dark red fruits, which are usually ready to harvest between late summer and early autumn. Apart from their delicious fruits, plants are magnets for insects, attracting bees and butterflies into the garden with their nectar-rich, white flowers.

CARING FOR LOGANBERRIES
Place containers in a sunny, open, sheltered site with protection from the wind. To keep plants producing, water regularly, especially during the summer, and feed plants with a balanced granular fertilizer in the spring.

Train plants against a sturdy support, as for tayberries (*see above*). In the fall, after the plants have cropped, cut down to the base all the stems that produced fruit.

Berries blue
Blueberry and honeyberry

Known as "superfoods" due to their high vitamin content, these delicious berries are produced on compact bushes that grow well in patio pots. Apart from the beautiful blue fruit, many offer a long season of interest, boasting attractive flowers and foliage, and fiery fall colors.

Plants used
Blueberry and honeyberry

Height and spread
Blueberry H & S 3ft (1m); Honeyberry H & S up to 5ft (1.5m)

Exposure
Sun or partial shade

Temperature needs
Fully hardy

Harvesting period
Summer

Suitable pot size
18in (45cm)

Suitable container material
Any non-porous material

Compost type
Blueberry: soil-based ericaceous compost; Honeyberry: soil-based compost

GROWING BLUEBERRIES

Healthy blueberries are the perfect fruit for a small garden or patio, providing a wealth of interest. In the spring, plants bear a profusion of tiny white flowers, followed by the blue summer berries, and, in some varieties, fiery scarlet autumn foliage.

Grow blueberries in pots of soil-based ericaceous compost, and water using rainwater from a water barrel—only use tap water as a last resort during periods of drought. While growing, give them a dose of balanced feed formulated for acid-loving plants every two weeks, and place pots in full sun or partial shade.

Select a plant from the many varieties available that is naturally compact and suited to a pot. Some are not self-pollinating, so you will need to buy two plants. In a large pot, you could team them with cranberries, which like the same ericaceous growing conditions and will extend the fruiting season until fall.

GROWING HONEYBERRIES

Native to Siberia, honeyberry plants are extremely hardy. They are grown for their large fruits that look and taste like blueberries, and the best results are achieved by growing two plants together. Honeyberries also do well in pots of soil-based compost, and you can use water straight from the tap. Apply a slow-release granular feed in the spring, and tomato fertilizer every two weeks after the flowers appear.

TOP TIP: PRESERVING

When they are ripe, remove berries from plants by gently pulling them from the stems. They are best eaten fresh or cooked in desserts. However, berries will keep fresh for several weeks in the refrigerator. Place them in a single layer in a storage container, ensuring that they do not rest on top of one another or the weight could cause bruising and result in rotting. If you end up with a glut, berries can also be frozen.

Blueberries need acid soil, but you can grow them easily in pots if your garden conditions are alkaline.

Berry selections

Blueberry 'Brigitta' *has richly flavored fruits that ripen at the end of summer. Grow another variety with it.*

Blueberry 'Earliblue' *is a vigorous bush that is covered with large, juicy berries in midsummer.*

Blueberry 'Toro' *produces a bumper crop of berries over the summer and has bright red autumn foliage.*

Honeyberry *bears long, oval berries in early summer with a blueberry flavor and a honey aftertaste.*

Delicious plump berries *grow in abundance in the summer, but birds also enjoy these juicy fruits. To prevent your crop from disappearing, cover plants with anti-bird netting.*

Late-summer delights

Once considered only suitable as orchard trees because of their size, cherries and plums are now available on dwarfing rootstocks. Plant one of these fruiting favorites in a warm, sunny, sheltered spot and enjoy a confection of beautiful spring blossom, followed by a heavy crop of sweet, juicy fruits from mid- to late summer.

Cherries

Plant used
Dwarf cherry

Height and spread
H 8ft (2.5m)
S 3ft (1m)

Exposure
Full sun

Temperature needs
Fully hardy

Harvesting period
Summer

Suitable pot size
Min. 18in (45cm)

Suitable container material
Terra-cotta, plastic, glazed ceramic

Compost type
Soil-based compost, e.g., John Innes No. 3

With breathtaking spring blossoms followed by glossy fruits in the summer, cherries make attractive trees for a garden or patio. They are available as freestanding bushes or space-saving, columnar towers, which bear fruit on short spurs along a single upright trunk rather than on spreading branches. You can also train a tree as a fan or cordon against a wall or fence.

Grow cherries in large containers of soil-based compost in a sunny, sheltered site. They flower early in the spring and the buds are vulnerable to frost damage, so if a severe frost threatens, bring the tree inside or wrap it in garden fabric.

ANNUAL CARE
Keep trees well watered, especially when fruits are swelling and during dry periods. In the late winter, feed them well by removing the top layer of compost and replacing it with fresh, mixed with a balanced slow-release granular fertilizer. Raise the container on pot "feet" to improve drainage. When fruits are ripening, cover trees with netting to deter hungry birds.

TOP TIP: SELECTING DWARF CHERRIES

Only recently has it been possible to grow cherries successfully in containers. Old-fashioned varieties were too vigorous to have their roots confined, but self-pollinating trees grown on modern rootstocks, such as Gisela 5, remain compact. Among the best cherries to try are 'Sunburst,' 'Crown Morello,' and 'Stella' (*left*).

Modern varieties of cherry will grow well and produce a good crop of fruit within the confines of a container.

Plums

Plant used
Plum 'Stanley'

Height and spread
H: 7ft (2.2m)
S: 3ft (1m)

Exposure
Full sun

Temperature needs
Hardy

Harvesting period
Late summer

Suitable pot size
Min 18in. (45cm)

Suitable container material
Plastic, terra-cotta, glazed ceramic

Compost type
Soil-based compost, e.g., John Innes No. 3

Plums were once the preserve of large kitchen gardens, where mature spreading trees would take up a huge amount of ground space. But plums on a full-sized tree are difficult to pick and protect from bird damage—as with cherries, you need to cover them with netting to ensure you get your fair share of fruits. Modern dwarf trees are much more garden friendly, and plums are now available as small pyramids, columns— which bear fruits on short spurs along a single, main trunk—or as fans or cordons trained against a wall or fence.

For the heaviest crops, position your tree in a sunny, sheltered location and water regularly, ensuring the compost in the pot never dries out, especially when the fruits are developing. Feed plants in late winter with a balanced granular fertilizer, and protect them from severe frosts (*for details, see cherries, opposite*). Plums can be heavy croppers, so check branches regularly for signs of imminent snapping, and have a supply of canes and ties ready for extra support.

CHOOSING ROOTSTOCKS

There are three rootstocks available: semi-dwarfing 'Pixy', which restricts growth to around 7ft (2.2m); the new 'VVA1' rootstock for trees that reach around 8ft (2.5m); and 'Saint Julien A', which produces slightly more vigorous 9ft (2.7m) plants.

Plum 'Stanley' is a self-pollinating tree that produces masses of blooms followed by deep blue plums.

CHOOSING VARIETIES OF PLUM

'Victoria' is an old favorite dating back to the 1840s. This self-pollinating plum produces masses of sweet, red fruit in late summer. A delicious dessert or cooked fruit.

'Warwickshire Drooper' has an attractive weeping look. Its yellow plums are sweet and juicy and cascade from the branches. Self pollinating, it crops in early autumn.

'Marjorie's Seedling' has good disease tolerance and is partially self pollinating. In late summer, its sweet, purple-blue fruits are ready to pick; enjoy them fresh or cooked.

'Giant Prune' is an American heirloom plum with very sweet oval fruits that are ready for picking in early fall. It has good frost- and disease resistance.

Orchard on a patio

With hundreds of apple varieties to choose from, in an assortment of shapes, sizes, colors, and flavors, it's well worth growing your own. Many favorites are grafted onto dwarf rootstocks, which means they produce full-size fruit on compact plants that are easy to grow in large patio containers.

TREE FRUIT

Plant used
Malus 'Fiesta'

Height and spread
H 6ft (1.8m)
S 3ft (1m)

Exposure
Full sun

Temperature needs
Fully hardy

Harvesting period
Late summer
to fall

Suitable pot size
18in (45cm)

Suitable container material
Terra-cotta, stone,
heavy-duty plastic

Compost type
Soil-based compost,
e.g., John Innes No. 3

You may not have space to plant an orchard in your garden, but you can still enjoy your own homegrown apples. Compact trees are ideal for large pots on a sunny, sheltered patio as long as they are not placed in a frost pocket or wind tunnel. Apples generally flower in late spring and are pollinated by insects that will be discouraged by strong winds.

The overall height and spread of an apple is largely determined by its rootstock. If grown on their own roots, apples become too large or produce disappointing crops. To overcome this, they are grafted onto a rootstock, which controls the growth rate and size of the tree. Plants suitable for pots are grafted onto 'M26' rootstocks, which produce trees 8–10ft (2.5–3m) tall, or you can opt for an 'M9' rootstock for a slighter smaller tree. To ensure good pollination, grow a few varieties in separate pots, or buy a family tree, which has several varieties grafted onto one rootstock.

BOOSTING FRUIT PRODUCTION

Water trees regularly during the growing season and give plants a boost in early spring with a slow-release granular fertilizer. Maintain their shape by pruning in winter, removing vigorous shoots and thinning congested stems. Large clusters of fruit result in small apples because they don't have sufficient space to grow. Although trees naturally drop some fruit in summer, help them by thinning them out. Remove the low-quality large central "king", along with any diseased or misshapen apples.

TOP TIP: STORING APPLES

Harvest apples when they detach from the tree with a gentle twist. Wrap in tissue paper and put in a single layer in wooden trays. Or store without wrapping in slatted plastic trays, ensuring that fruits do not touch. Store apples in a frost-free garage or shed, and check fruit regularly for signs of rot.

'Fiesta' apple trees are widely available on dwarf rootstocks, and produce sweet apples in the fall.

Apple choices

'Discovery' produces clusters of pretty white blossoms in the spring, followed by medium-sized, red-skinned apples that are usually ready to be picked between midsummer and early fall. The fruits are crisp and juicy.

'Red Falstaff' produces attractive round fruits that are ready to pick in the middle of autumn. Renowned for their superior flavor, these crisp apples store incredibly well, so you may still be eating them in the spring.

'Egremont Russet' is a highly popular apple with slightly rough, brownish-yellow skin and a sweet, nutty flavor when you bite into the creamy flesh. Harvested in early autumn, fruits will keep until midwinter if stored well.

'Pixie' produces medium-sized, sweet fruits with greenish-yellow skins that are flushed red. They look very pretty on the tree and are produced in abundance on small plants. They are ready for picking in mid-fall.

'Improved Ashmead's Kernel' is a heritage variety that produces highly aromatic fruits with pale yellow skins and a pearlike flavor. The sweet, juicy apples can be eaten raw or cooked, and they are ready in mid-fall.

'Ellison's Orange' is an old variety and many nurseries offer it on a dwarf rootstock. It produces apples with crisp, juicy flesh and a slight aniseed taste. The red-flushed, yellowy-green fruits are ready for picking in early autumn.

TREE FRUIT

Pears for pots

The wonders of modern, dwarfing rootstocks have made even the most vigorous of fruit trees, the pear, available to container gardeners. As easy to grow as apples, pears just need a little more warmth, sunshine, and frost and wind protection. That said, if you get the site right, your diminutive tree will reward you with bumper crops of sweet fruit.

Plant used
Pear 'Terrace Pearl'

Height and spread
H 4ft (1.2m)
S 3ft (1m)

Exposure
Full sun

Temperature needs
Fully hardy

Harvesting period
Late summer to fall

Suitable pot size
Min. 18in (45cm)

Suitable container material
Plastic, terra-cotta, stone

Compost type
Soil-based compost, e.g., John Innes No. 3

Dwarf pear trees may only grow to just above waist height, but they produces masses of foamy white blossoms in spring followed by a heavy crop of delicious pears. Perfect for a big container, the dwarf 'Terrace Pearl' is one of the smallest available. You can restrict the growth of others by training them as cordons, espaliers, or fans. Another option is to grow a dual-column, which bears two varieties of pear on short spurs up the trunk rather than on spreading branches.

Plant trees in large containers of soil-based compost, and water them regularly. Feed in spring with a slow-release, balanced, granular fertilizer, and remove any suckers from the base.

THINNING FRUIT

Pears naturally drop some of their developing fruit but will need further thinning. In the summer, remove deformed or damaged fruits to give those remaining more space to ripen. Fruit will be ready to pick between late summer and early fall. Gently twist ripe pears from the tree.

The dwarf pear 'Terrace Pearl' *produces a veil of white spring blossoms, and a good crop of juicy fruits on a tiny tree.*

TOP TIP: PRUNING DWARF PEAR TREES

Encourage trees to produce more fruit with careful pruning. In the summer, cut side branches to leave 5 or 6 leaves of the summer's new growth. Prune sideshoots growing from these branches to 3 leaves beyond the basal cluster (closely spaced leaves at the base of the shoot), and new sideshoots to one leaf beyond the basal cluster. Also prune in winter to shape the tree.

Choosing patio pears

'Concorde' is a heavy cropping pear renowned for its slender but juicy, smooth-skinned fruits.

'Doyenné du Comice' bears large fruits in mid-fall with pale russet, yellow-green skins. Grow in a warm area.

'Humbug' has green, yellow, and pink striped skin. The teardrop-shaped fruits are very sweet and juicy. Stores well.

'Williams' Bon Chrétien' has large, pale green fruits with delicious, juicy flesh. Ready to pick in early autumn.

Upright cordon pears are perfect for patio pots, producing a crop of fruits close to the stem on short spurs, rather than on wide, spreading branches.

Exotic fruits

It's surprising what you can grow in containers on a warm patio. If you love Mexican food, you could be harvesting your own homegrown tomatilloes, which are a key ingredient in the classic salsa verde. Or, for the health conscious, save a small fortune by growing your own "superfoods." High in antioxidants, the jewel-like goji and aronia berries are easy to grow and make attractive plants.

Goji berry

UNUSUAL FRUIT

Plant used
Goji berry

Height and spread
H & S 4ft (1.2m)

Exposure
Sun or partial shade

Temperature
Fully hardy

Harvesting period
Autumn

Suitable pot size
30cm (12in)

Suitable container material
Terra-cotta, stone, glazed ceramic

Compost type
Soil-based compost, e.g., John Innes No. 3, with extra sand

The red, oval fruits of the goji or wolfberry are displayed like jewels on the branches of this hardy shrub. As well as their aesthetic appeal, the berries are also crammed with antioxidants, vitamins, and minerals. Young plants are available in spring, ready to plant into pots of soil-based compost. To improve drainage, add extra sand and raise pots on "feet,"and boost plant growth by mixing a slow-release, balanced fertilizer into the compost. Water regularly, and lightly prune plants in the spring. The purple to pink flowers produced in summer are followed by fall fruits, but remember that plants won't crop until their second year. Shake berries from the branches rather than picking them off.

TOP TIP: DRYING BERRIES

Berries can be used fresh or dried. To dry them, spread the fruits in a single layer on a wire rack and allow to dry naturally in a warm and light place. Alternatively, dry the berries on a rack in an oven set on a low temperature. Avoid touching the fruits as their skins will discolor your hands.

Ripe goji berries *are full of health-giving properties. Enjoy them fresh or dried.*

Aronia berry *Aronia melanocarpa*

Plant used
Aronia berry

Height and spread
H & S 4ft (1.2m)

Exposure
Sun or partial shade

Temperature
Fully hardy

Harvesting period
Autumn

Suitable pot size
12in (30cm)

Suitable container material
Terra-cotta, stone, glazed ceramic

Compost type
Soil-based compost, e.g., John Innes No. 3

The nutrient-rich, black currantlike berries of aronia or chokeberries can be juiced or made into jam. In spring and summer, this deciduous bush forms a mound of glossy green foliage, but in the fall the leaves turn a fiery red, which is even brighter if plants are placed in full sun. The small, white, spring flowers are followed by dark purple autumn berries.

In their native habitat, aronias are found growing in damp, acid soil, but they will thrive in a range of soil conditions. Plant in pots of soil-based compost, such as John Innes No. 3, and keep plants well watered.

WHAT TO GROW
The wild species produces prolific crops of berries, but more compact cultivars, such as 'Iroquois Beauty' ('Morton') and 'Hugin,' are better suited to the cramped conditions of a container.

Aronia berries contain high levels of antioxidants.

Tomatillo

Plant used
Tomatillo 'Toma Verde'

Height and spread
H & S 3ft (1m)

Exposure
Full sun

Temperature
Not hardy below 32°F (0°C)

Harvesting period
Late summer

Suitable pot size
8in (20cm)

Suitable container material
Plastic

Compost type
Soil-based compost, e.g., John Innes No. 3

Tomatilloes are related to Cape gooseberries.

Related to the Cape gooseberry, tomatilloes have plump fruit hidden inside a papery husk, only in this case they are green. Vigorous, tender plants, tomatilloes produce masses of large, yellow flowers, followed in late summer by the fruits, which are used in Mexican cooking.

STARTING FROM SEED
Sow seed thinly in small pots in late winter and early spring, transplanting the seedlings into individual pots when they are big enough to handle. Plants can go outdoors in a sunny, sheltered area after the last frost, but they will crop better in a sunroom or greenhouse. Tomatilloes aren't self-pollinating, so you will need more than one for pollination. Like cordon tomatoes (another relative), their stems need to be tied to canes to support the weight of the fruits. Don't overwater or you'll ruin their flavor, and feed occasionally with a balanced liquid fertilizer. Harvest fruits in late summer, when the husks split and the tomatilloes are still green.

UNUSUAL FRUIT

PLANTING GUIDE

In this chapter you will find advice on some of the best methods for planting and growing ornamentals, such as trees, bushes, and perennials, as well as techniques for sowing vegetable seeds in containers. Pests and diseases can undo all your hard work and ruin your plants and crops, so check out ways to prevent attacks and tackle any problems that may arise.

Sow vegetable seeds carefully *to reap the rewards, and keep all your containers well watered to produce healthy plants. Recognize common pests and diseases, and help to conserve moisture in pots with mulch.*

Planting shrubs and perennials

Planting beautiful containers of flowers and shrubs is surprisingly easy if you follow this tried-and-tested method. The key is to choose your pots and compost carefully, and check that they will suit the final size of your plants and the conditions they thrive in. And unless the temperature falls below freezing, it's a job you can tackle at any time of the year.

1 Choose containers with drainage holes in the bottom. Then, to prevent the compost from clogging them up, cover over the holes with some pieces of broken clay pot or styrofoam packaging.

2 Add a deep layer of compost, choosing the type your plants prefer. If you are using terra-cotta pots, you can line them first with bubble plastic to help protect them during freezing conditions.

3 Add some slow-release fertilizer granules to the compost. Check the instructions on the packaging for application rates. These granules will sustain most perennials and bushes for a full growing season.

4 Give your plants a good soak. Stand them in their pots in a bucket of water; wait until bubbles stop rising to the surface before lifting them out to drain. Arrange them, still in their pots, in the container.

5 Once you're happy with the arrangement, remove the plastic pots and reposition your plants, packing compost around their root balls. Plants should go in at the same depth as when they were in their original pots.

6 When planting, ensure that there is a 2in (5cm) gap between the compost's surface and the rim of the container to allow space for watering. Place your pots in a location appropriate to the plants' needs, and water regularly, aiming the spout of your can or hose at the compost rather than spraying the foliage and flowers.

Planting bulbs in pots

Pots brimming with spring bulbs lift the spirits after the long dark days of winter. Plan ahead and plant up pots in the fall, and for a truly dazzling display, combine a collection of different flowers in one large container.

1 Prepare your container as for bushes and perennials (*see step 1, opposite*). Add a layer of compost and arrange the largest bulbs, such as daffodils, on top. Plant them twice as deep as the height of the bulb.

2 Cover the bulbs with a layer of compost, then plant slightly smaller bulbs, such as tulips. Ensure the pointed tips of your bulbs are facing up, and space them closer than recommended on the packet.

3 Cover the bulbs with a layer of compost, then plant small bulbs, such as grape hyacinths (*Muscari*) on top. Cover with compost, and set the pot on "feet" to prevent waterlogging. Place in a sunny spot to flower.

COMPOST TYPES

MULTI-PURPOSE
This light, soil-less compost is easy to transport and ideal for many containers. Some formulas contain sufficient nutrients to feed plants for up to six weeks. Peat-free brands are available.

SOIL-BASED
Sometimes referred to as "loam-based," this contains sterilized soil which makes it heavy. It retains water and nutrients more efficiently than multi-purpose and is ideal for long-term plantings. The John Innes formulas also contain extra plant nutrients.

AQUATIC
Sterilized garden soil with added sand gives this mix stability in the water. A low nutrient content helps maintain good water quality.

HOUSEPLANT
Similar to multi-purpose, it is formulated to maintain the health of a wide range of houseplants. Composts are also available for particular plant groups, such as orchids and cacti.

Ericaceous multi-purpose and soil-based composts are formulated for acid-loving plants.

Choose bulbs that flower simultaneously for a dramatic burst of color in the spring. This display blooms in mid-spring.

Planting trees in containers

Small trees make elegant features when grown in large containers on a patio or as a focal point in a garden. Choose a small or compact type, or one grafted onto a dwarf root stock, and plant carefully. Remember that you will need to feed your tree each year in spring, and you must ensure that the compost never dries out.

1 Buy a large container with drainage holes in the bottom. Place pieces of broken clay pot or styrofoam packaging over the holes. Stand your tree in a bucket of water to soak the root ball.

2 Add a deep layer of soil-based compost, such as John Innes No. 3, to the bottom of the container and mix in some slow-release fertilizer granules at the rate specified on the packaging.

3 Leave the tree soaking until bubbles have stopped rising to the surface of the water. Lift out to drain; slip off its pot, and gently tease out the roots. Stand the tree in its new container, ensuring the stem is upright.

4 Check that when the tree is planted, its root ball will sit at the same depth as it was in its pot. Fill in around the root ball with compost mixed with slow-release fertilizer, firming it with your fingers as you go.

5 Leave a gap of at least 2in (5cm) between the top of the compost and the rim of the container to allow space for watering. Firm the compost around the root ball, checking once again that the stem is straight. Water the tree well, and keep the compost moist at all times. Feed annually in the spring by carefully removing the top layer of compost and replacing it with fresh, mixed with a slow-release granular fertilizer.

Planting a hanging basket

Plant a large hanging basket with a medley of different colors and textures for interest all year round. In the summer, you can create glorious spheres of flowers and foliage (*as shown here*); for the colder months, replace tender plants with hardy types, such as grasses, bulbs, and violas. Hang your basket at head height on a patio, deck, or balcony on a sturdy metal bracket.

1 Sit the basket in a pot while you work. Position your chosen liner in the basket. To help retain moisture, lay a small circle of plastic, punched with a few holes, over the bottom and cover with gravel.

2 Cut slits in the shape of a cross in the liner, just above the plastic. Add a layer of compost. Wrap the leaves of trailing plants with plastic and thread them through the liner, one plant per slit.

The plants used here are *Verbena* 'Derby' and *Verbena* 'Peaches 'n' Cream', together with trailing blue lobelia, *Lotus berthelotii*, *Dichondra argentea* 'Silver Falls' and a pink-colored diascia. A summer basket like this will need watering every day, even if it has been raining. In the fall, remove the plants and compost them, and plant the basket with some evergreen grasses, spring bulbs, and dainty violas for an autumn to early spring display.

3 Fill the basket to just below the rim with compost, then add the rest of your plants. Work from the center out, with the tallest plant in the middle, and small or trailing plants set evenly around the edge.

4 Fill in around the plants with more compost mixed with some slow-release fertilizer granules. Water the basket well, and add a layer of gravel over the compost to help retain moisture and suppress weeds.

TOP TIP: ATTACHING BRACKETS TO A WALL

To attach a hanging basket bracket securely to the wall, place it in position and use a level to check that it is perpendicular. Mark the locations of the screw holes, then remove the bracket and use an electric drill with a masonry bit to drill holes through the center of your pencil marks. Push an anchor into each hole, and line up the bracket with the holes on the wall. Insert a washer and coach bolt and screw it into the wall. Repeat for the second hole, and tighten up both bolts.

Caring for container plants

Plants in hanging baskets, pots, and planters require more hands-on care than those grown in the ground, where their roots have greater access to soil moisture and nutrients. Plants confined to containers require you to supply all their water and food needs, but there are some useful tips that you can follow to make these jobs a little easier and to save time.

Watering

Keeping thirsty plants supplied with water is essential if you want to maintain their health and growth. If you don't have time to water every day in the summer and during dry spells, choose large containers, which hold more compost and, therefore, correspondingly larger volumes of water. Small terra-cotta pots need watering the most frequently, while tall containers made from plastic or other man-made materials will require less attention. Covering the compost with a layer of mulch will also help to seal in moisture (*see opposite*).

When planting, ensure that you leave a gap of 2in (5cm) between the top of the compost and the rim of the pot to allow space for water to accumulate and filter down to the plants' roots. Aim your watering can or hose onto the compost, where it's needed, rather than the leaves.

Top: **A good soaking** once or twice a week, making sure the water reaches the roots at the bottom of the pot, is more effective than a light sprinkling every day.

Right: **Hanging baskets** need watering once or twice a day in summer. Use a long-handled hose to make the job easier.

Automatic irrigation

If you work long hours, are going on vacation, or have lots of patio containers to look after, consider installing an automatic watering system. Most systems come in kit form, consisting of a timer, which you attach to an outside tap (there are also kits available to fit rainwater barrels), and a network of tubes into which you insert feeder pipes and small drip nozzles that deliver water directly to your pots.

Some systems are a little complicated to install, and you will need to read the instructions carefully. If you are finding it difficult to attach the feeder pipes or drip nozzles, soak the tubes in hot water for a few minutes to soften the plastic. Also, check your plants every few days to ensure that they are not being over- or under-watered and adjust the flow or watering period accordingly.

Top left: **Run a main pipe** alongside your containers, cut it where it meets each pot, and attach a feeder pipe at that point with a connector.

Top: **Attach drip nozzles** to the feeder pipes, and lay them on the surface of the compost.

Left: **Fit the timer** on your tap, and set it to water early in the morning or in the evening when it is cooler and evaporation rates are low.

Feeding plants

There are three basic nutrients that plants require to maintain good health. These are nitrogen (N), which is needed for leaf and shoot growth; phosphorous (P), required for good root development; and potassium (K), which helps flowers and fruits to form. All-purpose fertilizers usually contain a balance of all three nutrients, but those that are formulated to promote good fruit or flower production will have a high potassium content, while fertilizers for leafy crops or foliage plants contain high levels of nitrogen.

CHOOSING FERTILIZERS

Trees, shrubs, and perennials that will live in their pots for a few years benefit from an annual application of all-purpose fertilizer in spring. Granular fertilizers labeled "slow-release" or "controlled" are best, as these are easy to apply and will continue to feed plants over the whole growing season. If you want to boost flower or fruit production, give your plants additional doses of a potassium-rich liquid fertilizer as soon as the flowers start to form. Tomato fertilizers are a good choice for any flowering or fruiting plants. If you are growing plants with specific needs, such as orchids or citrus trees, buy a fertilizer formulated for that particular plant.

Mulching

A mulch is an organic or inorganic material (*see options, below*) that you spread over the top of your compost to seal in moisture and lower the rate of evaporation from the surface. Before applying your chosen mulch, water your containers thoroughly to soak the compost.

A layer of mulch that is thick enough to exclude light will also help to inhibit weed growth. On an aesthetic level, mulches add a decorative finish to containers, particularly when a single-stemmed plant, such as a tree, is surrounded by bare compost.

MULCHING OPTIONS

The best mulches for containers are both practical and beautiful. Good choices include washed gravel, colorful crushed glass that has been milled to take off the sharp edges, or dyed and crushed sea shells, which are a by-product of the seafood industry. For larger containers, try using smooth pebbles, slate chips, or finely shredded bark. Mulches are excellent for all plants, but are especially effective for those, such as alpines and drought-lovers, whose stems must be kept dry.

Apply a layer of gravel around summer bedding or alpines. As water runs off it into the compost below, it will help to keep the plants' stems dry, preventing them from rotting.

Decorative mulches, such as sea shells, add to the aesthetic appeal of your container displays. You can use almost any material as a mulch, including nut shells, glass beads, or even buttons.

Sowing vegetable seeds

If you thought seed sowing was just for the experts, think again. Most vegetables germinate quickly and easily, requiring only a little care and attention to get them off to a good start. The technique shown here is for sowing seed directly into containers outside; to sow tender crops, such as tomatoes, see specific plant entries (*see pp. 156–191*).

1 Prepare your container as for shrubs and perennials (*see Step 1, p. 234*). Fill it to within 2in (5cm) of the rim with an equal mix of multi-purpose and soil-based composts. Sow seeds as specified on the packet.

2 Water the container with a watering can fitted with a fine rose to avoid disturbing the seeds. Place in a sunny, sheltered spot, and keep the compost moist. Most seedlings will appear within a week or two.

3 When the seedlings have produced four leaves or more, remove the weakest to allow the others sufficient space to develop. Check packets for spacings; you can usually grow plants a little closer in pots.

4 Keep your seedlings well watered; if they are allowed to dry out, their growth will be inhibited. At the other extreme, you must also safeguard against waterlogging, so stand seed pots on "feet" or pebbles.

5 When crops are mature and ready to harvest, gently remove them from their pots with a hand fork; for plants such as lettuces or Swiss chard, simply cut off their stems with sharp scissors. For quick-maturing crops, such as radishes, sow some seeds every few weeks to maintain your supply throughout the summer.

Growing tomatoes in growing bags

The compost in vegetable growing bags is specially formulated for optimum growth, but it can dry out quickly. To overcome this problem, increase the volume by inserting open-ended pots into the holes in the top of the bags, and then fill them with good-quality multi-purpose compost. The extra compost gives the plant roots more space to develop, and holds more water.

1 Using a knife, make drainage holes in the base of the bag and cut three large circles in the top. Insert bottomless plastic pots (make your own or buy ready-made) into the openings and fill with extra compost.

2 Transfer your tomato plants to the growing bag when their first flowers are about to open. Plant one tomato per pot, positioning the root ball just below the top of the compost, and water them in well.

3 Add canes for support, and pinch off all fast-growing sideshoots that appear between the leaves and the main stem, as they divert energy away from fruit production. Apply a weekly dose of liquid tomato fertilizer.

4 As the main stems grow, tie them to the canes with soft twine. Prevent the plants from growing too tall by removing the uppermost tip, two or three leaves beyond the last cluster of fruit on the stem.

5 Keep your tomato plants well watered throughout the growing season; the fruits may either split or succumb to disease if they do not receive sufficient moisture. If you are growing tomatoes in a greenhouse, or you have a number of containers to care for, consider installing an automatic watering system (*see p. 238*).

Keeping pests and diseases at bay

The risk to plants from pests and diseases can be reduced by growing them in the conditions they enjoy and checking them at regular intervals so that you can nip any problems in the bud. In addition, where a plant is particularly prone to a disease, choose a resistant variety, and if pests are causing problems, encourage predators in to track them down.

Reduce the risks

Healthy plants will often resist attacks from pests and diseases, so ensure yours are not under stress by growing them in appropriate conditions and watering regularly. Feed plants according to their needs, but avoid overfeeding, as aphids love the resulting soft growth.

Inspect your plants regularly for signs of attack. Shriveled or distorted leaves and branches are often a sign of aphid infestation, while holes in leaves will be most likely due to slugs and snails. Check flower buds and the undersides of leaves, and either pick off the culprits, in the case of slugs and snails, or, with a gloved hand, wipe off aphids or use a spray hose to wash them off. Prevent diseases by sterilizing pots and tools when growing seeds, and pick off any infected leaves, flowers, or stems.

Drought-stressed plants grow below par and are at risk from pest attacks. Keeping plants well watered will help prevent problems.

Choose healthy plants

Above: **Rosa 'Graham Thomas' ('Ausmas')** is prized for its blooms and disease-resistant foliage.

Right: **'Sungold' tomatoes** have been bred for their sweet fruits and resistance to diseases and viruses.

To ensure that pests and diseases are not unwittingly brought into your garden, check plants carefully before you buy them. Reject any that are wilting, have yellow or marked foliage, or have weeds that may be carrying diseases growing on the compost surface.

In addition, where possible, select disease-resistant plants. Roses, for example, suffer from several diseases, including black spot, mildew, and rust, but scan through catalogs and plant labels, and you will find many that offer resistance to these infections. Many new types of tomatoes and other vegetables also provide resistance to viruses and blight.

Check with experienced horticulturalists at your local garden center for plants that are recommended for your area. National organizations for specific varieties can recommend disease-resistant varieties as well.

Encourage pest predators

Adult ladybugs and larvae of ladybugs, lacewings, and hoverflies will all help to gobble up aphids, while frogs and toads like nothing better than a slug feast. To lure these useful creatures into your garden and encourage them to stay, plant nectar-rich flowers, and install a pond or a barrel pool on your patio. Leafy ground cover plants will provide a hiding place for amphibians.

*Top: **Ladybugs** have a voracious appetite for aphids and will actively seek out infested plants.*

*Above: **Frogs and toads** eat slugs and flies, and will visit your garden if you have a small pond or pool.*

Use physical barriers

They may not be the most attractive additions to your patio display, but if you are growing crops you may need to cover them with bird- or insect-proof netting at key times to guard against pests. To deter slugs and snails, wrap copper tape around containers—it gives the pests a nasty electric shock.

*Net **strawberries** and other fruit before birds eat them; wrap a strip of copper tape around containers to ward off mollusks.*

Houseplant problems

Protected from most outdoor pests, houseplants still succumb to a few that find their way inside. Many are brought in on new plants, so carefully inspect potential newcomers before buying. Diseases and other problems increase when plant care and hygiene are neglected.

Mealybug is a sap-sucking insect with a protective waxy coating that attacks cacti, succulents, and other houseplants. It causes leaf and stem distortion. Use the biocontrol, *Cryptolaemus*, or spray with thiacloprid, acetamiprid, fatty acids, or plant oils..

Whitefly and their whitish-green nymphs suck sap from indoor plants and greenhouse vegetables. They excrete sugary honeydew, which attracts sooty mold. Use the parasitic wasp, *Encarsia*, as a biocontrol, or spray with an appropriate insecticide.

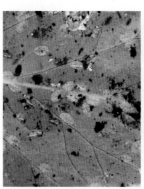

Scale insects affect many houseplants. The adults, which are covered with protective, flat, circular scales, suck plant sap. A bad infestation can seriously weaken plants. Spray with thiacloprid, acetamiprid, fatty acids, or plant oils.

Gray mold rots plant tissue and covers plants with a gray, fluffy fungus. Flower petals may also develop small brown spots. Keep your home well ventilated and water plants in the morning to reduce humid conditions, which the fungus loves.

Ornamental plant diseases and pests

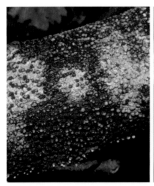

Coral spot is commonly seen on the dead twigs of trees and shrubs or woody debris. In damp weather, small pink or red eruptions appear on infected bark. The fungus can infect through open wounds and, once established, kills branches rapidly. *Acer*, *Elaeagnus*, figs, currants, and gooseberries are often affected. Cut out diseased wood promptly.

Powdery mildew causes a powdery white coat to appear on any part of a wide range of plants, distorting the infected tissue. The leaves may drop, buds die, or stems die back. Watering during dry periods and improving air circulation by pruning or ventilation will help, as will spraying with an appropriate fungicide.

Rust affects a wide range of plants and causes pustules of powdery spores to appear on the underside of leaves and stems with corresponding pale spots on the upper surface. Plants such as rhododendrons, roses, and fuchsias develop orange-brown spores. Leaves often fall prematurely. Destroy these leaves and do not compost to help prevent the disease from spreading.

Rusts spread by rain splash, wind, or animals. Spores need a moist environment to germinate and infect, and so rust infections are generally at their most severe in damp conditions. Spray infected plants with an appropriate fungicide; some plants, such as fuchsias, are sensitive to sprays, so check the labels of fungicides carefully.

Rose black spot causes dark brown or black blotches to appear on leaves from late spring onward. The affected leaves will fall prematurely, which can weaken the plant, but encouraging vigorous growth will help. Initial infection is mainly from spots on stems in which the fungus *Diplocarpon rosae* has overwintered. Severe spring pruning helps to remove this tissue, as does thorough leaf raking in the fall and mulching in the spring.

Various fungicides are available to help kill black spot, and alternating applications of different active ingredients will allow you to find the most effective product. Spray plants immediately after spring pruning, and then spray once again when the leaves open.

Camellia yellow mottle virus causes bright yellow or creamy-white blotches or speckling on the dark green leaves. The virus may also cause flower discoloration. The plant's vitality is not affected, but prune out affected branches to help prevent the virus from spreading. The virus is spread by the grafting of infected nursery stock.

Leaf miners are usually fly or moth larvae, but there are also leaf-mining sawflies and beetles. All eat through leaf tissue leaving distinctive colored lines or blotches in the foliage where they have tunneled. Leaf miners do not seriously harm plants, but you can cover plants with garden fabric to shield them from attack.

Ornamental plant pests

Lily beetle eats the foliage of lilies giant lillies, and eucomis, as well as damaging the flowers and seedpods. The adult beetle is ¾in (8mm) long and bright red, with a black head and legs. The grubs are often completely covered with their own wet, black excrement. Damage occurs from spring to early autumn. Remove the beetles by hand.

Rose leafhopper causes a coarse, pale mottling to develop on the upper leaf surfaces of rose leaves. The insects suck sap from the underside of leaves, especially on roses grown in sheltered places. Adult rose leafhoppers are pale yellow and ⅛in (3mm) long, and jump off the plant when disturbed. Control them with insecticide.

Aphids suck sap from most garden plants using their needlelike mouthparts. Heavy infestations stunt growth and soil the plant with their sticky excrement and resulting sooty mold. When they need to move on to another host plant, winged aphids develop. Control aphids with an appropriate biological control or insecticide.

Earwigs hide in dark places during the day. At night, they emerge to eat the soft foliage and petals of flowers such as dahlias, chrysanthemums, and clematis. In some years earwigs can be particularly abundant and damaging. Trap them in pots loosely stuffed with grass, or spray plants with an appropriate insecticide.

Flea beetles eat small, round holes in the upper leaf surfaces, and attack brassicas as well as ornamentals. Heavy attacks can kill seedlings and stall the growth of older plants, so protect seedlings by sowing when weather and soil conditions will allow rapid germination and growth through the vulnerable seedling stage.

Sawflies are caterpillarlike larvae with seven or more pairs of clasping legs on their abdomens. The larvae often feed together in groups and can quickly devour the foliage of certain trees, shrubs, and herbaceous plants. Other sawfly feed as larvae inside developing fruits or as leaf miners. Remove the larvae by hand.

Slugs and snails feed by scraping the surface of leaves, stems, and flowers with their "tongues." They prefer cool, dark conditions, and do most of their feeding at night or after rain. Seedlings and soft young growth are particularly vulnerable. Pick off by hand, use slug pellets, or deter with copper tape (see also p. 98).

Vine weevil grubs are up to ½in (10mm) in length, creamy-white, and legless. (The adults look like black wingless beetles.) They eat plant roots and bore into begonia and cyclamen tubers from fall to spring, and can kill plants, especially those in pots and containers. Use a biological control or an appropriate insecticide.

Vegetable diseases, disorders and pests

Blossom end rot in tomatoes is caused by calcium deficiency and is often seen in acid soils or inadequately watered soil, which prevents the plant from absorbing calcium. A sunken, leathery, dark brown to black patch appears at the fruit's flower end. If blossom end rot does develop, pick off affected fruits and improve the watering routine.

Clubroot is usually introduced on seedlings brought into the garden. It causes vegetable roots to thicken and distort into a swollen mess; plants become stunted and leaves may wilt on hot days, recovering overnight. Improving drainage and using good-quality soil-based compost in your vegetable containers will help to prevent clubroot.

Tomato blight causes fruit to discolor and rot rapidly, with brown patches developing on the leaves. Outdoor plants are particularly at risk. If fruit is picked from diseased plants, keep for five days to see if rot develops. If nothing happens, it is safe to eat. Prevent by spraying with a copper-based fungicide or one based on mancozeb.

Potato common scab causes scabby spots to develop on the skin. The tubers look unhealthy, but the damage is not serious. It occurs in light soils that lack organic matter and is worse in dry years. Use a good-quality, soil-based compost, and water plants regularly when the tubers are forming. Resistant varieties of potato are available.

Potato blight causes dead patches to appear at the tip of leaflets, which enlarge to kill the leaf; the rot is a hard, reddish-brown patch. It spreads rapidly in wet conditions, and airborne spores can infect plants even when no diseased material is present. Affected tubers will rot when stored. Spray foliage with fungicide before blight appears.

Brassica downy mildew is usually most severe in seedlings, and the seeds may be infected. Yellow patches appear on the upper leaf surfaces with white fungal growth underneath the lesions. Improve ventilation by giving plants more space. Buy resistant cultivars and use fresh compost each year, because the fungus can survive in the soil.

Tomato viruses typically cause mottling and distortion of leaves, stunting, and poor fruit yields. Tomato mosaic virus (TMV) is highly contagious and serious: fruit can fail to set and young fruit is "bronzed" or streaked. If symptoms are seen, destroy plants immediately. Tools and hands should be cleaned well, and pest control is important.

Tomato moth caterpillars are brown or pale green with a thin yellow line along the sides. They are up to 1½in (40mm) long and between mid- and late summer they eat the foliage and fruits of tomatoes. When fully fed, the caterpillars go into the soil to pupate. Remove the caterpillars by hand or spray with pyrethrum or bifenthrin.

Vegetable pests

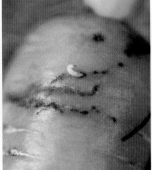

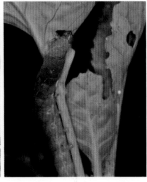

Cabbage whites are most dangerous to crops at the larval stage, when the yellow and black caterpillars devour the outer leaves. Prevent the butterflies from laying eggs by growing cabbages under fine mesh netting. Pick off caterpillars or control with pyrethrum or bifenthrin, but not those feeding inside cabbage heads.

Carrot fly larvae are slender, pale yellow, and up to ½in (10mm) long, and they tunnel into carrots, parsnips, and parsley roots. No effective insecticide is available. Protect plants by growing under garden fabric or in tall pots (the pest flies close to the ground). Some cultivars, such as 'Flyaway', and 'Resistafly' are less susceptible.

Brassica flea beetles can attack all brassicas, as well as related plants such as turnip, rutabagas, radishes, and arugula. These tiny, mostly black, beetles eat small holes in foliage and can kill seedlings. Encourage seedling growth by watering well. If necessary, spray crops with bifenthrin, thiacloprid, or pyrethrum to control the pests.

Cutworms are brownish-white caterpillars of various moth species. They live in the surface layers of the soil and eat cavities in root crops and potato tubers. They also kill seedlings and lettuce by eating through the roots. There is no effective treatment—if a plant wilts, search through the soil around the base and remove the pest.

Wireworms are mainly a problem in new gardens. The slender, orange-yellow grubs are up to 1in (25mm) long with three pairs of short legs at the head end. They kill seedlings and bore into potato tubers, onion bulbs, and other root vegetables. There is no insecticide available for their control, but numbers decline after a year or two.

Leek moth caterpillars are whitish green and up to ½in (11mm) long. They live as leaf miners and also tunnel into the stems and bulbs of leeks and onions. Small plants develop secondary rot and may be killed. There is no effective insecticide available; protect plants from the pests by growing them under garden fabric.

Pea moth eggs are laid on pea plants from early to midsummer. The caterpillars bore into pods and feed on the developing pea seeds. Early or late sowings of quick-maturing pea cultivars that flower outside the moth's flight period avoid damage. Mid-season peas can be protected with bifenthrin a week after the onset of flowering.

Pigeons devour the foliage of peas, cabbages, and other brassicas. Damage can occur at any time of year, but often increases in the winter. Growing vulnerable vegetables under netting will keep pigeons away from the foliage. Scaring devices are likely to give only temporary protection against the ravages of this bird.

Fruit and herb diseases and disorders

Brown rot affects many fruit trees. Spots of soft rot appear on fruits and rapidly enlarge. Rings of buff spores appear on this tissue and initiate more infections. Rotten fruits remain on the tree, and the fungus can then grow back into the branches. Prune out the diseased wood, and remove all rotten fruits from the tree to prevent infection from spreading.

Pear scab causes blackish-brown, scabby patches to appear on the skin of fruits, and greenish-gray spots on the leaves. The fruits are often small and misshapen and are prone to splitting and then spoiling. Rake up and destroy infected leaves and fruits. Prune out cracked and scabby branches, and apply an appropriate fungicide.

Canker grows on apple and pear trees near buds or wounds, which become elliptical with concentric rings of shrunken bark. Spores enter through wounds. Prune out small cankered branches; on larger limbs, chisel back to green wood and apply wound paint. Spray with a copper fungicide after harvest and again after half the leaves fall.

Peach leaf curl affects peaches and apricots. Red or pale green blisters develop on new leaves, which swell and curl, and are later covered in white spores, some of which overwinter on dormant shoots. Remove diseased tissue and apply copper fungicide as buds begin to swell in midwinter, and again two weeks later. Also buy resistant cultivars.

  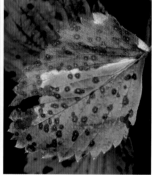 

Apple bitter pit causes brown spots to appear within the flesh, or sometimes on the skin of apples, giving a bitter taste. The spots on the skin are usually slightly sunken, but otherwise the fruits are normal in shape and size. Feed, water, and mulch trees to prevent the disease, and spray developing fruits with calcium nitrate solution.

Strawberry gray mold enters through flowers and remains dormant until fruits mature, where it can be seen as grayish growth. It spreads by contact or airborne spores, surviving on plant debris or in the soil. Remove infected plant parts and debris promptly. Mulch around plants with straw and remove weeds, which may carry spores.

Strawberry leaf spot is caused by a fungus that creates white spots ringed with purple. It is spread by rain splash, and lesions occur on flowers, fruits, and stems. Its effect on plant growth is not severe, although it spoils the appearance of foliage. To control it, remove plant debris on which the fungus overwinters and use resistant cultivars.

Pear rust causes bright orange spots to appear on the upper surface of leaves in the summer. Fruits and twigs can also be infected. The fungus causes perennial swellings on juniper bushes, which release spores in the spring. Removal of affected junipers may help, but spores can still travel. Treating for pear scab can help to control rust too.

Fruit and herb pests

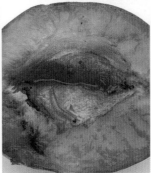

Mice eat the developing corms and seeds of germinating peas, beans, and sweet corn. They also eat crocus corms and orchard fruits, both in gardens and when produce is being stored. They can be controlled by setting mouse traps. If traps are set in gardens, place under a log or brick shelter to reduce the danger to birds and pets. Rats cause similar damage.

Apple sawfly larvae feed inside apples at the fruitlet stage, causing them to fall in the early summer. Those that stay on the tree develop a long, brown-yellow scar by late summer. Remove damaged fruitlets. If the tree was heavily attacked the previous year, spray with bifenthrin at petal fall to control the hatching larvae.

Plum moth caterpillars feed inside the fruits of plums, damsons, and greengages in late summer. Choose varieties that ripen later in the season, as moths tend to attack early fruits. This pest is hard to control; effective insecticides are not available, but pheromone traps can be used in early summer to capture male moths.

Gooseberry sawfly larvae feed on gooseberry and red currant foliage and can cause complete defoliation. The caterpillarlike larvae are up to ¾in (20mm) long and pale green, often marked with black dots. Two or three generations occur between spring and the end of summer. Search for the larvae and spray with an appropriate insecticide.

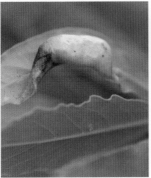

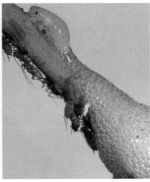

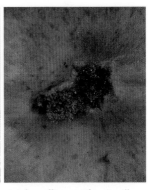

Rosemary beetle and their grayish-white grubs eat the foliage of rosemary, lavender, thyme, and sage. Damage occurs from late summer until the following spring. The adults are ¼–⅜in (7–8mm) long, with purple- and green-striped wing cases. Remove by shaking the plant over a sheet of newspaper, or spray with insecticide.

Bay sucker nymphs suck sap from the underside of leaves, causing them to curl up and become yellow and thickened; damaged parts will dry up and turn brown. Two generations occur during the summer. The adults resemble aphids, have wings and are 1/12in (2mm) long. Pick off infested leaves or spray with an appropriate insecticide.

Cuckoo spit is a white frothy liquid created by immature froghopper nymphs. These sap-sucking insects surround themselves with cuckoo spit, feeding on the stems of herbs and garden flowers; the nymphs are especially attracted to lavender. Little harm is done to the plant, so insecticide treatment is not required.

Apple codling moth caterpillars feed in the cores of ripening apples and pears. By the time the fruit is ready for picking, the caterpillar has usually left by an exit tunnel. Pheromone traps may catch enough male moths to reduce the mating success of females on isolated apple trees, and so may reduce the number of apples with maggots.

Index

Acknowledgments

Martyn Cox would like to thank Alis, Louis, and Lily.

Dorling Kindersley would like to thank the following:
Kate Johnsen for Americanization; Helena Caldon for proofreading; Jane Coulter for indexing; Brian North for additional photography; Becky Shackleton for editorial assistance; Mel Watson for the use of her home and garden; Steve Crozier for assistance with image retouching.

The publisher would like to thank the following for their kind permission to reproduce their photographs:
(Key: a-above; b-below/bottom; c-center; f-far; l-left; r-right; t-top)

9 GAP Photos: Tim Gainey (br); Graham Strong (bc). **10 Marianne Majerus Garden Images:** Marianne Majerus (br). **Photolibrary:** Ken Hayden (c). **10-11 Photolibrary:** Pernilla Bergdahl. **11 The Garden Collection:** Nicola Stocken Tomkins (bl). **Photolibrary:** Clive Nichols (cb). **12 GAP Photos:** Richard Bloom (r). **The Garden Collection:** Derek Harris (bl). **13 GAP Photos:** Jonathan Buckley - Design: John Massey, Location: Ashwood Nurseries (c); Friedrich Strauss (bl); Visions (tl). **14 GAP Photos:** J S Sira - Design Suzan Slater HCFS 2005 (bc). **15 GAP Photos:** Richard Bloom (bc). **The Garden Collection:** Marie O' Hara, Designer: Paul Williams (bl). **Photolibrary:** Flora Press (cl). **16 GAP Photos:** Suzie Gibbons, Design: David Letham (r). **Marianne Majerus Garden Images:** Marianne Majerus (clb). **17 Photolibrary:** A S Milton (t); Ron Sutherland (b). **18 GAP Photos:** Graham Strong (cra) (cla). **Marianne Majerus Garden Images:** Marianne Majerus (b). **19 GAP Photos:** Friedrich Strauss (bl) (t). **20 GAP Photos:** Heather Edwards (cr). **Marianne Majerus Garden Images:** Marianne Majerus (br). **21 GAP Photos:** J S Sira (cr). **Marianne Majerus Garden Images:** Marianne Majerus (bc). **22 GAP Photos:** Friedrich Strauss (br) (bc). **Getty Images:** Janet Kimber (tr). **23 GAP Photos:** Jonathan Buckley, Design: Robin Green and Ralph Cade (bc). **Marianne Majerus Garden Images:** Marianne Majerus (t). **24 GAP Photos:** Friedrich Strauss (r). **Photolibrary:** Friedrich Strauss (bl). **25 GAP Photos:** Nicola Browne - Design: Jinny Blom (t); J S Sira, Design: Foundation Degree Course and Landscape Design Students (Year 3) Warwickshire College (br); Rob Whitworth, Design: Jo Ward-Ellison & Janette Dollamore (bl). **26 GAP Photos:** Jerry Harpur, Design: Van Oordt (bl). **Harpur Garden Library:** Jerry Harpur (br). **26-27 Marianne Majerus Garden Images:** Marianne Majerus. **27 GAP Photos:** Jerry Harpur - Design Christopher Bradley-Hole (b). **28 GAP Photos:** John Glover (bl). **Photolibrary:** Lynne Brotchie (br). **29 GAP Photos:** Tim Gainey (bl). **Getty Images:** redcover.com (c). **Marianne Majerus Garden Images:** Marianne Majerus (bc). **Photolibrary:** Suzie Gibbons (cr); Ellen Rooney (t). **30 GAP Photos:** Clive Nichols (bl); Friedrich Strauss (bc) (br). **31 GAP Photos:** (tr); Lynn Keddie (bl); Friedrich Strauss (br) (cl). **Photolibrary:** Flora Press (tl). **34 GAP Photos:** Friedrich Strauss (bl). **35 GAP Photos:** Jerry Harpur/Design Nancy Heckler - Oyster Point (tr). **36 The Garden Collection:** Michelle Garrett (cr). **37 GAP Photos:** Friedrich Strauss (b). **38-39 GAP Photos:** Jerry Harpur/Design Geoffrey Whiten. **40 GAP Photos:** Jerry Harpur/Design Nancy Heckler - Oyster Point (r). **45 GAP Photos:** Neil Holmes (r). **48 GAP Photos:** Jonathan Buckley, Design: Christopher Lloyd (r). **49 GAP Photos:** BBC Magazines Ltd (cla); Visions (clb). **50-51 The Garden Collection:** Andrew Lawson. **51 Getty Images:** Martin Page (br). **53 GAP Photos:** Rob Whitworth (b). **Getty Images:** GAP Photos (t). **55 Clive Nichols:** (r). **62 GAP Photos:** Friedrich Strauss (r). **65 Getty Images:** GAP Photos RM (br). **70 GAP Photos:** Mark Bolton/Design Bob Purnell. **73 GAP Photos:** Friedrich Strauss (b). **74 GAP Photos:** Heather Edwards (r). **82-83 GAP Photos:** Friedrich Strauss. **87 Clive Nichols:** (bc). **89 Photolibrary:** Maria Mosolova (br). **92-93 Photolibrary:** Pernilla Bergdahl. **105 Raymond Evison:** www. raymondevisonclematis.com (tr) (bc). **108 GAP Photos:** Claire Davies. **109 Clive Nichols:** (t). **Thompson & Morgan:** (br/'Matacuana') www.thompson-morgan.com (bl) (fbl). **110 GAP Photos:** Jerry Harpur. **113 GAP Photos:** Brian North (bl). **114 GAP Photos:** Visions (r). **115 GAP Photos:** Friedrich Strauss (t) (b). **116-117 Marianne Majerus Garden Images:** Marianne Majerus/Susan Bennett. **118 GAP Photos:** Friedrich Strauss (r). **119 GAP Photos:** Friedrich Strauss (t). **120 GAP Photos:** Friedrich Strauss (b). **122-123 GAP Photos:** Friedrich Strauss. **129 GAP Photos:** Neil Holmes (br). **136 GAP Photos:** John Glover (b). **139 GAP Photos:** Friedrich Strauss (tr). **142-143 GAP Photos:** Juliette Wade. **143 GAP Photos:** Visions (tc). **145 GAP Photos:** Friedrich Strauss (t); Visions (b). **148 GAP Photos:** Friedrich Strauss (r). **152 GAP Photos:** Friedrich Strauss (bl). **154 GAP Photos:** Friedrich Strauss (bl). **155 Getty Images:** Kathy Collins (br). **160 Photoshot:** Photos Horticultural (cr). **162 GAP Photos:** John Glover (br). **163 Dorling Kindersley:** Airedale (b). **171 GAP Photos:** Friedrich Strauss (r). **179 GAP Photos:** Lynn Keddie (r). **180 GAP Photos:** FhF Greenmedia (r). **184 GAP Photos:** Howard Rice (r). **185 Brian North** (tr). **186 Brian North** (c). **189 Garden World Images:** Martin Hughes-Jones (bl). **190 GAP Photos:** Friedrich Strauss (b). **204 Photolibrary:** (r). **205 Getty Images:** StockFood (t). **206-207 GAP Photos:** Heather Edwards. **207 Getty Images:** Tim Hawley (cr). **Photolibrary:** Martin Page (tr). **210 Marianne Majerus Garden Images:** Marianne Majerus (r) (bl/Petit Muscat). **213 Blackmoor Nurseries:** www.blackmoor.co.uk (br/Tomcot). **Getty Images:** Inga Spence (t). **214 Marianne Majerus Garden Images:** Marianne Majerus (r). **215 Photolibrary:** Richard Bloom (b). **216 GAP Photos:** Friedrich Strauss (b). **217 GAP Photos:** FhF Greenmedia (b). **Photolibrary:** Photos Lamontagne (tr). **221 Getty Images:** Zara Napier (b). **223 Garden World Images:** Francoise Davis (r). **224 The Garden Collection:** Marie O' Hara (r). **225 GAP Photos:** Rob Whitworth (tr). **226-227 Getty Images:** Paul Debois. **229 Photolibrary:** Claire Higgins (cr). **230 Alamy Images:** Lou-Foto (b). **Getty Images:** Brand X (cr). **232 GAP Photos:** Sarah Cuttle (bc). **241 The Garden Collection:** Andrew Lawson (cr). **243 Royal Horticultural Society, Wisley:** (bc). **244 Getty Images:** Nigel Cattlin/Visuals Unlimited, Inc. (tr); Mark Turner (tc). **Royal Horticultural Society, Wisley:** (bc). **245 GAP Photos:** Sarah Cuttle (bl). **Royal Horticultural Society, Wisley:** (tl). **246 FLPA:** Nigel Cattlin (bl) (br). **GAP Photos:** Dave Bevan (fbl). **Royal Horticultural Society, Wisley:** (fbr). **247 GAP Photos:** Dave Bevan (ftr); FhF Greenmedia (fbl). **248 FLPA:** Nigel Cattlin (bl) (br). **Royal Horticultural Society, Wisley:** (fbr)

All other images © Dorling Kindersley
For further information see: www.dkimages.com